Developing Life Skills

A Learning Resource Manual for Trainers and Educators Working in Non-traditional Learning Environments

Gillian Squirrell

Russell House Publishing

Developing Life Skills

Russell House Publishing Limited

First published in 1998 by:
Russell House Publishing Limited
4 St. George's House
The Business Park
Uplyme Road
Lyme Regis
Dorset DT7 3LS

© Gillian Squirrell

British Library Cataloguing-in-Publication Data:
A catalogue record for this manual is available from the British Library.

ISBN: 1-898924-27-9

Design and layout by: Jeremy Spencer, London

Printed by Bookcraft, Midsomer Norton

Contents

About the author

Gillian Squirrell has worked as a teacher and continues to work as a trainer for ied and non-qualified teachers and trainers in a variety of learning situations. She has a cal and research background in teacher education and induction, formative assessment evelopment of personal competences and in developing learning and assessment opportun ith marginalised learners.

Acknowledgements and thanks

Work in preparing and writing several of the modules was undertaken by Jacki n. Neville Williams contributed significantly to Managing Money. The often diffic k of word processing the modules was undertaken by Vivienne Nelson. A number of coll have contributed various ideas, field tested and helped revise the modules.

What are 'life skills'?

The term 'life skills' covers the host of skills which all people need to develop in order to negotiate their lives successfully and to help themselves have a more fulfilled time. They are the essential building blocks for 'quality of life'.

The life skills that are explored in this manual form a whole mesh of inter-linked skills, beliefs and ways of managing the world and oneself. They cannot be treated as separate skills divorced from one another. So working on one area will be key to improving many other areas of life skills. For example, problem solving will be relevant to developing job search skills, managing debt or improving interpersonal relationships.

Life skills are skills, understandings and ways of approaching things which *can* be learned and *can* improved upon.

Why work on 'life skills'?

As a trainer you will need to be convinced that working on life skills is of value. You will also need to be able to explain, explore and defend the learning activities to the learners as being productive use of learning time. To help you, this section outlines some of the assumptions on which this manual is based.

Everyone will face various challenges, crises and critical situations in their lives in addition to needing to negotiate day-to-day matters. To be effective in managing day-to-day living and in dealing with larger life issues everyone requires the skills and knowledge to so do. Having such skills and knowledge, and understanding the importance of learning from past experience, are central to feeling in control of ourselves and our lives. Feeling able to take control, to make some decisions, to change personal direction, to create plans, to ask for help, to stand back and reflect are all part of the process of using and developing life skills. Being able to do all of these things, and to have some impact both on personal life and what is going on around us, gives us a sense of greater well-being than if we feel powerless and driven by circumstance or other people.

The skills to manage life are therefore keys to greater mental, emotional, spiritual and physical health and well-being. They are the keys to greater self-esteem, self actualisation and to deriving more from life. Importantly they are the skills which also enable us to be able to give to others and to their communities. Having sufficient life skills to be able to give to others and the belonging which comes with this, helps stimulate the upward spiral of developing positive self-esteem.

This manual is grounded on several principles:
- young people and adults continue to change, develop and grow. These experiences are not the prerogative of the young. So, you *can* 'teach an old dog new tricks'
- learning is something everyone does every day of their lives. Without learning we could not deal with new technologies or ways of looking at the world, and could not cope with everyday events or imposed changes. The learners you work with should be encouraged to understand that learning is an inevitable part of everyone's life
- life skills are skills which can be learned. Helping people to develop such skills is crucial to helping them to improve the quality of their lives, their chances and their relationships with others.

This manual has been written on the assumption that people can be helped to help themselves and change their behaviours. Each of us can be encouraged through various learning activities, for example role-play, self-assessments and brainstorming, to make explicit the beliefs, values and assumptions that underlie our behaviours and perceptions of the world. Once explicit, the consequences and limitations of such attitudes, values or beliefs can be examined; and they can then be altered to become less self-limiting or less damaging to ourselves and others.

The manual assumes that learners can be encouraged to:

- think about, analyse and explore issues
- think about changes or developments which would serve themselves and others better.

It works to develop better cognitive and self-management skills which are a key part of the action planning and review processes in each module. This encourages assessment, analysis, problem-solving and the consideration of behaviours and aspirations as well as planning, anticipation and execution of organised actions and, eventually, their review.

The work on improved social interactions is further explored in the companion volume, *Developing Social Skills*.

Support and development in your work as a trainer

Developing Life Skills is an invaluable resource in whatever training context you are working and it is designed to help if you:

- have little or no experience of training others, but your workplace role now includes 'becoming an effective trainer
- have had some experience of the trainer's role, and want to develop your competencies and deepen your understanding
- are involved in designing training programmes for trainers and educators, you will find it a useful reference and support resource.

Whatever your level of experience, devising programmes of structured and planned activities for learners in non-traditional contexts can pose challenges for both new and experienced trainers. Support in this work can be obtained from the companion volume *Becoming an Effective Trainer* which:

- provides information on developing and managing effective learning opportunities
- encourages you to think about your training style
- encourages you to develop as a reflective practitioner, and become someone who thinks seriously about how to execute your role as a trainer, and how to develop your role in the future
- gives you greater confidence about your management of learning situations
- enables you to feel more competent in working towards the realisation of appropriately determined learning goals
- offers guidance on undertaking the evaluation and marketing of learning activities
- offers guidance on working with other trainers.

To develop the training that you can provide by using *Developing Life Skills* there are three companion volumes which draw on the practices promoted in *Becoming an Effective Trainer*. They describe and resource learning activities in key areas of *Developing Social Skills, Addressing Anti-social Behaviour* and *Confronting Offending Behaviour*. These learning resource manuals each carry trainer's notes to support the activities and can therefore be used as stand alone items; however, they are most effective when you have developed an understanding of how learning takes place and how best to promote and manage learning. This is described in *Becoming an Effective Trainer*.

In planning the learning and development routes for individual learners, therefore, trainers may wish to select appropriate modules from several of the manuals. Each manual emphasises the importance of the learner engaging with their own situation and taking responsibility for making changes. All the manuals are available from Russell House Publishing.

How to use this manual

An overview

Each life skill topic and many of the learning activities are free-standing. This enables you to sample and use a range of activities with the learners. However, to gain greatest benefit learners should be exposed to a thorough investigation of a life skill area and encouraged to consider how the information and approaches can be applied to their situations. A brief and random exposure to life skills activities will not enable such learning to be consolidated.

The manual is in four sections:

- *Section One: Starting points* puts life skills in context.
- *Section Two: Introducing life skills to the learner* contains exercises which explore life skills with the learner and begins to identify learning needs.
- *Section Three: The life skills modules* is the bulk of the manual and contains the thirteen life skills modules each divided into a number of 'sessions'.
- *Section Four: End notes* contains some notes on evaluation and self-assessment, notes on valuing what the learner has done, and discussion of the 'tools' used in the training sessions.

In each module there are:

 Guidelines on time needed for each of the sessions within the module

 Valuable links to other modules

 Descriptions of the types of activities covered in the module

 Trainer's notes

The introductory part of each module raises learners' awareness and encourages a review of some of the issues. The middle parts rehearse various themes and issues and encourage further awareness raising. They also explore techniques and skills that the learners can develop and integrate into their lives. The final part asks the learners to review the main ideas and skills covered thus far and often requires the learners to produce a final learning plan or summary plan.

In some modules the sessions follow in a sequential and developmental way. In other modules there is both progression through sessions, and sessions that cover discrete areas. For example, the module *Developing learning skills* progresses through general learning skills to the importance of learning to manage life, as well as containing a more specialist five hour session on developing 'study skills'. It is important to familiarise yourself with the content of the modules so that you can select the parts and activities that are most appropriate to particular groups of learners.

In constructing a life skills learning programme you should note the importance of working through several complementary modules and of reminding the learners of how learning in one life skills area will support learning in another.

For example, developing positive attitudes links with work on:

- developing personal support networks
- developing self-esteem
- goal setting
- effective time management and planning
- managing stress
- an awareness of good nutrition
- effective money management
- improving appearance
- improving personal chances
- improving job search skills
- effective management of relationship at home, work, with authority and in social situations
- improved communication skills
- exercise
- developing relaxation skills.

The trainer is therefore directed at the beginning of most modules to several others within *Developing Life Skills*, and to some modules within the companion volume *Developing Social Skills*. It is important to help the learner realise that improvements in one life skill area will have an impact on developing other life skills. This realisation should encourage the learner and provide a further reason for the effort and honest self-appraisal that working on life skills often requires.

Managing the learning activities

At the start of each module is a list of the learning styles that the module involves. The trainer should be aware of the possible pitfalls, and the particular demands of managing and steering the activity. (Guidance can be found in Section Four of this manual and in *Becoming an Effective Trainer*).

In some cases the 'trainer's notes' offer a full explanation. For example, how to run a brainstorm, its purpose and how to complete the action planning process.

Guidance is given on suitable questions and the sequencing of questions to support many of the role-play and hot-seating activities. The questions should encourage the trainer and the learners to gain more detailed insights from the activity by pushing the learners to analyse what has happened more fully.

Where appropriate there are warnings to trainers about activities which will need to be handled with particular sensitivity or that could pose special difficulties, for example practical activities in the kitchen.

When introducing an activity it is essential that you describe what is wanted, provide clear instructions and tell the learner what outcome is needed. For example:

"At the end of the small group discussions there will be a three minute presentation of the five key ideas which have emerged from these discussions. A spokesperson will be needed from each group to give this presentation. It may be helpful to write these five points on flipchart paper."

If clear instructions are not given the learners will drift off into idle talk or other activities, the learning atmosphere will be damaged and the group momentum will slow down. If this happens the group may well be lost to the trainer.

The trainer needs to know:

- **why** an activity is being undertaken
- **what** it contributes to the overall exploration, discussion and learning
- **how** the activity builds on to or links with a preceding activity or with the one to follow.

Much of the learning will take place during the activity sessions. However, and it will depend on the learners' environments and any other constraints, there are some learning activities which suggest that the learners undertake work outside the session. For example, collecting information on a given topic from various sources and evaluating it. This type of activity encourages the learners to undertake an activity within a real life context and so implement what they have learned.

There are also occasions when the learner should work with the trainer to devise and review an action plan. The importance of one-to-one surgeries should not be underestimated. They encourage a close working relationship, make the learner feel more valued and so encourage them to work on the plan because it is being taken seriously. These planning or review meetings help develop understanding, help the trainer to know more about the learner and help identify any particular learning needs.

Some learning activities should be subject to review within a week or so of them being implemented by the learner in order to:

- consolidate the learning
- encourage the learners to adapt and modify the learning points by applying them in their own lives
- enable the learners to share with others what they have done.

A note about literacy

The trainer needs to be alive to any problems in the group with literacy, and of numeracy in the money management module. Learners may be:

- struggling with written instructions and completion of worksheets
- slow to put pen to paper
- cover their work
- try to copy others
- become obstructive
- exhibit other blocking behaviours when a worksheet or reading task is presented.

The trainer should, for clarity of instruction-giving and helping with any literacy problems, go through each worksheet activity explaining what is required, checking understanding and, as appropriate, working an example on the flipchart.

Learners who experience problems in completing worksheets should not be penalised or stigmatised. They can work with the trainer or with a partner. The importance of discussion and exploring concepts are opportunities that should not be closed to a learner just because he or she currently experiences problems in recording answers. If possible, the learners should use a tape-recorder to make notes on key learning points or action plans and the tape could become an important part of the learners' portfolio.

Referrals to help learners improve upon literacy must be made and the trainer needs to know how to do this.

Resources

The resources needed may be as simple as having a flipchart and pens available for a brainstorm or for writing up a couple of questions for discussion. Resourcing may mean copying the learners activity sheets that are to be found at the close of the module. They are all numbered and this reference number appears in the learning activity to which it relates. Sometimes you may need an overhead projector and have to make a transparency from one of the OHT templates found at the back of a module. Occasionally assembling appropriate resources may mean collecting together magazines for collage work.

To ensure that this manual is as comprehensive as possible, all the practical 'tools' that you will need have been included (handouts, checklists, questionnaires, action plans and OHTs – over 200 in all). In order to provide these valuable resources in a volume that is not too bulky and at a sensible price, we have reduced these 'tools' from A4 to A5 size. To restore them to their original size you will need to photocopy them using the standard 'enlarge' feature (normally 141%).

Alongside the delivery and management of the learning activities the trainer should build up a database of useful local and national referral addresses and telephone numbers. Some are included in this manual. Others should be found locally. Such contacts and referrals may be an important part of discussion about future work or training opportunities or home safety.

The trainer should also develop a resource bank of public information and other leaflets. For example, collecting materials from the Employment Service, jobcentres, local health education authorities, local government departments, supermarkets, chemists and DIY stores.

The trainer's role

Full discussion of the roles of trainer and learner can be found in the companion manual *Becoming an Effective Trainer*. The following paragraphs are a reminder to the trainer of the importance of the relationship and responsibilities of both trainer and learner.

While care has been taken to provide clear guidance for the trainer and to include some notes on training techniques at the close of the manual it has be stressed that the trainer needs to be:

- familiar with the material before attempting a training session
- able to explain what is wanted or the concepts behind an activity in various ways appropriate to the learner
- familiar with the techniques to be used
- aware of learners' needs, concerns and possible areas of vulnerability
- able to supplement an activity with additional resources where this is indicated e.g. providing magazines or newspapers.

Developing Life Skills makes a number of assumptions. The trainer should:

- be in charge of the training session and should therefore create a safe learning environment for all group members
- have prepared the learning activities and materials in advance of the session
- create group groundrules with the group and not be afraid to challenge behaviours which contravene these
- provide clear explanations about activities and feedback to the learners. Learners need to understand why they are doing something and how they are performing
- assist, guide and keep on task. Small group activities are not an occasion to leave the learners alone and to do something else
- check on learners' understanding of the task, and make use of effective questioning to encourage deeper analysis of an issue or to encourage the learner to address it from another perspective

- run the group and not relinquish control to the learners
- be fully cognisant of the processes of active learning and the learning cycle and action planning
- be consciously improving their communication skills
- make use of learners' evaluations to inform later planning or session delivery
- cultivate the skills of reflection and self-assessment
- believe in the possibility that people are able to make changes in the ways they live and that the skills and strategies for so doing can be learned. Everyone has the right and the capacity for such learning and therefore for making changes
- encourage the learners to take some responsibility for what they are learning and how they implement what has been learned.

The learner's role

Each learner in the group has a number of responsibilities, as an individual learner and as a group member. This should be made explicit to the learners:

- in the creation of the group contract or groundrules
- in the creation of group and individual learning plans
- through the whole process of working together in an active and experiential way
- through the heavy investment of time in self-assessment check-lists, considering past experiences and aspirations and dwelling on the power of the individual to take control over personal development and make life changes.

The learning activities require a seriousness on the part of the learner to take what they can from the activities and to share insights, skills and interests with others, through discussion, role-play, listening or questioning.

The learners should be encouraged to:

- take themselves seriously as learners
- support others in their learning activities
- develop their learning skills and willingness to try a range of learning activities
- apply learning from the training sessions to their lives
- be self-analytical
- be self-critical
- try out learning activities and plans and accept that they do not always work and that this is itself part of the learning process
- accept and give feedback
- consider their performance, skills, qualities and interests. Develop the skills to discuss and to describe them.
- understand the importance of working with others and treating fellow learners with tolerance and respect
- understand such issues as health and safety of the learning environment
- understand and work within the group's own rules
- understand the ways in which they and others learn.

The learning process

The life skills modules are written to:

- explore the learner's current understandings, practices and values

- encourage the learners to engage in broad-based exploratory thinking
- receive new information
- test out and challenge ideas through such medium as role-play, practical applications or discussion
- consider how to incorporate changes and undertake planning processes.

The learning activities:
- work from and build on from the learner's own starting points
- encourage an active handling, testing and manipulation of ideas
- encourage reflection of learning activities
- encourage planning about how to make use of the learning
- where possible, encourage evaluation of learning after it has taken place.

The activities acknowledge the importance of experiential, contributory and active learning. There are few occasions of information giving. Where possible learning is reinforced by practical activity and subsequent reflection.

Chapter 2 of the companion volume *Becoming an Effective Trainer* explores the conditions in which adult and young adult learners learn most effectively. The trainer is referred to this section and encouraged to review the material on the nature of learning and the learning process.

It is suggested that each learner has a 'Learning File' and that the materials from sessions are stored in it (handouts, worksheets, evaluations, action plans and self-assessment checklists). The learners will need to retain self-assessment materials and action plans. They will be a source of reference about starting points and so a means to measure progression, and a reference about aspirations and their achievement.

The file will also contain material which can be used for completing personal statements, application letters and a CV.

Throughout the modules it is important to emphasise that learning is a process of small changes, of exploration, and of mistakes as well as successes and larger changes.

Section Two: Introducing life skills to the learner

 This introductory section is divided into two parts.

1. Defining life skills and setting group parameters (3 hours 50 min)

2. Working on group and individual learning plans (1 hour 20 min plus time for individual learning).

There is much material on the significance of the first session and guidance on running the first session in *Becoming an Effective Trainer*.

You will need to schedule the first session to meet the time you have available, but you will need to include:

- ice-breaking activities
- an opportunity to talk about practical matters
- work on brainstorming life skills
- initial activities on life skills designed to engage participants' interest, to encourage a sense of having begun the course and to help identify learning needs
- finding out the learners' hopes, expectations and concerns about the course
- an evaluation of the first session.

Trainer's notes

It has several functions. It is:

- a chance for you as the trainer to get to know something about the group you will be working with
- a chance for you, as the trainer and for the learners to identify areas which individuals and the group would like to know more about or indeed, need to know more about
- an opportunity to clear the ground and to encourage all the group members to explore any prejudices they have about learning in this way
- an opportunity to find out about any prejudices the learners have about working on their life skills
- an opportunity to explore the practical matters of running the programme, for example:
  - attendance times
  - any out of course work
  - modes of assessment
  - roles and procedures for goal setting and review
- opportunities for individual meetings between learner and trainer
- an opportunity to explore the range of styles of learning and training through which the programme will be delivered
- the chance for individuals to record early on any particular expectations, hopes or concerns about the course
- a chance to engage the learners in active learning opportunities and evaluation of the part of the programme they have sampled.

Defining life skills and setting group parameters

Introductory activities (20 min)

These early sessions may well be ones of apprehension or tension, as both trainer and learners need to find out: about each other; why they are there; how the power is distributed in the group; what parameters surround behaviours and what expectations there are of each other. The activities at this stage need to be clear and focused. With all the other activities of sorting things out is going on, the learners will not be able to process too many or too complicated things.

Opening activities should include welcoming the group, some comments about practical matters, such as break times and any health and safety instructions. The trainer should make a few comments about himself or herself and the programme.

Useful 'ice-breaker' games are the Name Game with the learners talking to each other in pairs and introducing the person they have spoken with to the whole group or Throwing the Ball (see Endnotes and the manual *Becoming an Effective Trainer* for further discussion of the first session).

A chance to talk about the programme (20 min)

Whatever their status, the attendees should all be treated as learners who have much to offer and to gain from the programme. Whether volunteers or directed to attend, they will all have concerns about such things as what they are expected to do: why they are on the programme; what they might gain from it; whether they will be pushed beyond their limits and so exposed, or made to feel vulnerable in some way. There are various ways to solicit such concerns from the group. Exercises for so doing can be found in *Becoming an Effective Trainer*.

This part of the session should enable you to offer information to the learners. You may want to reinforce this with the key information on a single sheet of paper.

During this session it may be useful to know what publicity material the participants have received about the programme. Ideally they should have received material outlining the course. This should include:

- times of sessions
- content of the programme
- anticipated outcomes of the course
- the potential activities of the course

If this has not happened before they arrive then the group will be starting completely cold and time should be taken to rehearse these points. Time should be available to check on any questions or misunderstandings.

Exploring life skills
a. Brainstorm (10 min)
This session addresses the questions:

> **What are life skills?**
> **Why are life skills of value?**

Write these two questions on a flipchart or project on an OHP so that the whole group can read them.

Ask the group to work in pairs or threes to suggest some answers to these questions. As this is a brainstorm exercise emphasise that finding as many ideas as possible is of more value than finding right answers (10 min).

b. Feedback (20 min)

Bring the group back together pool, the ideas on the flipchart. Write up exactly what is said by group participants. Use their words not yours. Ensure you write clearly so it can be seen. You may be given suggestions like:

What are life skills?

- cooking
- printing
- plumbing
- DIY skills
- getting on with people
- looking after yourself
- looking after your money
- ways to cope in life
- getting and keeping a job
- staying healthy

The group participants may not come up with all the areas which this manual covers. Some of the things may be repetitive or not clear, ask for some explanation of what is meant but do not silence either the individual or the whole group by doing this. Maintaining the speed of generating ideas and their enthusiasm is most important. Try to encourage everyone to contribute.

If the group is flagging or ideas are becoming very repetitive move onto:

Why are life skills of value?

- helps you cope better in life
- can do more things for yourself
- makes you able to look after other people
- can care for your children/partner/self better
- saves you money doing things for yourself
- don't have to depend on other people
- can feel proud of yourself for doing things yourself
- being self-sufficient
- know more about how the world works
- know how to find things out
- ways to get on better in life
- people can respect themselves if they can look after themselves

Again, try to draw out as many ideas a possible.

There is information and guidance on managing group discussion and brainstorming in the manual *Becoming an Effective Trainer* and in the Endnotes.

During discussion about the areas of life skills and their value a number of prejudices and assumptions may become clear. For example, that certain life skills are gender-related or that within their experience certain life skills are just not considered of value, such as budgeting or managing time. Such issues can be discussed but not too intensively. This information should certainly be considered by being woven into later activities. From observations of the learners in pairs and within the whole group work you will have many clues about the ways in which the learners are beginning to function. It is important during an opening session not to pigeon hole and to label people. If you begin to expect to behave in certain ways then you will reinforce certain behaviours which may be limiting both the learner and yourself.

Summary (10 minutes)

Ask each person to look at the two brainstorm lists and to consider

- What life skills they may want to develop.
- Why life skills, or the particular ones they have chosen to work on, may be of value to them.

Ask for the top three skills to be noted. They will be coming back to these ideas later. Take no more than five minutes on this. Ask for volunteers to share their thoughts with the group. List these.

From the general activity, move to more individual experiences and expectations. Before beginning the individual work there may be a chance to have a break. Try another ice-breaking game or change direction by looking at the hopes, concerns and expectations activity below.

Hopes and expectations about the course (20 min)

Ask the learners to complete the IN1 sheet on which they record their hopes, expectations and concerns about the programme they are starting. Work through the four questions on the sheet and ask them if they understand what is meant. In so doing collect some answers. These could be recorded. The learners should retain these sheets for future reference and to help in the planning session.

Taking stock: self-assessment checklists (40 min)

Information on managing checklists in included in the Endnotes. There are several checklists which the learners can work through to give them some ideas about how they would rate themselves on several areas of life skills (these are IN2-3). Before letting the learners work on their own go through the checklists to ensure that they understand what is wanted and to discover if any learners are experiencing any difficulties. Some learners may want to work in pairs or to work with you.

Check that the exercise is proceeding well by looking at individuals' progress. Check some of the responses by asking for examples of why they have ticked certain columns.

While going from learner to learner as they completed the sheets you would have discovered much about:

- levels of understanding about life skills
- areas they consider strengths
- areas they consider weaknesses
- the kinds of evidence they used to support their statements of being good or bad at something.

You will have reached some conclusions about what the group as a whole needs to address and what particular learners need to work on. The summary sheets should help you in deciding on a programme to meet collective and individual needs.

Summary activity (20 min)

Once the learners have completed the checklists then read through IN4 with them. This is a summary sheet and asks them to evaluate what they have found out from the two sets of checklists.

Feedback (20 min)

Ask the learners to compare what they have written with the three life skills areas which they selected earlier. Find out how many have selected the same or a different three and why this may be so.

Ask for the life skills areas which merit attention to be called out in order that a collective list can be produced. You may find that some areas consistently appear or that there may be a wide ranging set of identified needs.

Re-charging the group (10 min)

Most of what has taken place has been sedentary; listening, discussion and pen and paper exercises. Use a game to to re-energise the group. It might be appropriate to try Throwing the Ball as a way to help them remember each other's names, but have them standing up, or try Fruit Bowl to force the learners to move about the room. Details are in the Endnotes.

Drawing the threads together (10 min)

Go through with the group what life skills are and why they are of value. Discuss with the group what else they would like to add to their first two brainstorms. Ask the learners to see if they want to add anything to their 'hopes concerns and expectations' list following the checklist work and discussions. Explain that in terms of the learning about life skills and developing a programme that there will be some one-to-one reviews and creation of a learning plan in a subsequent session. Check that every learner is clear about what has taken place and what will happen. Explain that the remainder of this session will look at the way the group functions.

Group ground rules (30 min)

This activity is necessary if the learners are going to meet regularly to work through the programme. It is more effective for group management and self-regulation if the group agrees its own rules rather than has rules imposed upon it. There may be some rules which have to be observed, for example health and safety or the institution's equal opportunities policies. There may be rules which you as a trainer or as a member of a team of trainers would wish to see in place. These may include such as:

- no feet on tables or chairs
- being punctual
- only leaving the session at break times unless otherwise agreed
- not smoking in session
- not defacing others' learning materials

The group should generate some rules which may include:

- everyone having the right to speak
- everyone being expected to speak
- everyone having regard for everyone else
- not making personal comments or being critical

A draft could be produced at this early stage and then after a couple of sessions checked by the group to see if it works or is in need of revision. The group should then have it in final printed form, each group member could sign it and have it as part of their learning file.

Discussion and examples of groundrules can be found in the book *Becoming an Effective Trainer*.

Working on group and individual learning plans

The group will have identified a number of areas which it wished to work on as part of the group feedback session following the individual work on checklists. This group-generated list is a useful starting point for developing a group learning plan. It is however a list of self-identified concerns which has been fashioned after exposure to a few ideas about life skills.

This session takes the form of giving information to the learners in order that they can make better judgements about what learning they need to undertake within a life skills programme.

IN5 offers a list of life skill areas. All of which are covered in this manual and some are covered in more detail in the manuals *Developing Social Skills* and *Dealing with Anti-Social Behaviour*. These include work on developing communication skills, managing relationships and emotions.

Information giving and discussion (30 min)

Work through the list **IN5** and discuss what each area means. Ask the learners for examples of each life skill area. Ask if there are any other life skills which are not on the list which they would like to add. There should be a number of other skills which the group could add.

Completion of life skills list and feedback (30 min)

Ask the learners to complete the list and then to prioritise the top five life skills which they wish to develop.

Ask each person in the group to offer these five skill areas and develop a collective list. Suggest that the learning programme will include the most frequently listed, but that this may change after review of individual learner's needs.

A group learning programme will need to be produced with the life skill areas to be covered, the dates of sessions, expected running times and other local information. In producing this, other information may need to be taken into account. For example, the learners may not have identified communication skills but it may be a particular area which the institution wishes the group to develop further experience of and exposure to.

In devising the group programme it may be that some learners need not attend certain sessions. The ways in which a group programme will be implemented, the possibility of an individual learner opting out of one strand of a life skills programme and taking other more relevant sessions in another programme will depend upon local timetabling arrangements, the availability of resources and trainers. The more, however, that a learner perceives of value in a particular learning area the more likely they are to be predisposed to be engaged with the learning activity.

Individual reviews (allow 20–30 min for each learner)

Ask the learners to bring with them all their documents to date. The process of discussion and review and the information which has been previously gleaned about the learner while watching and listening in the training sessions will form the basis of the learning plan. There may be areas of work which others have recommended that the learner undertakes, having identified various learning needs in other situations. These may be part of what can be covered during a life skills programme or may be best covered in others sessions, for example work on dealing with addictions needs specialist help not the more general work on thinking about well-being.

A proforma for the learning programme should be created for the individual learner and signed (see **IN6**) A copy of this should be kept by both learner and trainer along with any individual learner compacts which are required to have been made. An example of an individual compact can be found in *Becoming an Effective Trainer*.

Evaluation (20 min)

An evaluation form (**IN7**) should be completed at the close of the first session. The purpose of evaluation and the uses to which forms are put should be explained. Learners should also be made aware that comments should be fair, reasonable and not personally attacking of tutor or other learners. It should be stressed that what is included on evaluation forms is not going to be used against the learner but rather to improve the quality of the programme.

IN1: Hopes, concerns and expectations

1. My feelings about doing this course are ...

2. My greatest concerns about this course are ...

3. My greatest hope is that this course will give me a chance to ...

4. By the close of the course I would expect to have gained ...

Name: _____   Date: _____

IN2: Managing your resources

Work through the checklist, tick the column which applies to you. Be honest and you will then be able to work with your trainer on the areas where you need most help.

	Like to know more about	Yes	No

Yourself

Your health

Do you take any regular exercise?

Do you eat well – protein, vegetables, fruit and fibre?

Do you fry a lot of food/eat fried food?

Do you tend to overdrink?

Do you limit how much sugar or salt you eat?

Do you smoke?

Have you had a dental check-up recently?

Are you registered with a doctor?

Have you had your eyes tested recently?

Have you weighed yourself recently?

Do you know how fit you should be for your age?

Do you take medicines frequently – painkillers, tranquillisers etc?

Do you know when to stop?

Do you often feel under pressure and close to your breaking point?

Can you relax?

Is your sleep interrupted or do you find it hard to sleep?

Do small things sometimes get on top of you?

Do you know when you need to find help or talk to someone?

If you get in difficulties do you know where to go for help?

Your resources

Your money

Do you make a budget for your income and spending?

Do you feel you manage your money well?

Do you have money for an emergency or a luxury you want?

Do you 'shop around'?

Does the way you manage money get you into trouble or difficulties?

IN3: Checking your skills

Tick the yes/no answer which applies to you and if you want to know more.

	Like to know more about	Yes	No
Can you wire a plug?			
Can you decorate your home?			
Could you measure up for carpet or curtains?			
Can you repair your clothes?			
Can you look after your clothes – wash, iron and keep them looking good?			
Can you read timetables?			
Can you understand a map?			
Can you use a library?			
If you want information about something would you know where to go?			
Can you word process or use a computer?			
Can you prepare and cook food for yourself and others?			
Do you feel you understand how to eat well and keep yourself healthy?			
Have you been able to find work or to change jobs recently?			
Can you manage your money?			
Can you make the best of your situation?			
Can you get what you want from life?			
Can you talk positively about yourself?			

IN2: Managing your resources continued

	Like to know more about	Yes	No

Your time

Do you feel you make the most of your time?

Can you balance work, home, social and leisure activities?

Are there often things you put off doing?

Are there often things you wish you could do if you had the time?

If you were looking back over your life would you regret things that you had not done?

Do you feel under pressure a lot of the time to get things done?

Do you have time for yourself or time for a leisure or other activity?

How much of your leisure time do you think you waste?

Your view of others and the world

Developing relationships

Do you make time for other people?

Do you listen well?

Do you confide in people?

Can you show others your feelings?

Do you often get into conflict with people when you do not mean to?

Can other people rely on you?

Do you often feel isolated or lonely?

If you were in trouble have you got people who would help you?

Your view of the world

Do you always tend to see the worst in people and situations?

Do you think a lot of things are your responsibility?

Are you often ready to take the blame for something?

Do you think most things which go wrong are others' fault?

Can you stand back from a situation and look at it again?

Do you feel more positive about yourself than negative?

IN5: Life skill areas

Read through the list of life skills and ✓ those which you want to develop. Put numbers 1-5. No. 1 being the one you want to work on the most.

Managing myself
Improving my appearance
Improving job search skills
Getting better at learning new things
Getting better at managing changes
Improving my study skills
Improving on planning and goal setting
Being able to think more positively

Managing personal resources
Managing time better
Managing my money
Knowing how to budget
Managing relationships a little better

Getting on better with other people
Knowing how to get on with people at work
Managing phone calls better
Thinking more about how things are to others
Thinking about what can be offered to others

Developing other skills
Getting better at reading
Working on writing and spelling
Improving my maths
Writing job applications
Managing interviews

Caring for myself and others
Knowing more about personal hygiene
Knowing more about exercise
Finding out about cooking
Finding out what I should eat
Knowing more about safety at home
Knowing about home improvements

Other skills

IN4: Summary sheet

Working through these lists I find I am happy with my skills in the following areas:

I am less happy with the skills I have in the following areas:

I would like to improve my skills in these areas:

IN7: Evaluation of first session

Could you please help me get the programme off to a good start by answering these five questions.

1. What have you enjoyed about this first session and why?

2. What have you not enjoyed and why?

3. Is there anything about which you still feel concerned or feel that you still need to know?

I am concerned about _____

I want to know about _____

4. What has been the most useful part of the session?

5. What are you particularly keen to find out about now you are doing this programme?

Thank you for completing this

Name: _____   Date: _____

IN6: Learning plan

Name: _____

Priority areas for life skills work	Reason	Date of sessions

Agreed between: _____   Date for review: _____

On: _____

Section Three: The life skills modules

Identifying and managing stress

 This module is divided into five sessions:

1. Raising awareness about stress (1 hour 15 min)

2. Myths and facts about stress (45 min)

3. People can make themselves more stressed (2 hours 15 min)

4. Getting stressed and the consequences of stress (2 hours)

5. The effects of stress and getting stress smart (2 hours 45 min)

 The work on stress links well with:

- Developing assertiveness skills in the manual *Developing Social Skills*

- Develeloping communication skills

- Exercise and well-being

- Food and nutrition

- Developing and maintaining positive attitudes

and sections of modules such as Relationships in the workplace.

 The module includes activities such as:

- brainstorming

- discussions

- completing stress checklists

- information giving

- role-play and scenario activities

- completing personal stress management plans

 Trainer's notes

This module is intended to:

- help the learners develop a clearer understanding about the causes and management of stress

- help learners to identify any of their **own** stress symptoms and look for causes of their **own** personal stress

- help the learners discover the consequences of too much or too little stress in their lives

- help the learners to think about ways they may more effectively manage their own stress and begin to set up an action plan for so doing.

If this is the first time you have met your group then you may want to formally introduce yourself and ask them to introduce each other. Try ice-breaker activities such as the Name Game or Throwing the Ball. It is however to be hoped that you worked through some of the activities in the Introductory Session to life skills with the group. If the group has already met, consider a warm-up game to get attention, some group cohesion and interest.

Session One: Raising awareness about stress

Opening brainstorming activity
Working alone (15 min)
Ask the learners to work on their own using the spider diagram **ST1** on what stress means to them.

Ask them to consider:

- What is stress?
- What does stress feel like?
- What does stress do for them or to them?
- What causes them stress?
- How do they react to stress?

Each answer or sets of answers can be a branch on their spider diagram.

If the learners are floundering then ask them to move into pairs to complete the exercise.

Group activity (30 min)
Bring the group back together and then complete a group brainstorm, asking for ideas so everyone participates. All course members will have had the opportunity to think through some of the issues but may not want to offer personal comments. Encourage these learners to contribute to the discussion of what may cause stress for others and how other people react when they are under stress. Use a flipchart and divide into quarters, putting one question in each in order to record the group's responses.

What is stress?

What causes stress?	What does being stressed feel like?
What are people like or how do they behave to others and to themselves, when they are stressed?	How do people cope with feeling stressed?

Bring their discussion to a close by encouraging the group to summarise what has been said into three, one sentence statements:

1. Stress is ...
2. When people are under stress they may ...
3. Stress can be caused by ...

Brainstorm (10 min)
Ask the learners to brainstorm:

> **In what ways can stress be a positive thing?**

Ask for examples of ways in which stress may be valuable or experienced as positive.

Experiences (20 min)
Ask the learners with a show of hands to indicate if:

- stress is currently a problem for them
- stress has been a problem for them
- stress has never affected them

At this stage there is no need for significant disclosure about what causes them stress, or discussion of how they respond to stress. Record the numbers affected by stress currently or in the past.

Given that stress may have been or may currently be a problem ask the learners to suggest some of the areas they would like to cover and some gains they would like to make from the work on stress. List these on the flipchart and retain the list.

Session Two: Myths and facts about stress

Trainer's notes

Having gained the group's attention and involvement, the rest of the module explores some of the facts and myths about stress. This will add to the learners' current knowledge about stress, help them to become more effective managers of their own stress and responsive to others' stress. It is important to encourage the learners to add less negative coping strategies to the ways they tackle stress. For example, taking exercise rather than alcohol.

Comments from the early brainstorm will give some clear ideas about the ways in which the group thinks about stress. They may consider suffering from stress as:

- a sign of personal weakness
- something others experience but which they do not
- the result of a whole lot of external forces – no money, poor housing, their neighbours or a lack of opportunities. In fact as a result of anything and everything except themselves.

It will be important to encourage the learners to understand that stress is a normal part of life and not a sign of weakness. It will be important to encourage the learners to realise that they can take some control of things which make them stressed and of their responses to stress. It will be important for the learners to become aware that they can also create or contribute to their own experience of stress. This last point is the focus of Session Three.

Lecturette: what is stress? (35 min)

Use the following notes about stress and give out ST2 to help the group develop an effective understanding of stress.

Stress can be a highly individual response

It is important to emphasise that stress can be both positive and negative in its consequences and that the same stress can be experienced by different people either positively or negatively. Not everyone responds in the same way and individuals do not always respond to stress in the same way at different times in their lives.

Stress is the relationship between internal or external demands and pressures and the individual's responses to them. It is this which makes stress an individual response and which makes the same person respond differently at different periods of their lives. This is not to deny that there are events shared by a number of people which provoke a range of stress reactions or that certain occupations or situations for occupational groups cause stress.

Ask the learners for some examples of:

- situations which a lot of people find stressful
- stresses which may be more particular to individuals
- times in life when people may be more prone to experience something as stressful

Too little stress can be bad

People with too little stress may not be encouraged to take action or get on with doing things. Too little stress can lead to a general slowing down and to tasks taking a significantly greater period of time to be completed than if the person experienced some sense of pressure or urgency. Under-demand and boredom can in themselves be stressful. The individual can feel unproductive, not challenged and useless. Ask the learners for some examples of these sorts of situations.

Some stress can be good

Stress is a feature of everyday life. It is an essential for motivating people to do things.

Too much stress is bad

If people feel overloaded by demands and pressures they can become unable to function well if this goes on for too long. The following diagram shows the importance of some stress for performance and then the negative consequences of overload. We need some stress to function well but we all have a certain point after which stress becomes painful and no longer helps us to be productive.

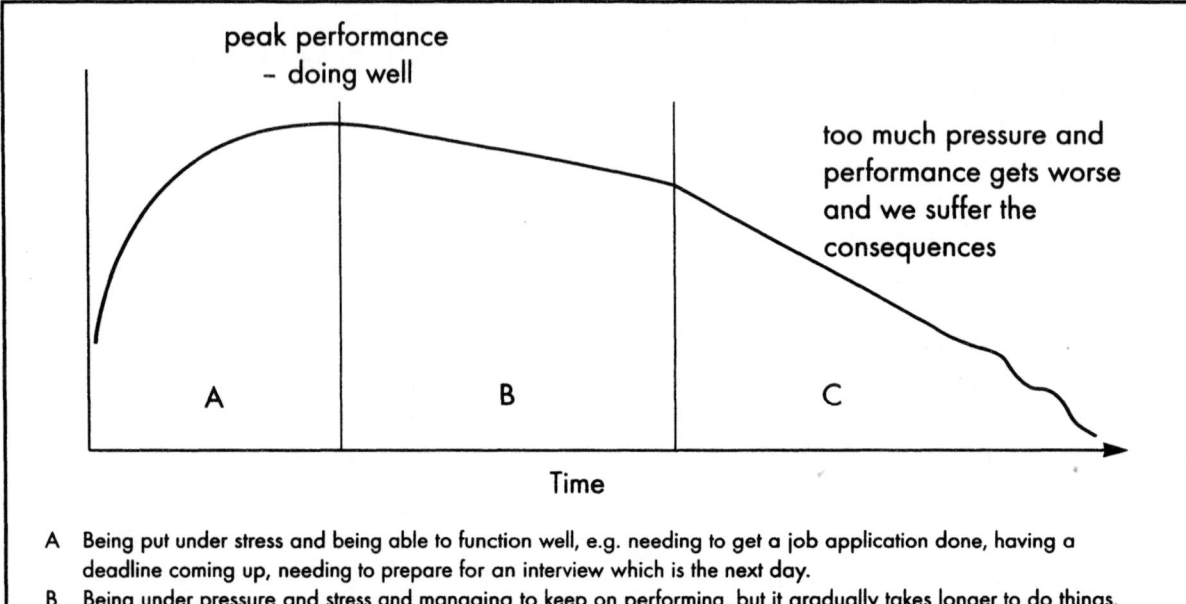

A   Being put under stress and being able to function well, e.g. needing to get a job application done, having a deadline coming up, needing to prepare for an interview which is the next day.
B   Being under pressure and stress and managing to keep on performing, but it gradually takes longer to do things, more mistakes are made, people begin to feel and function less well.
C   Stress has gone on for too long and exhaustion, fatigue, ill-health are the results.

The diagram should be drawn on a flipchart and the learners may like to think how examples from their own lives illustrate the ABC phases of the diagram. Check that the learners are happy with the information which has been discussed. Conclude this session with a brainstorm.

Brainstorm (10 min)

Ask the learners to brainstorm:

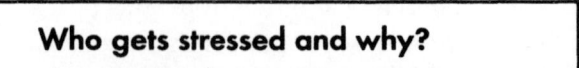

Who gets stressed and why?

Write the answers on a flipchart. Prompt the group if it gets stuck. Prompts could include such things as:

- occupational groups
- times in people's lives
- events which happen to people

The group should be prompted to cover every age of person, every occupation, life events and activities which people try. These should be listed on the flipchart. In brief *anyone* can get stressed.

Session Three: People can make themselves more stressed

From the starting point that everyone may suffer stress the group can analyse what people do to make their own experiences of stress worse and to cause themselves stress. Explain that you are going to look at three types of people:

- Type A people
- People who create stress and have poor personal management skills
- People with poor coping strategies

1. Type A people (25 min)

Type A people are prone to high stress experiences and often these are of their own making. They are keen to be productive, to do a lot of things at once. They are tense, nervy sorts of people who take very little in their stride. They are considered very likely to be heart attack victims. They are often highly enthusiastic and able to carry other people along with them.

The opposite of Type A behaviour is Type B behaviour. These people are often laid back, may be easier to be with but they may get little done or may just allow things to drift. These people may find it hard to get themselves motivated or to encourage others to get on with things.

There is a questionnaire for learners to complete to think about their own behavioural responses. Ask the learners to complete ST3: Stress questionnaire 1.

Feedback (20 min)
Find out how many rate themselves as Type A people. Ask those who are Type A people to give some examples of their behaviours, what it feels like to them and how they think others experience such behaviour. Record these ideas. Ask those non-Type A people to say what they think about Type A behaviour and what it is like to be around such behaviour. Record these ideas. Then ask if any can suggest what Type A people can do to reduce their experience of stress. Record these suggestions on a flipchart and ways in which they can be implemented. For example, part of dealing with the self-created stress of Type A people would be to deal with the behaviours of rushing, interrupting others, being pushy and being hostile to others.

2. People who create stress and have poor personal management skills (20 min)

Another group of people likely to get stressed are those who have a particularly negative outlook on life or who feel little able to take control over their lives.

Ask the learners to work through ST4: Stress questionnaire 2. This questionnaire should highlight particular attitudes or ways of viewing the world which can cause individual learners to experience the world as a more stressful and overwhelming place than it need be.

Feedback (20 min)
Ask the learners to indicate their scores. Pick a few of the items on the list and ask the learners what they think these mean and for examples of the ways in which these might happen. Ask the learners to then suggest ways people could avoid falling into the traps, e.g. of being put upon or having negative ways of thinking and record these.

Find out how any learners would value work on areas such as:

- developing positive attitudes

- work on self-esteem
- becoming more assertive

Note this for future group and individual programme planning.

3. People with poor coping strategies (20 min)

The third way in which people can cause themselves stress is through the ways in which they cope with their lives and manage situations. Some people make or add to the stress they experience by the ways in which they go about their lives. They put themselves under pressure by putting things off to the last minute, by getting over-committed and doing too many things at once. These people, for example, do not allow enough time to complete a task e.g. complete a form or job application or to complete a journey.

Some people respond to setbacks, such as traffic jams, being in a queue in a shop, having to wait for information at a Job Centre, Benefits Office or hospital by getting aggressive, anxious about the delay and by looking at their watches or pacing up and down. These may be Type A behavioural responses or the product of not having allowed enough time to complete the task in hand. None of these things makes anything happen faster. It just makes the person feel worse. These ways of responding need to be dealt with.

Poor management of personal resources: time, money, relationships, personal emotions and poor management of oneself with others can all lead to unnecessarily stressful situations. Ask the learners to complete ST5: Stress Questionnaire 3. This can be used to help highlight any problems people have in these areas.

Feedback (10 min)
Ask what issues or areas the learners have identified as being ones which could be worked on. Record these and consider how this information may be used to further shape the group's learning programme.

Summary activity (10 min)
Ask the learners to look back over their Stress Questionnaires 1–3 and to then complete ST6, the Learner's summary sheet.

Feedback (10 min)
Ask for examples of ways in which stress is self-created and ask for examples of solutions for such stress. Discuss the suggestions and find out how the learners will put the proposed solutions into practice. Encourage the learners to think about the ways in which they can benefit from sharing these ideas. Allow a couple of minutes for anyone to add to their summary sheet or for learners with similar problems to identify each other.

Session Four: Getting stressed and the consequences of stress

This session focuses on the consequences of stress – the psychological, physical, behavioural and social consequences of stress.

Role-play activity: getting stressed and what happens (1 hour)

Divide the learners into groups of four and give each group one of the suggested role-plays on activity sheet ST7. Remind the learners of all the work they have done on why people get stressed and how they respond. Allow ten minutes for the characters to get in role and decide on their role play.

Presentation and discussion

Ask each group to present their role-play to the whole group. This will take a few minutes, then spend the remainder of the ten minutes for the group members to question the various characters while they remain in role.

Encourage those who are watching to ask:

- What did it feel like to be so stressed?
- Had you not been stressed what would have happened?
- What did the stress lead you to do?
- What was it like trying to communicate/to be with someone so stressed?
- How did their stress make you feel?

Ask the actors to be their real selves and to comment on any differences and similarities between their reactions to the situation of the role-play when they are in role and not in role.

Ask the learners how they felt becoming stressed or being near a stressed character. Draw out the points and record them on the flipchart under the headings suggested below.

What did the stress feel like?	Where did being stressed lead the character?
How was the situation changed by the stress response?	How was the stress experienced by the other characters?
How did the stress response cause damage?	What could have been done if the character had not been stressed?

As a group, analyse the points which are on the flipchart. Decide what were the consequences of stress and record or highlight these. Decide what could have been avoided or done differently and highlight these points

Personal responses to stress (30 min)

The following activity should help the learners to think about the ways in which they respond to stress situations.

Give the learners a set of cards, ST8. They should sort through the cards selecting about ten cards which are their usual reactions to stress. If their usual responses are not on the cards then they should write them on the backs of some of the printed cards.

Then they should begin to complete their stress response sheet (ST9), finding common patterns of how they respond to stress, thinking about how they appear to themselves and to others. This can be done with a drawing or by writing down any images or words.

These activities are intended to encourage the learner to think about their own responses, how they make themselves feel when under stress and how they appear to other people. Raising awareness in this way will then move the learner on to thinking about steps to change and to discovering better ways to deal with stress.

In pairs (15 min)

Ask the learners to work in pairs and to compare their top ten responses and the effects that these have on themselves and on the way they feel about and are seen by others. Ask the learners to consider which reactions to stress they would like to change and to list these. Ask the learners to consider in their pairs how they might do this.

Feedback (15 min)

Ask each pair to offer two responses they want to change and their suggestions for changing them. Ask the rest of the group to add to the list of proposed suggestions.

The learners should have time to record these ideas.

The trainer should take note of areas which the learners would like to tackle and to consider what referrals may be needed, further sessions or how to get other help for individuals. This thinking will be needed for the final session.

Session Five: The effects of stress and getting stress smart

What happens if stress is not dealt with? (15 min)

Ask the group to think about the effects of stress and brainstorm as a group what happens if stressful situations go on. Try to collect ideas under the headings of:

Physical effects of stress	Psychological effects of stress
Social effects of stress	Behavioural effects of stress

While the group may think about the effects of stress on the individual you may want to encourage the learners to also think about effects on families, friends, workmates and others. Record ideas about the effects of individuals on other people.

ST10 lists some consequences of stress. This handout can be a reminder to learners of the symptoms of stress. Work through the handout on these consequences of stress. Ask the learners if they agree with the list or can think of other consequences.

Tackling stress: brainstorm, explanation and discussion (1 hour 25 min)

Ask the group to think of the positive and negative ways in which they do or could deal with stress. Record all the answers on a flipchart. Do not pass any comments at this stage about any things which are positive or negative. Allow ten minutes for this.

After the brainstorm work through the thirteen points with the group on ST11.

As each point is explained:

- review what it means to the learners
- ask for examples of similar things which they have done and how well they worked
- ask how they would implement any of the points in their own lives

Summary (15 min)

Ask the learners to work alone on S12, the module summary sheet for ten minutes. Share some of the points which the learners have made.

Taking action (40 min)

Give out ST13, Action plan, and go through the headings to ensure the learners know what is wanted. Ask the learners to complete their own action plan. One-to-one help should be provided while the learners are completing the form. Some learners may need help with referrals and addresses of useful agencies. The learners should be encouraged to discuss their plans and seek other ideas from a fellow learner. Suggest that some learners may want to work with each other to support each other's change plans.

Closure (10 min)

Close the session with an activity to bring the group back together, e.g. 'Rain forest' or 'Counting to ten'.

Thank the learners for their work.

ST2: Information sheet – what is stress?

Stress is the collection of feelings and responses which are the result of external and/or internal demands or events and an individual's ability for dealing with them.

Everyone deals with situations differently and experiences them differently, so while some people may experience stress others may not.

Sometimes an individual finds something just too much. At other times that person takes the same thing in their stride. How a person responds and copes with a demand or event will depend on:

- their state of health
- how well or badly other things are going in life
- if the event is basically positive and wanted, e.g. a new baby
- if the event is seen as negative and a bad thing, e.g. a death, loss of job, being in prison
- if the person understands the demand or event
- if the person has previous experience which can help him or her deal with the stressful event

The person's basic personality will also affect how stressful something is. Some people make things more stressful for themselves by worrying, leaving it all to the last minute, or by not confronting problems so they get worse.

Stress can be caused by good things, e.g. a new job, getting a pay rise or promotion, having a new relationship or moving to a new house. Stress can be caused by bad things, e.g. loss of job, loss of home, death, break-up of a relationship or family, getting ill.

Stress can be caused when something changes or more or different demands are made on you. Dealing successfully with stress means finding ways to get things back into balance again, by dealing with the stressful event so it is no longer so demanding or by coming to terms with it so it is no longer destructive.

We all need stress to be able to function well. Without stress we may not get round to doing things, may take a long time to do something simple or may not do it as well as if we were under some pressure.

ST1: What does stress mean to me?

- What causes stress for me?
- How do I react to stress?
- What does it feel like?
- How do others experience my response to being stressed?

- Do I like stress?
- What causes stress for others?
- How do others seem when they are stressed?
- Do I need stress?

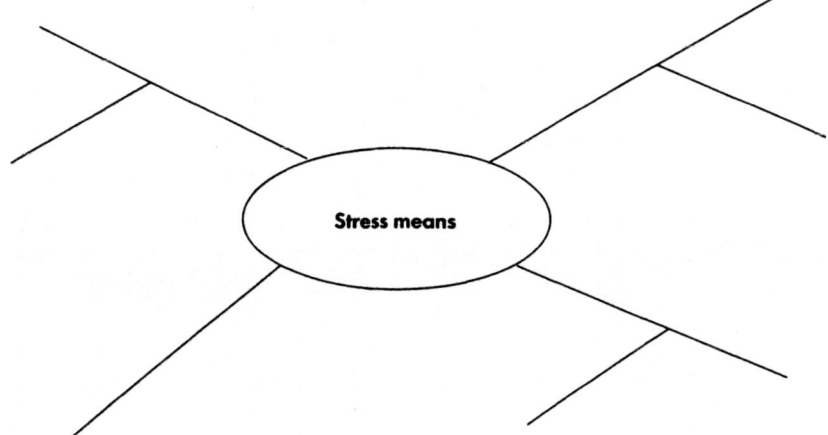

Jot down words or phrases in answer to these questions. Add more lines as needed. Write down as many ideas as possible

ST3: Stress questionnaire 1

Are you a type A person?

Tick any statement which applies to you

	Yes	No
Do you hide your feelings?		
Do you try to do several things at once?		
Do you have several jobs on the go?		
Do you think that you walk faster, talk faster, eat faster than others?		
Are you ambitious?		
Do you want others to notice you?		
Are you competitive?		
Do you hate waiting for things to happen?		
Do you often finish other peoples' sentences or interrupt them?		
Do you get impatient with people?		
Do you want to get conversations round to your own interests?		
Do you take yourself seriously?		
Do you tend to be tense?		
Do people find you bossy?		

The more ticks in the yes column, the more likely you are to be a Type A person

How do you think others feel being around you? Write a few words about each situation.

- at home
- in a shopping queue
- at work

ST4: Stress questionnaire 2

Do you find yourself prone to stress?

Read the following statements and ✓ Yes or No

	Yes	No
1. Are you negative about yourself?		
2. Are you negative about others		
3. When things go wrong do you tend to feel overwhelmed?		
4. Do you see change as difficult or as likely to create problems?		
5. Do you think when things go right it is fate?		
6. Do you often feel put upon?		
7. Do you blame other people when things go wrong?		
8. Do you often feel tense or anxious for no real reason?		
9. If you have a problem do you keep on thinking about it?		
10. Do you set yourself clear and realistic goals?		
11. Do you know how to get what you want from life?		
12. Do you often do things you do not want to do?		
13. Do you often say 'no' to other people?		
14. Do people think of you as fun to be around?		
15. Do you feel in control of yourself and your life?		
16. Can you easily enjoy yourself?		
17. Do you ever praise yourself for succeeding?		
18. Do you ever praise yourself for succeeding?		
19. Do you take things in your stride?		
Total		
Overall score		

Score 2 for every Yes you answered for questions 1-9. Score 0 for every No for questions 1-9.

Score 2 for every No you answered for questions 10-18. Score 0 for every Yes you answered for questions 10-17.

The higher your score the more you need to think very carefully about your attitudes towards your life and other people.
If you are generally negative, serious in outlook, anticipate problems and do not take control over yourself, then you are more likely to experience stress.

ST6: Learners' summary sheet

On the following scale mark X where you place yourself

I do not create stress
for myself

I create a lot of
stress for myself

I have found out that I create stress for myself by:

I can improve on this by:

ST5: Stress questionnaire 3

Do I create stress by the ways I deal with life?

Read the statements and ✓ Yes or No depending on how they apply to you

	Yes	No
Do you leave things to the last minute?		
Do you fall behind with repayments?		
Are you often running to catch a bus or train?		
Do you get to work, training programmes or meetings on time?		
Do you have enough money at the end of the week or month to stay in credit?		
Do you have enough friends to help you if you have problems?		
Do you put off important decisions?		
Do you try to tackle everything that has piled up at once?		
Have you got into difficulties for not paying TV licence, car tax or rent?		
Do you have a clear sense of what you want to achieve?		
Do you know how to check whether you are making progress towards your goals?		
Do you write yourself lists of things you need to do?		
Do you have a diary?		
Do you keep a budget?		
Do you know where to find important phone numbers?		
If you can't do something do you just leave it?		
Do you ask for help if you need it?		
Have you missed a job or collecting benefits because you did not send off for details/completed form?		

List areas with which you feel you could benefit from some help.

Pick out your ten most frequent reactions to stress

Drink more	Smoke more	Do more drugs
Eat more junk food	Sleep more	Sleep less
Think about my problems	Spend more time alone	Spend less time with friends/family
Try to find other things to take my mind off it – the riskier the better	Spend more money	Go out more and run away from my problems
Give up and feel a failure	Get weepy and less able to cope with things	Feel moody

Photocopy onto thin card and cut out each of the cards

ST7: Role plays

Give each group one of the following four scenes.

1. It's Phil's first interview after five months of applying for over fifty jobs since his last and unsuccessful interview. In all he has been out of work for nine months. The situation at home is tense.

2. You and your new partner have just moved house and you discover an ex boy or girlfriend lives two doors away. How does this affect you and your new partner? How is the ex-reacting?

3. "But I thought you said you could get the money – now what are we going to do?" One friend is angered by the other's financial problems. They are trying to run a business together.

4. You are sent to prison on suspicion of receiving stolen goods. What effect is this having on the person remanded and their family?

Not want to eat	Want to hide from other people	Feel more tired
Spend time indoors away from others	Give up on outside interests	Get involved in any other activity to stop dealing with the stressful one
Loss of interest in hobbies or activities	Become unreliable, e.g. not going to work, not seeing friends	Feel bad about myself
Spend more time watching TV	Feel everything's against me	Feel a failure
Feel down and uninteresting	Denying that there's anything wrong	Feel that no-one gives me a chance

Photocopy onto thin card and cut out each of the cards

Not make an effort about how I look	Seek help and guidance from people who can help me	Take it out on people close to me
Cut myself off from others	Get obsessive about what is causing me stress	Not listen to other people's suggestions
Feel anxious, panicked and tense	Get into arguments, conflicts or fights with others more easily	Have poorer communication skills
Take it out on myself, cut myself or damage myself	Feel people are quick to pick on me	Get into rages and tempers easily
Try to find out how to deal with the stressful situation	Keep talking to others about my problem often in the same way	Keep thinking about my problems

Photocopy onto thin card and cut out each of the cards

ST10: Being under too much stress for too long

The following are some of the ways people react to stress. The effects get worse or more of an established habit the longer the stress goes on. These consequences of stress get harder to manage and harder to change the longer that stress goes on.

See Zone C on the diagram below

Physical	Behavioural	Social	Psychological
Headache	More drinking	Relationships suffer	Poorer concentration
Backaches	More smoking	Not being interested in others	Not listening properly
Mysterious aches and pains	Using drugs to get less tense	Not paying attention to work	Poorer decision-making
Pains in the chest	Having more accidents	Becoming isolated	Depression
Poor sleep	Having more outbursts of emotion	Letting other people down	Being irritable
Digestive problems including ulcers	Being more compulsive		Feeling anxious
Conditions such as asthma, skin troubles and diabetes get worse			Suffering fatigue

peak performance – doing well

too much pressure and performance gets worse and we suffer the consequences

a little stress motivates people — A

stress goes on and performance gets a little worse – more mistakes, slower working — B

C

Time

ST9: My stress responses

My usual ways to respond to stress are to:

-
-
-
-
-
-
-
-

When I'm stressed other people will see me as:
Write a few words or phrases or draw an image of yourself

When I'm stressed I will see myself as:
Again, write down some words or phrases or draw a picture of what you look like

When I am stressed I have the following feelings/thoughts about other people:

ST11: Tackle your stress

These thirteen points will help you to think about new ways to manage stress.

1. Can you change it?

Can you look at the situation differently?

Can you change how you feel, or feel less strongly about it?

If you can't change something can you change your attitude, thought patterns or responses?

You may find stepping away from a situation, spending less time on it or discussing it with someone not directly involved in the situation, will help you.

2. Think about your coping strategies

How many are negative ones which may make you feel worse? e.g. alcohol, smoking more, more drug use, taking little rest or sleep, worrying and going over issues.

How many are positive? e.g. taking a break from the problem, talking things through with others, taking time to look after yourself, get rest and exercise, eating sensibly, looking for alternative solutions.

3. Are you looking after yourself?

Are you: eating a balanced diet?

           taking exercise?

           getting sufficient sleep?

           being positive about yourself?

           trying to make yourself do the impossible?

4. Get people around you who can help

Look for people who could help with difficult situations or who may just be able to talk things through with you.

5. Are you seriously finding solutions or just going over the same ground?

Are you, e.g. have you found someone to talk to help you better manage the stressful situation; have you worked out what is making you so stressed?

6. Are you managing to find time for others or doing things for others?

Being stressed often makes people very preoccupied and self-concerned. In the long-run stress ruins relationships and destroys friendships.

---

7. Are you managing the feelings which are part of stress, recognising what they are and finding ways to cope with them or to get rid of them?

For example, storing anger, feelings of hurt, feeling ill-used or rejected will all become more powerful if left to fester, and possibly they will become increasingly unrelated to the stressful event or incident which caused them.

8. Are you making the stress worse for yourself?

- Are you brooding on the events which caused the stress?
- Are you failing to look for solutions and feeling like a victim?
- Are you abusing yourself with drink, drugs and other self-medication?
- Are you losing sight of the reality of the stressful situation or event?
- Are you cutting yourself off from other people?

If you are answering yes to any of these, then you need to be trying to do the opposite. For example, stop taking it out on yourself, see other people, talk about something other than the stress-making problems.

9. Take a break

Take a holiday for a few days, do something different, do something to escape – go to see a film, go for a long walk.

10. Acknowledge you are stressed

Know what signs to look for and find out the cause of the stress then,

11. Tackle it

Break down the problem into manageable chunks.

12. If you cannot tackle it, then think about making the problem not a stressor.

Accept or acknowledge it or remove yourself from the problem.

13. Get a range of different things in your life.

Try to balance the stressful activity or demand with other things. They may be distractions or may be other stressful or challenging activities but ones which are positive.

ST13: Action plan

My action plan for reducing stress

The following situations are causing me greatest stress at the moment:

The things about these situations which cause me most stress are:

I plan to tackle these situations by taking the following actions. (Write down action steps and dates for each situation.)

Action steps	Start date

ST12: Learner's summary sheet

Think about all you have learned so far and complete the three boxes below

So far I have found out the following new facts about stress and its causes:

I would add the following new ideas to the ways I usually manage my own stress:

I would like to tackle the following stressful situations in my life:

S T13: Action plan – continued

I am going to help myself by: Write down a list of the:

- Ways you can support yourself
- Who can help you and how?
- How can you reward yourself for dealing with these stresses?
- What will you do to give yourself a break while you are dealing with your stressful situation?
- How you can measure your own progress in dealing with the stressful situations.

The date on which you will review your progress will be _____

Managing change

 The module is divided into five sessions:

1. Exploring change and types of changes (2 hours 30 min)

2. Dealing with forced changes (2 hours)

3. Positive thinking (3 hours)

4. Planning changes and taking charge (2 hours 30 min)

5. Progressive and involuntary changes and closing activities (1 hour 30 min)

 The trainer might like to link this module with *Exercise and well-being, Identifying and managing stress* and *Developing positive attitudes*.

 The module requires that the learner be familiar with the following learning activities:

- role-play and hot seating

- brainstorm

- discussion – whole and small group

- self-assessment tasks

- using choice cards

🍎 *Trainer's notes*

This module looks at change and its management from the perspective that change is a natural and normal part of everyday life. Managing change is not simply dealing with the one-off major positive or negative event such as having a new child or the death of a parent. Change management is about dealing with day-to-day changes such as managing new technology, managing the changing patterns and demands of work and understanding changes in children's lives.

Changes are a fundamental part of every area of our lives. Becoming able to manage change has many benefits for the individual, knowing when to change, to develop new or alternative skills makes someone *change-aware* and knowing what changes to make and how to make them, makes someone *change-smart*. Effectively managing life means becoming change-aware and change-smart.

This module aims to raise the learners' awareness of the main types of change:

- progressive changes which are a normal part of life

- the sudden or crisis type of change

- planned changes

The module aims to help learners by:

- encouraging a sense of being competent and confident to manage change

- developing the skills to manage change and to evaluate personal success in negotiating periods of change and sustaining a change

- encouraging an awareness of the differences between externally imposed change and self-generated changes and the strategies to manage both and feel empowered

Session One: Exploring change and types of change

🍎 Trainer's notes

The session opens the issue of change to examination by the group. The learners may think of change only as dealing with major life events, and so think of change only in negative terms such as crises or as externally imposed upsets over which they have no control. While these are indeed life changes, this opening activity should encourage the learners to consider other types of change such as:

- change as a natural part of life, e.g., dealing with new technologies or coming to terms with ageing
- change as something which they as individuals can plan, can make happen and can manage

Three opening brainstorms: identifying change and types of changes (35 min)

Ask the group to brainstorm the following question for 15 min:

> **What is change?**

Ask the group to give some examples of change and encourage a wide range of examples. Try to get examples of personal changes common to most people, world events and technological changes. Their lists could include:

- getting married
- the Internet
- making use of solar panels and wind power
- death
- divorce or splitting up with spouse
- computer literate children
- microwaveable food
- new job

- Berlin Wall coming down
- wars
- being unemployed
- getting older
- advances in space travel
- electronic tagging
- scanning images
- barcode readers in supermarkets

Ask the group to look at the list and to work out what types of changes they can find. Help them to identify the three types of change:

- inevitable changes, ageing, the fact that things change
- sudden changes, personal or in the world, e.g. a war or a death
- planned changes, e.g. stopping drug use or drinking, taking a new training course on computers

On the flipchart paper separate out the different types of changes and add any new examples the group thinks of (10 min).

Progressive change/ Inevitable change	Sudden change	Planned change

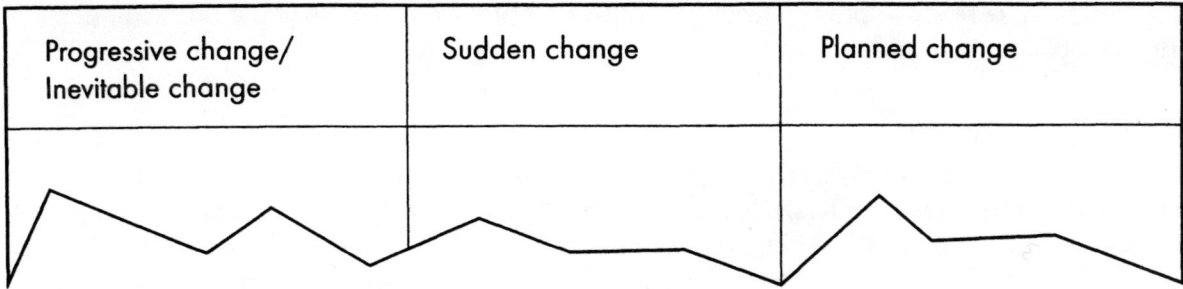

Consider with the group the question for the final 10 minutes:

Is change good or bad?

You should try to get examples of why some are good changes and some are bad, and that even seemingly good changes, for instance getting a new partner, having a child, can create problems, while changes which seem bad, such as loss of job or splitting up with a partner may have some good outcomes in the longer-term.

Individual starting points

 Trainer's notes

This activity encourages the learners to think about the types of changes which they have experienced and their responses to change. At the close of the activity the learners should have some views about their own current powers to manage change.

Working alone (20 min)

Ask the learners to work alone for ten minutes, completing MC1 on change in their lives. After ten minutes ask if anyone wants to read out a few of the changes they have put down. This may help the others in the group to complete their change lists. Now read through MC2 with the group and check that the learners understand it. Ask the group to work alone for ten minutes, complete MC2 thinking carefully about a few of the changes they have listed on their spider diagrams. The trainer will need to move around the room checking and helping individual learners to think about the changes they have experienced and how they have managed them.

Working in pairs or threes (30 min)

As the exercise (MC2) is completed ask the learners to get into small groups of three or into pairs. Ask each learner to select a change and to talk about:

- Do the others agree that the score is about right?
- Do they agree with the suggestions for other ways to manage the change?
- Would they have done the same?

This sharing of experiences should not be used as a chance to criticise each other but as a chance to show people if they are being overly hard on themselves or to explore how others would have managed the change. This sharing activity may show other ways to manage changes and so expand the individual's understanding of ways to manage changes.

More work on the change stories (15 min)

After they have exchanged change experiences ask the small groups to be ready to look at all the experiences listed on MC2 to find:

- some examples of changes which went well and the sorts of reasons the change went well
- some examples of changes which did not go so well and some of the reasons why this was the case

Ask the groups to be ready to provide feedback some examples to the whole group but without identifying individual group members.

Group feedback (20 min)

On the flipchart draw three columns for changes working well, changes working badly and the reasons for why it works well or badly. Note the examples of the changes and the reasons. Some groups may give an example as working well, others that it was a bad change, e.g. getting married, having a child or moving. The differences of the experience will come back to such reasons as the change being planned or not planned, wanted or not wanted, accepted or not. This should provide good material for discussion about the power of individual's perceptions.

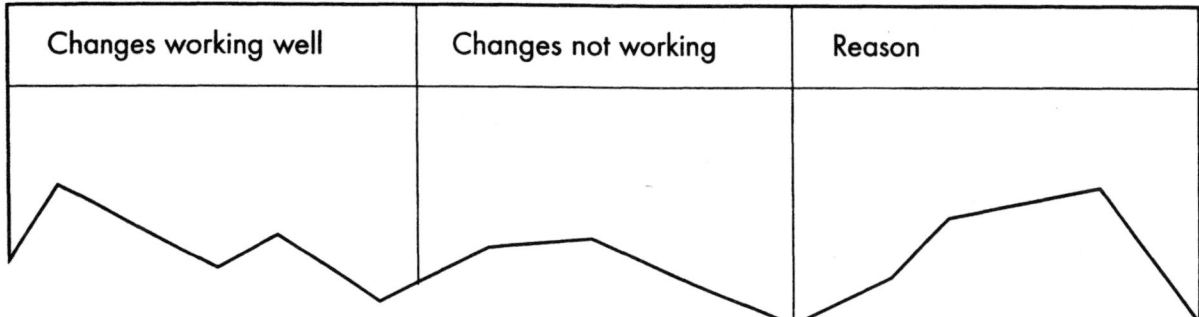

Changes working well	Changes not working	Reason

Some examples are listed below.

Why do changes work?

- want them, e.g. getting married
- plan for them, e.g. going on holiday or moving house
- happening gradually and time to get used to it
- not too big a change

Why do changes not work?

- not want them, e.g. being made redundant
- not prepared for them, e.g. house fire
- resist them, e.g. someone who is ill and dying
- not be able to manage them, e.g. birth of new child
- becomes a cause of conflict, e.g. splitting up with partner

Drawing the threads together

This has two parts. Firstly ask the learners to work alone using MC3 and then have a whole group feedback.

Individual work: MC3 (10 min)

Go through MC3 and ask the group if they understand what is wanted. Ask them to complete it. The learners will need to keep this worksheet to use again.

Feedback (20 min)

1. Ask the group to volunteer some things they have written. They do not have to give their individual marks, but it would be useful to know:
   - what they have learned about change
   - what they would like to work on – come back to this list when you cover point 3 below.

2. Summarise the main points from the opening session:
   - different types of change
   - change is a normal part of life so needs to be managed
   - people may manage some types of change better or worse than they manage others
   - some reasons for successfully managing change
   - some reasons for less successfully managing change

3. Ask what the learners would like to consider in a module on change. Record this and ensure that the expectations are met or referrals are made.

4. Outline the remaining sessions which will be covered. Link this with the learners' voiced expectations.

Session Two: Dealing with forced changes

Role-play and hot-seating (up to 1 hour 15 min)

Ask the participants to form into groups of three or four and give out the scenarios on **MC4**. Each group will need a different scene. The scene offers a few details about a situation which could be thought of as a disaster by some but which others may see as a chance for making positive changes. Let each group decide how it interprets its scene and acts out what can be done.

Allow each group ten minutes to prepare and then ask each in turn to role-play their scene. At the close of each, tell the characters to stay in their roles and then ask them, and encourage those in the audience to ask questions such as:

- How did it feel when ...?
- Did it seem fair ...?
- Do you think that was a reasonable/understandable reaction ...?
- What will you do next and why ...?
- What do you think will happen next ...?

Out of role the learners can be asked to say what they may have done or how they may have reacted had they been faced with a similar situation.

Group discussion (45 min)

Discuss with the whole group once all the scenes have been played out, how many groups dealt with the situation positively, how many negatively and why this was so. Question the groups to find out what characteristics those who responded *positively* showed. Contrast these with those shown by people who responded *negatively*. Record these positive characteristics or behaviours on the flipchart. However, if no group responded positively then ask each to re-form into their original small groups and ask them to work out a positive outcome.

Ask for one group to volunteer to enact their scene positively. Then question the characters as follows:

- How did it feel to be positive rather than negative?
- How do you feel about yourself in this more positive scene?
- How likely is it that someone would be positive?
- What would stop someone responding positively?
- How do you prefer yourself, as positive or negative?

Discuss the attributes which each group identified as important in the positive outcomes and write these on the flipchart. The features or qualities which the learners identify as part of a positive response may include:

- not being afraid to change
- humour
- sense of perspective
- having friends/people to talk to
- having inner resources
- not giving in
- not panicking
- seeing a challenge and taking it
- being prepared to have a go
- not being defeated
- trying again

Session Three: Positive thinking

 Trainer's notes

From the previous activity it should have become clear to the group that even when confronting a forced change there are ways to respond to it and then manage it successfully. This session on positive thinking links managing changes of whatever type with planning life goals, problem-solving, thinking creatively, decision-making and self-esteem. It should be stressed that positive thinking is a powerful tool which learners may choose to use.

You may face some opposition and negativity when you try to explain what positive thinking is. Comments may include such as:

- "so what if I think about making changes – I can't afford it/they won't go along with it."
- "it doesn't matter what I want I won't get it."
- "people like me don't get such a chance to make changes to their lives."

Positive thinking – lecturette with group providing examples (45 min)

Use an OHT (**MC1**) to support your lecturette. The key points you need to make are:

1. Positive thinking means playing the key part in your life and not letting others write your life plan for you. You need to see yourself taking charge of your life and making the changes you want to get the life that you want.

2. The opposite of positive thinking is negative thinking. People say to themselves:
   "I can't do ..."
   "It won't work if ..."
   "People like me just don't ..."
   "I never had a chance ..."
   "I will never be able to ..."

   These negative statements are very powerful excuses to do nothing, not to take risks and to make no changse. People manage to make themselves stay in situations they do not want or like, or manage to make themselves fail because they have become so good at negative thinking.

3. Ask the group to give you some examples of negative thinking and the phrases which people often use and which they themselves may say. Write these on the flipchart. These may include:
   - "I always fail when ..."
   - "Last time I tried ... it went wrong"
   - "I don't want to look an idiot in front of the others, so ..."
   - "It's better if I don't go to ..."
   - "Someone else is bound to get the job ..."
   - "There's always someone better than me ..."
   - "There's no point in me applying ..."
   - "I can't save ..."
   - "I can't stop drinking ..."
   - "No-one is interested in my so why ..."

   The fact that the group can come up with so many examples will give a clear idea of how powerful negative thinking is.

4. Positive thinking is the reverse of negative thinking. It is:
   - saying positive and encouraging things to oneself and others
   - brainstorming and having lots of ideas to try out

- looking at a situation as a puzzle or a problem and thinking how to tackle it
- thinking about past successes
- not thinking about past failures
- fantasising about or imaging success
- writing lists of things that can be done
- not giving up and feeling hopeless
- having a clear image of yourself with everything you want falling into place
- stopping people around you thinking negative things about you or your situation
- moving away from people who are going to be negative
- remembering other times when problems were solved
- rewarding yourself for achievements

5. Positive thinking has to be more than a fantasy about things going right. While the individual should act as if things are going to be right and they should have clear action steps to follow to make the positive changes happen.

When doubts from others or self-doubt creeps in the individual should have phrases to say to affirm what is being done or what is to be achieved. The individual should combat doubt by looking for progress and making progress steps in a visible way, e.g. ticking things off a list. The individual needs to have a clear statement or picture of what is to be achieved. This can be read and re-read as a positive reminder. The individual needs to regularly visualise success and visualise taking the steps towards being successful.

Check that the group has understood these basic points. Discuss the group's views about these ideas:

- do they think they are reasonable?
- have they had experiences of using positive thinking or visualisation?
- have they stopped themselves through negative thought?

Explore the group's thinking and experiences so everyone is comfortable with the basic ideas.

Record the key points from the discussion and descriptions of experiences. Try to get the group to a position of agreeing that there is something of value in thinking positively.

Brainstorm (15 min)

Ask the group to think how to link the power of positive thinking with managing change.

- they can think about concrete experiences
- they can think about the process of managing change
- they can think about the ways in which positive thinking may help them to realise they can make changes

Record the ideas on the flipchart.

Consider with the group how many examples have been about making planned changes and how many about dealing with an enforced change.

Brainstorm

Ask the group to list out some ways in which positive thinking could be used:

a. in a situation of planned change
b. in a situation of unplanned change

This brainstorm will be needed for the remaining activities in this session.

Managing unsort changes: role-play (1 hour)

The group needs to get into smaller groups of 3–4 and each group needs a copy of MC5 which outlines a situation of a relationship breaking down. The groups will need to prepare their scene for ten minutes and then each group should perform it.

After each performance hot seat the characters while they are still in role. Trainer and audience should ask questions examples of which are below. All the groups will be dealing with the same situation and their different approaches will give rise to further questions about similarities and differences in managing the change.

- Why did you decide to deal with the situation like that?
- How did it feel to do that?
- What else could you have done?
- How might that have felt?
- What will happen next?

Group feedback (20 min)

Each group will have played out the same situation. As a group decide on the similarities and differences in interpreting and then in managing the situation. Record these on the flipchart. Ask the group to consider the role played by positive and negative thinking in interpreting and managing the situation. Consider alternative outcomes if a more positive approach had been taken.

Managing sort changes through positive approaches (20 min)

Working as a group ask them to give some examples of situations where positive thinking would help in managing a change situation. Put this list on the flipchart and ask for examples of positive thinking to manage those situations, e.g.

Event	Examples of positive thinking
Give up drinking	- Tell myself I can - Don't think about past failures - Find a supportive group, e.g. AA to tell me I can - Have an image of myself as a non-drinker and act that way - Think about what I can do with the money I would have spent on drink and reward myself - Be clear I and not the bottle am in charge - Don't allow other people to undermine my resolve - Think of it as someone else's problem, what positive advice would you give - Think of it as a step at a time, decide how each success will be rewarded

Summary (10 min)

Ask the learners to each offer a key point for them from the session. These should be recorded on the flipchart under the headings *Managing change* and *The role of positive thinking*.

Session Four: Planning changes and taking charge

🍎 *Trainer's notes*

This session continues the theme that change is something which the learners can control, can initiate in their lives and can manage. It encourages the learners to think about areas in life where they might like to make changes.

This session links with work on:

- Healthy living (see also *Addressing Anti-social Behaviour*)
- Managing relationships with others (see also *Developing Social Skills*)
- Managing time
- Managing money
- Developing assertiveness skills (see *Developing Social Skills*)

The session will help learners to consider what holds people back from making changes, and encourages them to consider factors such as fear, guilt, unreasonable demands from others, lack of self-esteem and self-awareness in their own cases.

Brainstorm: Do we have to wait for disaster to strike? (20 min)

Ask the group to think carefully and brainstorm the following questions:

> **Do changes only happen at time of crisis or upset?**
>
> **Why are changes likely to happen then?**
>
> **When else might changes happen?**

Try to move the group away from thinking about change as part of a causal relationship between calamity and change, and towards the idea that people may decide to make changes in their lives without first experiencing a major upheaval.

You may get a list of changes happening because:

- you get fed up with your own behaviour
- you get fed up with the consequences of your behaviour, e.g. being drunk, being broke, wasting time, being locked up, not having a job, not having a relationship
- your behaviour is putting your partner/family at risk
- you think you could do better for yourself
- you are bored

This brainstorm may also help the learners to distinguish between personally generated motivation for change and changes which others want. A change because someone is fed up with the consequences of their own behaviour may be more effective than a change which occurs because someone is threatened with loss of a relationship or job. Consider with the group the possible changes which may come about because an individual responds to pressure and changes because an individual identifies that they need to take action. Relate this back to the role-play of the difficult relationship.

How ready or willing are you to make changes? (15 min)

Ask the group to work alone with MC6. Ask them to select those cards which apply to them and then to work out what their choices suggest to them about their attitudes towards and willingness to make and manage changes. They should record what they find in a few sentences. After working alone ask the learners to share their findings with one or two other learners.

Feedback – willingness to change (20 min)

Brainstorm the question:

> ### Why are some people more ready to change than others?

From working with the change cards and talking in pairs or threes, the learners should be able to generate a list of issues like:

- less fearful
- more used to change
- had successes when change happened before
- have high self-esteem
- have self-confidence
- optimistic

- belief in self
- people who can support the person
- know why they are changing
- know what they want to achieve
- are motivated
- can see the benefits of change as they go along

These are all the positives aspects of change which have to be part of any change plan.

If the group gets stuck then ask them to brainstorm the question:

> ### Why do people not make changes?

Their answers may include:

- fear of the unknown
- a lack of imagination
- feel trapped – no money, qualifications
- no help
- partner would not like it

- the familiar past is more comfortable
- not got the money etc.
- didn't realise that change would be beneficial
- make excuses

From one or both brainstorms there should be a long list of reasons why people do want to change.

What would I want to change? (20 min)

Ask the learners to consider whether there are any changes they would like to make to their own lives and why? They can work on this by trying an individual or group brainstorm. The group brainstorm may get some ideas flowing but will not lead to the personal disclosure which the learners will need to consider their own changes. MC7 is a personal change brainstorm activity.

The learners may like to consider change from another perspective, that of imagining that they are now 65 and looking back over their lives and asking themselves three questions:

- I wish I had ...
- I wish I had not ...
- I wish I had made the effort to change ...

These questions are on MC8.

Once the learners have identified several things they would like to change, they need to consider the creation of a change plan.

Making changes (40 min)

Remind the learners what helps to make change successful and what makes changes fail. Remind them of their own attitudes to change from the card selection exercise. Go through points such as:

- no clear idea why
- fear
- easier to stay as it is
- benefits seem a long way off
- guilt – it would upset someone else

Remind the learners that some of the things people say to themselves are very powerful in keeping people where they are but they do need to be tackled. This session will help learners to tackle their own negativity. Ask the learners to volunteer one thing from their own change brainstorm. Record this on the flipchart. Ask the learners to offer reasons for the change and what may stop the change. Layout the flipchart sheet as below:

```
┌─────────────────────────────────────────────────────────────────┐
│                                                                   │
│  The change I want to make is:                                    │
│                                                                   │
│                                                                   │
│                                                                   │
│  The reason for the change is:                                    │
│                                                                   │
│                                                                   │
│                                                                   │
│  The things which may stop me are:                                │
│                                                                   │
│                                                                   │
│                                                                   │
└─────────────────────────────────────────────────────────────────┘
```

Ask the rest of the group to help the learner to add to their list of reasons for change and the things which may stop the changes. Record these. Now ask the group to think of ways to deal with or find solutions to the things which may stop the changes. Having practised this as a group ask the learners to try working on an individual change plan by asking the group to complete the first half of MC9. Once the group has completed this ask them to work in pairs or threes to compare plans and to see if they can help each other to find more ways to deal with any difficulties.

A change plan (25 min)

Ask the learners to complete the rest of their change plan, MC9. Before starting to complete these plans check that the group understands what is required. Ask for examples of what each heading wants. Remind the learners about the ways to be successful:

- saying positive things to themselves
- having small and clear steps to follow
- knowing when progress has been made

You will need to help the learners to complete the action steps towards change.

Explain to the learners that they will need to be ready to deal with others' doubts and disbelief as well as their own. They will need to have rewards for themselves as they make progress. These need to be part of the plan.

Once the plans have been completed, remind the learners that they may find it useful to work with someone else. Two or so people may want to make the same changes and so can share, e.g. the problems and pains of giving up smoking. Or they may just want the support of someone else who is trying to make a change and can share the process and difficulties.

Ask the learners to look at their plans in pairs or threes to see if anyone else can offer any good ideas and to see if it is possible to set up 'change partnerships' to support each other. Explain what a change partnership is (MC10).

Drawing the threads together (10 min)

Find out how many have decided to set up change partnerships and check that they know how to make these work.

Ask the group to repeat for a final time what will make their change plan work. Write these suggestions on the flipchart, e.g. positive attitude, visualising success, ticking off progress, using problem-solving skills, explaining to others what is being sought and seeking their help and support.

Suggest the group members try the change plans for one week and then review it.

Session Five: Progressive and involuntary changes and closing activities

 Trainer's notes

A final area of change to consider are changes which everyone experiences and to which your learners will have to acclimatise. These include *personal* changes such as:

- ageing
- changes to health as a result of ageing
- normal life events which we all experience and for which people can prepare, such as loss, moving home

and *external* changes such as:

- changes in technology which affect leisure and entertainment, travel, the sense of the world and workplace skills
- changes in the world of work

This session need not take long but it is a useful way to round off the previous work on change which has considered dealing with sudden changes, e.g. death, health and unemployment and planned changes, e.g. terminating a relationship, dealing with a substance abuse habit, re-training for new employment. These inevitable and progressive changes are ones with which they need to come to terms. They are ones which have an impact on their everyday lives. These changes need to be managed like the more dramatic ones or the ones which they plan. If they do not come to terms with and find the means to manage these changes then they will be failing to have control over areas of their lives.

Brainstorm activity one (10 min)

Ask the learners to:

> **Identify changes which occur, over which we have little control but which will happen anyway**

You may need to prompt the learners to consider areas of life beyond themselves. Their thinking may be limited if experience of work, current affairs and a sense of the wider world have been constrained. Asking the learners to think about changes over the last ten years or to compare their lives with their children's or their parents' may be an easy way for them to grasp the significance of technological, political, social and economic changes on everyday life.

Try to generate a broad and long list of changes. Then ask the learners to try to classify the types of changes as:

- personal – part of life
             – effect of ageing

- social

- economic

- political

- technological

Brainstorm activity two (10 min)

Brainstorm with the group:

> **Why should we keep up with the changes in the wider world?**

Again, encourage a breadth of responses. These may include:

- to understand what is going on and why

- to gain employment

- to be able to help my children

- to have things to talk about

- not to be victimised or left powerless because I don't understand

Brainstorm activity three (10 min)

Brainstorm with the group:

> **What frightens people about inevitable and progressive changes?**

On the flipchart write down the suggestions on the left hand side and some examples (see the example below). Once the group has finished listing its suggestions make use of the right hand side of the chart to record their suggestions for dealing with these fears.

Try to encourage the group to consider ways in which they need not feel left behind by changes or weakened by changes. Encourage the group to find ways to find out about changes before they happen or know how to get help when they do happen.

Fears	Sources of help/ways to deal with these fears
Being alone, e.g. death	
Being alone, e.g. being ill or immobile when old or after a relationship break-up	
Being poor, e.g. old and not able to earn, as a result of unemployment	
Not understanding, e.g. technological changes	
Not earning, e.g. not having the workskills needed in my home town anymore	

Drawing the threads together (10 min)

Go through the key ideas from the session about inevitable changes. As they are part of everyday life, the learners need to know they are skilled to deal with them.

Closing activities

This session briefly recaps the main points about managing change and is a chance for one-to-one review of the change plans.

A round robin on change (10 min)

Ask each of the learners to identify one thing from the work on change which they have found interesting or useful or both. Go around the room trying to encourage everyone to speak. If learners need to repeat what someone else has said that is fine, but try to get the learner to add a little more about what it meant to them personally. You might compare this list with the things that the group wanted to cover in Session One.

Deal with change (10 min)

Review on the flipchart as a brainstorm with the group:

> **why managing change is important**
>
> **what stops people dealing with change and what skills they must or need to have to deal with it**

One-to-one change plan reviews (30 min)

Conclude the Change module with one-to-one surgeries to look at the change plan. Help the learners to set or modify their targets, provide reinforcement for successes however partial and set further reviews and rewards with the learners. Encourage the setting up of change partnerships.

MC1: My life changes

Think about some changes which have happened or are happening in your life and write them on the spider chart.
Add more lines to the chart when you want to include more changes. Consider the types of changes you may have experienced, e.g. imposed changes, planned for changes and your response to these changes.

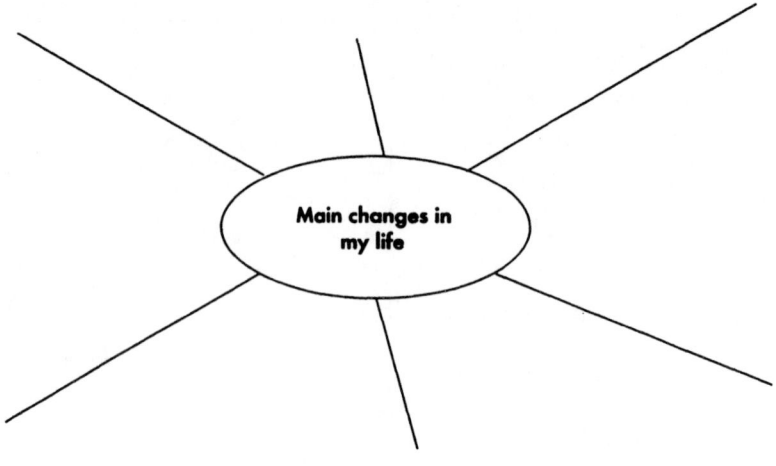

MC2: Managing changes

Think about a few different changes and complete the table below.
Some changes you may feel good about and feel that you managed well, others you may feel less good about

The change	What type of change – sudden, chosen, etc.	How did you feel about it then, some time later	How well do you think you handled it? 1=bad, 10=good Would you have done anything differently?
		Then:	1 2 3 4 5 6 7 8 9 10
			I would have done:
		Later:	
		Then:	1 2 3 4 5 6 7 8 9 10
			I would have done:
		Later:	
		Then:	1 2 3 4 5 6 7 8 9 10
			I would have done:
		Later:	
		Then:	1 2 3 4 5 6 7 8 9 10
			I would have done:
		Later:	

MC4: Dealing with forced changes

1. Joe was an experienced double-glazing fitter. He had been in his job for five years but went into work this morning and was told his company had gone bust. He was told that he and the other fitters were to be laid off. Each man took home statutory redundancy money.

   Joe has a young family. His wife Carole has not been able to get work since the youngest, Ben, was born.

2. Paula was out with her mates for a Friday night drink. On the way home from the pub she was knocked over by a drunk driver. The police arrested the driver and he awaits trial. Paula meanwhile remains in hospital. She will be referred to a Long Stay Hospital for more specialist care later this month. She is without proper use of much of her left side. Some of her body is badly scarred. She was an active athlete and had many out of work interests.

3. Roger and Jane had been married for three years. They both worked and earned a reasonable income. When Jane gave birth to their son Larry he was found to have a rare form of childhood cancer. They had spent much of Larry's first year of life in the local children's hospital. This year Larry has been less ill and at home for longer periods.

4. Your job has changed a lot over the years, but you have always managed to keep up with the changes, even going to an evening class to learn about computers in the workplace. Your boss has now offered you a big promotion, but your new job is situated 150 miles away. Your partner's job isn't very well paid but they love it and they don't want to move.

MC3: Dealing with change

Three things I have discovered about changes and the way I deal with them are:

1.

2.

3.

Overall I rate myself in dealing with changes in my life as:

1 = Poor   10 = Good

1   2   3   4   5   6   7   8   9   10

Because:

Some things I would like to do better when managing changes are:

Select those cards which best reflect your feelings about change.
There are a few blank cards if you want to write down any more feelings

Hope	I like chasing after new things, jobs, experiences, people	I prefer to always know what I am doing
I never mind a challenge	Usually change is for the worse	Like the thrill of new things
I'd rather sulk about things than confront issues	New things are exciting	Let sleeping dogs lie is my motto
I think most change is just change for change's sake	I am tired of so many changes	Don't like change
I like to plan things well in advance – I don't like sudden change	I like to know where I am going in life	I don't like being around people who stir things up
I don't like anything different for lunch	There is nothing wrong with the way things have always been done	I get scared in new situations

Photocopy onto thin card and cut out each of the cards

MC5: Role play

The characters

Two people who have been in a relationship for five years.

A friend who frequently offers advice on the relationship and is full of their own opinions.

Optional character – a close relative of one of the two partners in the worsening relationship.

The situation

The relationship has been worsening for a long time – there is distance between the two, frequent bickering and rows over very little. The two do not talk. Friend and relative often pour out their views on one or other of the partners and the relationship.

This weekend things came to a head, one of the couple has said they have had enough and want out.

- How will this situation be managed?
  - What happens next?
  - What can be done?
  - What should be done?

MC7: Making changes

Complete the spider diagram with the changes you would like to make and your reasons for making them.

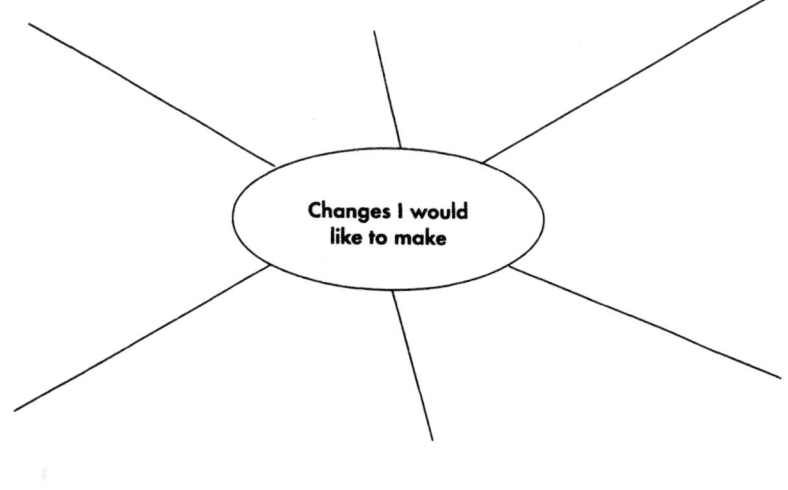

Changes I would like to make

I don't like feeling out of control – change does that to me	I'm not bothered by having to change	I like learning new things
I hate moving	Change can never be good	You can't plan for change it just happens to you
I like to have control – so I initiate changes	I plan to be in this house/job/relationship all my life	I like meeting new people
I don't like growing older	We have always done it this way – so I do	I hate changing jobs
New people just won't like me	I'm not comfortable changing cars/jobs	I always buy the same brand
Change is okay if you do it with someone else	It didn't work last time why should it now	I prefer being settled
	I might be exposed in a new situation	

MC9: Change plan

The change I want to work on is:

My reasons for making this change are:

The benefits from making this change will be:

To make the change I am going to take the following steps:

Action step	Date by which action is to be taken	People who can help me	My reward for completing this step will be
1.			
2.			
3.			
4.			

I will review my progress on: _____

MC8: Looking back I wish that I ...

Imagine that you are now 65. Look back over your life so far. Consider the phrases below and complete them to make sentences

1. Looking back I wish I had

2. Looking back I wish I had not

3. Looking back I wish I had made the effort to

Look at what you have written. Decide what changes your imagined 65 year old self would tell you to make to your life now. Write these below.

Changes I could make	Why I should make it
1	
2	
3	
4	

MC1: Positive thinking means

1. Being the person in charge of your life and not letting others drive what you do.

2. Thinking positively and not having negative thoughts about yourself, what you can do, achieve and change.

3. Deciding that you can do things for yourself and take charge of yourself.

4. Encourage yourself by thinking about all the things you can do, all the good qualities you have, all the times you have been successful and repeating these things to yourself.

5. Do not discourage yourself by thinking about things which may have gone wrong in the past or by concentrating on the things which you do not like about yourself.

6. Remind yourself that there is no such thing as a person who is a failure. There are only occasions when things which have been tried have failed.

7. Think about yourself succeeding. Imagine how it feels. Imagine what you will be doing, saying and how you will look. Now act like this.

8. Imagine how you got to the point of success. What things did you do on the way? Now do those things.

9. Have a clear image of yourself as successful. Have an image or a statement to repeat to yourself to remind yourself what you are aiming towards.

10. Do not listen to doubt, either your's or other people's. Have phrases to stop the doubts.

11. Reward yourself when you achieve something. Praise yourself and acknowledge you have done something well.

MC10: Change partnerships

Change partnerships are special and supportive. These are groups of between two to four people who:

• have come together to help one another through a period of change

• are supportive and encouraging about progress

• are not negative about a relapse or slow progress, but who praise the person for trying again

• are not afraid about being honest

• have practical ideas to help keep up progress

• respect each other for trying

• can be called on to help at time of doubt or relapse

• can share the rewards of keeping to the change plan

• can be relied on

• are honest with each other about successes and difficulties

• are not critical of one another

• maintain confidentiality

Developing learning skills

 The module is divided into seven sessions. These are:

1. Why learn? What's in it for me? (3 hours 15 min)

2. Thinking before doing (3 hours 20 min)

3. Making an action plan and taking action (2 hours)

4. Learning how to ask for and make use of feedback (2 hours 15 min)

5. Learning through listening, questioning and developing discussion skills (2 hours 55 min)

6. Some study skills (5 hours 10 min)

7. Review (1 hour)

It makes use of such activities as:

- brainstorming
- goldfish bowl
- small group discussion
- large group discussion
- self-assessment checklists
- evaluation of learners' progress and learning needs

Trainer's notes

This module asks the learners to challenge an area which may be difficult for some of them. For some it will require looking at an area which has in the past been one associated with failure, getting things wrong or not understanding what is wanted or why something is wanted. Few of those in the group will have an image of themselves as learners, let alone as successful learners.

Learning is however part of everyday life. The group members are learning all the time, even if they do not recognise it as such. Learning may be defined as follows:

> *Learning is about change and growth. Changes in and growth in knowledge, ideas, skills, behaviours, attitudes and beliefs. Learning is unstoppable otherwise people would not cope with the myriad of new situations which they face. Some learning is however planned and continued.*

The group members may need some persuading to think about themselves as learners and to think about learning. The ideas from the following quote may be of value.

> *To learn successfully is to be more in control, to have more choices in life. Examples of lifelong learning illustrate not only that learning can take place effectively at any age in life, but also that it is a continuous, cumulative process throughout life, once people have learned to learn.*
>
> (Roberts and Horton, 1996)

The module aims to encourage the participants to see learning as something everyone does, as a normal part of life, as something in which they have had success and as a tool to help in future. The module seeks to make the group participants aware that there are many ways to learn and styles of learning. The module will help you to work with learners:

- to analyse their experiences of learning, addressing positive and negative experiences of learning and discovering ways in which they learn best

- to become aware of the various ways in which learning may take place and to develop an appreciation that learners already have many learning skills

- to appreciate that learning is happening throughout everyone's life and that developing skills as a learner are essential if an individual is to manage life and the changes in life
- to develop some key skills for learning
- to develop some study skills if appropriate (Session Six)

Session One: Why learn? What's in it for me?

 Trainer's notes

This session seeks to raise awareness of the value of learning and the range of learning which the group members have already undertaken. By the close of the session the learners will have identified areas of competence, learning activities they would like to undertake and a learning plan.

Opening activity (15 min)

Ask the learners to complete **LS1**. Encourage them to think about learning a range of activities, facts and skills, and developing all kinds of understanding throughout their lives when they complete the activity sheet. Ask for one or two examples from the group before they start. Encourage the learners to think about informal learning rather than things which are traditionally called formal learning.

Group feedback (20 min)

Ask the learners to share some of the six items they have on their lists. Write these on the flipchart. Explore the range of activities and the different ways in which they were learned.

Ask occasionally:

- how old was the person when they learned the thing?
- why they learned it?

Emphasise that:

- learning takes place throughout life
- it is a natural event
- it is not just something which takes place in a classroom
- often learning takes place because of a need to know or interest
- learning may happen accidentally

Best and worst learning experiences (15 min)

Read through LS2 with the learners. Once they know what is required ask them to work alone to complete the activity sheet. Emphasise that the learning experience can be any type of learning. Check on learners' progress.

Small group discussions (15 min)

In small groups ask the learners to compare their experiences. Ask for small group feedback. Were there common experiences or patterns to the learning:

- where did most of the best learning experiences take place?
- when people did not want to learn happen?
- were the best learning experiences always those initiated by teachers?

Feedback (15 min)

On the flipchart draw out some examples from the small groups of the positive and negative learning experiences. Ask the whole group are there any patterns to their learning experiences?

It is likely that the best learning experiences will have some of the following:

- a desire to know
- learner initiated
- activity based learning
- informal learning
- feeling positive and excited by the learning
- sense of personal achievement
- not necessarily a normal learning situation
- not necessarily teacher involved

It is likely that worst learning experiences may include:

- feeling humiliated or not served well by the teacher
- not learning what was wanted
- being forced to do something
- not clear what was wanted or how it should be done
- formal learning situation
- theoretical, no obvious application or need to know or chance to apply the learning

Brainstorm (10 min)

What conclusions can be drawn from the experiences?

Emphasise that the learners have shown they can learn, that learning does not have to be a formal activity. Explain that they are different types of learners – some who like to learn by doing and finding out, others by thinking before acting and others who learn from experience. There is no one way of learning and no right way.

Brainstorm and feedback (15 min)

Using LS3 ask the learners to list several things they have learned recently. Ask for examples from the group. Write these on the flipchart. Then ask the learners to pick one or two things on their lists and explain how they went about learning them. An example may need to be worked through for the group. Again, ask for one or two examples to be shared with the whole group and ask why they were pleased or not pleased, and what may have been done differently.

Learners' questionnaire (15 min)

Ask the learners to complete the learning questionnaire LS4. Go through the questions before starting so that the learners understand what is wanted. Ask for some to volunteer what they have found out about themselves.

Learning cycles (20 min)

Explain to the learners that there is no one way to learn and no right way but that the work so far has demonstrated many ways to learn. Emphasise that there are many ways to learn – alone, from books, through discussion, by trying things out, by thinking about experiences and activities and working out what went well or badly. People will have different preferences for how they like to learn.

Explain that all learning is a cycle of four processes:

1. Thinking about something, finding out and having ideas about it.
2. Actually doing it and trying out the ideas.

3. Thinking about what has happened.
4. Modifying what to do next in light of what has happened (use LS34)

Explain that all four processes have to go together because:

   a. If people never try anything and just think about it nothing would get done.

   b. If people just rush in and do not think then they would be likely to make mistakes.

   c. If people do not think about what has worked or has not worked and why they will just repeat mistakes and not improve.

   d. If people do not plan the next stage of what they do then they will not have learned from experience and thought how to do something better next time.

Learning is about making small changes, modifying and adding to what you know and can do. Learning is not just about making huge changes or taking great leaps forward (use LS35).

Ask learners if there are any questions about these explanations. Check to ensure that everyone understands.

Sharing anecdotes (20 min)

Ask the learners to work in threes. Ask them to:

   1. share some examples of when they have used the learning cycle as a whole or in part.

   2. share some examples of when they have not used several parts of the learning cycle e.g., not learned from experience; not thought before acting.

   3. ask the small groups to be ready to share some examples with the whole group.

Group feedback (20 min)

Write up some of the examples and draw some lessons from the importance of the learning cycle.

Drawing the threads together and outlining the module: Explanations (15 min)

Recap on the following:

   • learning is about modifying what is already known and done and adding new ideas and skills

   • learning helps people to manage and care for themselves and others better

   • people are learning all the time

   • there are many ways to learn: through activities, through thinking about experiences and through more formal learning, like classes or training sessions

   • they have already learned many things and have learning skills

   • there are a number of parts to the learning cycle

Explain that the module will review:

   • looking at thinking and making decisions

   • planning and approaching problems

   • reviewing and feedback

   • learning from talk and discussion

   • learning alone

   • collecting and using information

By the close of the module the learners will have further ideas about themselves as learners and what they might like to do in future.

Session Two: Thinking before doing

🍎 *Trainer's notes*

This session focuses on a key part of the learning process, that of thinking about an issue or problem *before* acting. This thinking process requires:

- stating the issue or problem
- exploring the issue or problem – what is involved in the issue or problems, how many parts does it have, describe the problem
- being open to alternative interpretations
- collecting information and evaluating it
- considering the solution/solutions
- considering alternatives and being open to possibilities
- considering ways to achieve the solution
- evaluating the implications of various courses of action

This session focuses on a number of these aspects in order to raise the learners' awareness of the importance of perception in understanding and defining a problem, considering alternative positions and meanings, stating the problem and considering solutions and their implications.

The session is divided into five parts:

1. Finding the issues.
2. Perception and possibilities.
3. Thinking more creatively.
4. Considering the implications of actions.
5. Collecting information and using it.

1. Finding the issues

Trainer's notes and introduction (15 min)

Often people do not tackle the real issues: they think or assume they know what the problem is. They may deal with a problem or part of a problem with which they feel more comfortable or with an issue which is a symptom of the real problem.

> **To tackle a situation it needs to be established:**
> **What is the issue or issues?**
> **What are the facts?**

> **To deal with a situation it needs to be established:**
> **What outcome is wanted? How achievable it is**
> **What will help reach that outcome?**

The facts then need to be reviewed to see what will help to move the situation along. The learners should use three types of thinking – being analytic, making judgements and being creative in approach problems.

Read through LS5 with the learners; encourage them to consider the stages and check that they understand the sequence of activities.

Considering an issue in pairs (25 min)
Present the learners with the problem solving activity LS6. Read through the case with the learners and ask them what stages they need to go through. Ask them to apply the stages on LS5 to it to solve the problem.

Feedback (15 min)
Discuss with the group how they found using the steps to think about action before moving onto taking action. What problems might they have in applying such a procedure in their own lives? Explain that the next activities will focus on aspects of looking at thinking and problem or issue solving, thinking creatively and considering perceptions.

2. Perception and possibilities
Learners can get stuck with one view of the world and not be open to different possibilities. These activities challenge this tendency and expose the learner to a realisation that people may view the same thing differently.

Images and perceptions (10 min)
Ask the learners to look at LS7 and to decide what they see.

Feedback (20 min)
The group should have a number of suggestions about the objects and about what is happening with the two men running. Encourage the learners to offer as many suggestions as they can.

Finally show **LS36** and ask the learners what they see. Explain that some see a half empty glass others see that there is a half full glass. People's perceptions are coloured by the ways in which they view the world. If appropriate, refer to work on positive attitudes, negative thinking and self-esteem.

One thing which the learners may want to do is to consider how they typically see the world and try to challenge it.

LS37 – People read what they expect to see.

Finally ask the learners as a group the following two questions.
- What colour are fridges?
- What do cows drink?

The learners should be thinking about white fridges and images of fridges and so say "cows drink milk". They will not have properly heard the question but will be responding to what they expect.

3. Thinking more creatively
This section moves on from expectations in formal thinking and usual patterns of thinking to encourage the learners to approach a problem as having several possible solutions and to certainly as not necessarily being what it seems.

Problems and solutions 1 (15 min)
Ask the learners to consider the problem on LS8. They have ten minutes to solve the problem alone. Then ask them to work in pairs for five minutes to discuss their answer.

Group feedback (10 min)
How did the group arrive at their answers? What helped them and what hindered their thinking? Presumably the two names, so well known, put an image in learners' minds of the two people from the Shakespeare play. Getting caught by what we expect often traps us into one way of

viewing a problem and not finding alternatives. The group may know of other problems of this kind and it may, if time is available, be enjoyable for the group to share more of these problems.

Problems and solutions 2 (10 min)

Ask the learners to work alone to find how many ways they can get from point A to place B on the diagram on LS9. Ask how many each learner found. Work though the various combinations on an OHT or flipchart. This exercise should show that there are often many ways of tackling a problem.

Problems and solutions 3 (10 min)

Ask the learners to work on LS 10 to find ways to join the circles. The learners may try to invent rules for themselves which make it hard to complete the activity. For example the line has to cut through the centre of each of the circles or the lines can only be the same length at the shape made by the circles. The learners will probably restrict their solution finding by using rules found from elsewhere. Find out what rules they create and what constrains their thinking.

4. Considering the implications of actions

Explanation and example (15 min)

Before learners embark on any plan of action they should think about all the consequences of possible actions and what may be driving them. They may find it useful to use spider diagrams or mind maps as a way to explore possible solutions to a problem and the consequences of solutions. An example is worked as LS11. This looks at the problem, possible solutions and the consequences of dealing with not having enough money. Put the problem to the learners and work through a mapping exercise on the flipchart. LS11 can be an aide-memoire and discussed with the learners.

Mind mapping a problem and its consequences (15 min)

In pairs the learners should consider as many solutions and their consequences to one of the following problems:

- not getting on with partner
- want to find a new job
- feeling stressed
- not coping with training course
- bored most of the time

The learners should complete their mind maps on A1 paper and be prepared to display them.

Feedback and display (10 min)

Ask one pair to volunteer to explain their mind map and how they found the process. Display the others and allow time for the learners to read them through them.

5. Collecting information and using it

Group brainstorm (20 min)

Brainstorm with the learners:

> **Why should you collect information before making decisions?**

The learners should list such reasons as:

- finding out alternative actions/solutions
- finding out the consequences e.g. costs

- knowing how to choose between things which look similar
- feeling confident you have made the best choice

Brainstorm with the learners:

Where can you get information to explore and solve problems?

Ask the learners to list a number of types of situations, problems or issues for which they might want further information.

Encourage the learners to consider such sources of information as written, non-written information, libraries, the Internet, family, friends, agencies and voluntary organisations.

Find out how many of the learners would like to know about how information sources work or would like additional help.

Out of session activity

Ask the learners to suggest seven topics about which they would like more information. List these on the flipchart. Ask the learners to each select one issue and then to collect as much and as wide a range of information as possible. They should make use of the suggestions from the previous brainstorm. The information should be brought to a later session and the range of types of information considered. Those who have selected the same issue can compare the range of material they have collected.

Information summary (10 min)

LS12 offers a flowchart for collecting and using information. This should be given to the learners and each stage discussed to consolidate understanding.

Session Three: Making an action plan and undertaking action

 Trainer's notes

A key aspect of the learning process is that of planning (remind yourself and the learners of the learning cycle LS34 and LS35) the action or the learning activity. Many learners will rush into an activity or experience without preparation. It may be a formal learning activity like writing an assignment, an activity such as preparation of a meal to demonstrate understanding of nutrition or a personal project such as looking for a new job.

The modules in this manual and the companion ones all require the learners to undertake some action planning activities as a means to manage and support the change process.

This section considers:

- why learners should plan and organise
- how to make use of the plan while undertaking a learning activity
- some basic organisational skills

Action planning is discussed at length in the manual *Becoming an Effective Trainer*.

Opening activity: why plan? (20 min)

1. Ask the learners to brainstorm:

Why plan before acting?

Their suggestions may include:
- to save time by not doing the wrong thing
- to have a sense of direction
- to know clearly what the goal is
- to have a structure
- to not make mistakes
- to act purposefully
- to know when a goal has been achieved

The learners may however not be able to think of reasons to plan, they may think it a waste of time, that it is something which slows them down or which takes the fun out of an activity. If this is so turn the brainstorm round and ask them to consider what happens if they do not plan.

2. Ask the learners to offer examples of times when they have planned or not planned an activity and the consequences of this.

3. Give the learners **LS13** and work through the reasons why planning is useful.

The steps in an action plan
Explanation (20 min)
1. Use **LS14** with the learners to explain that there are steps in devising a plan and that these are based on questions the learners can ask themselves.

2. Explain the importance of clear goal setting. An action plan should include a defined goal which is both an achievable goal and one they would really like to meet.

3. Explain the importance of motivation to meet the goal and being able to visualise that a goal has been met. This section on action planning links with work on developing positive attitudes.

4. Explain the meaning of the acronym SMART.

5. Give the learners **LS15**. Explain that they need to break their goal into smaller action steps and to work on those action steps which are a coherent group which work towards realising part of a learning goal.

Check that the learners understand and discuss any issues.

Planning activity (20 min)
Ask the learners as a group to think of seven tasks or situations which they may face and write these up:
- looking for work
- finding somewhere to live
- taking a holiday
- buying a car/motorbike
- buying a video or household item
- changing jobs
- writing an assignment

Ask them to select one of these and to apply an action planning process to it. The learners will need to use **LS16** and **LS15** for this exercise. They should work alone for ten minutes and then compare their plans with another learner for a further ten minutes.

Group feedback (10 min)

Ask for one or two volunteers to work through their action plans on the flipchart for the whole group. The group can assist in adding in any more necessary action steps.

Checking on progress
Explanation (10 min)

1. Explain that there is little point in the learners having a plan if they then do not follow it once they begin the activity.

2. Explain that it is necessary to have a way of checking on progress and if necessary to change the plan.

3. Give the learners LS17 and work through each of the questions to ensure the reasons for checking are understood.

Checking activity (10 min)

Ask the learners to work in pairs and to select one of the action plans created in the previous exercise. The learners should then try to apply the questions to the situation in the action plan to see how they would work.

Feedback (10 min)

Check if the learners had problems in understanding what the checking process was for. This exercise will have been hard as it relies on much use of imagination.

Creating an action plan (20 min)

At this point or by the close of the module the learners should create an action plan based on a real personal goal. They should consider how they will check on their progress and set themselves a review date. The review should be undertaken with a trainer to give the plan and review status in the learners' eyes and to ensure the principles have been understood.

Session Four: Learning how to ask for and make use of feedback

 Trainer's notes

This session will encourage learners to appreciate the importance of asking for and making use of feedback to improve their learning. Remind learners that feedback is a significant part of the learning cycle, coming in as part of the review stage (use OHTs LS34-35 if appropriate).

While learners may be able to review what they have done, they may be too self-critical or not critical enough. They may fail to realise why something happened or did not happen in a particular way. Feedback can help with understanding interpretation of the learning which has taken place and so with laying more effective plans for the next stage of learning.

Asking for, receiving and giving feedback can be fraught. Learners often feel vulnerable and are liable to interpret comments as criticism. But learners want honest feedback, they know when a trainer is not telling the truth and the relationship of learner and trainer suffers as a result of such dishonesty.

This session outlines the skills needed for asking for and using feedback and its value in the learning process.

Introducing feedback (15 min)

Brainstorm with the learners what they understand by feedback in a learning situation. Put their ideas on a flipchart. Prompt them with questions such as:

- why is having feedback valuable?
- what would happen if you did not have feedback?
- how can feedback be used?
- who or what gives feedback?

Having collected these starting points explain the importance of feedback.

Positive feedback and negative feedback

Alone (10 min)
Ask the learners to work individually thinking about some examples of positive feedback and negative feedback. They will need to use handout LS18. Before the learners begin ensure all understand what is wanted.

In pairs (10 min)
Ask the learners to work in pairs and to pool their findings and answer the following questions:

- What were the forms that negative feedback most frequently took?
- Who offered most negative feedback?
- What were the effects of negative feedback on you and on your learning?
- What were the forms that positive feedback most frequently took?
- Who offered most positive feedback?
- What were the effects of positive feedback on you and on your learning?

Feedback (10 min)
Ask each pair to offer some of their findings. If a pair feels able to disclose experiences then ask for some examples of the positive and negative feedback and the impact on learning.

From this activity it should be clear how learning, in whatever form, can be helped or hindered by the type of feedback the learner receives.

When feedback is most helpful (15 min)
Ask each learner to think of a type of feedback or an occasion when they would find feedback helpful. Collect an example from each learner. Write these on the flipchart.

The statements should be displayed and if possible copied for each learner, to remind them that help and guidance can be sought. The statements are also a reminder for those trainers working with learners.

Asking for or giving feedback (30 min)
Tell the learners that they need to make an effort to encourage feedback from their trainer but they also need to give feedback.

Working in pairs (10 min)
Ask the learners to think about the sorts of questions which the people in the four situations (LS19) could use to receive or to give feedback which would help to change the situation.

Feedback (20 min)
As a whole group discuss the questions and decide what types of answers might be given and therefore help given to the learner. During the course of the activity record on the flipchart the key features of the types of questions which the group thinks are most useful.

The list may include:

- specific questions
- short questions
- questions which require clear and simple answers and do not allow woolly answers
- questions which focus the other person on the issues, ask for concrete examples and clear guidance and do not allow them to just be nice
- questions which ask for clear guidance on how to improve
- encourage the person giving the criticism to think clearly and check the reality of the criticisms

Giving yourself good feedback (35 min)

 Trainer's notes

The learners may or may not have identified themselves as a good source of feedback. If they are self-honest then they are a good source of information about what has happened and why. Ask the learners to each think of an example of a time when they had provided themselves with good advice, had 'given themselves a good talking to', had 'suddenly seen the light', had 'changed the error of their ways' or realised what they had been doing. After a few minutes' quiet thinking ask the group members for some examples.

After each example try to find out what was going on for each learner:

- was it time away from others to think?
- was it listening to someone for the first time?
- was it a desire to change and then being open to suggestions?
- was it taking courage to ask for help?
- was it standing back and watching themselves in action?

Write up the reasons on the flipchart.

Spend the final ten minutes with the group making a list of how people can give themselves good feedback. For example:

- what questions might they ask themselves?
- how could they make use of quiet time?
- how could they make use of diaries or making lists?
- how useful are checklists?
- keeping a record, e.g. on tape?

Drawing the threads together (10 min)

Conclude the session by asking the learners to summarise what they have learned and to offer others in the group one example of something they will try in future.

Session Five: Learning through listening, questioning and developing discussion skills

 Trainer's notes

This session focuses on the skills of listening, questioning and discussion. It aims to raise learners' awareness of the difficulties and the gains from talk-based learning activities. Many learners will not appreciate just how much information can be gained and shared through talk-based activities. Some may consider discussion a waste of time or to be easy. The session should encourage them to see that neither is the case. Others may consider talk-based activities intimidating or difficult. This session should help to reassure and encourage these learners to feel more confident in these activities.

Listening skills: a key to learning

The first part of the session has activities to focus on the importance of listening in learning.

Brainstorm (10 min)

Open the work with a brainstorm on:

> **How does listening help learning?**

The suggestions should include:

- knowing what is wanted
- finding out new information
- getting ideas to add to my own
- finding out what people feel about an issue
- finding out how to do something
- hearing about something which sparks off new ideas

Ask the group what happens if people do not listen properly. List the ideas on a flipchart.

Testing your listening skilss (15 min)

Read out the following paragraphs and ask the learners five questions about it. This should take about 15 minutes.

Daily Times Exclusives

CAR THEFT BACKFIRES

Jason, 20, and Darren Doyle, 17, stole a Vauxhall Senator from the Cleeve Lane Sainsbury car park. After Jason had been driving for some fifteen minutes the police began to give chase. The car went out of control after it joined the motorway at Junction 19. Bouncing off the crash barrier it overturned and led to a three car pile up. Jason Doyle was cut from the wreckage. Part of his leg was mangled by the steering column. Darren Doyle died from head injuries.

Of the other cars involved, one driver, John Brown, sustained minor injuries and some damage to his car. There were two fatalities in the car that collided directly with Doyle's out of control stolen vehicle. The police won't release names before the relatives have been informed. The final car, a Morris Metro driven by Julie Keen, was badly damaged and she has been taken to St Martin's with whiplash, facial injuries and injuries to her ribs and arms.

Doyle is being questioned by police and will face charges. This is his second involvement in a joy-riding accident and he is known to police for his various car-related offences.

Report by George West and Janet Brown

---

1. What were the names of the two brothers and which brother was driving?

2. Where was the car stolen from?

3. How many fatalities were there?

4. What were the two makes of cars mentioned?

5. What were the reporters' names?

Ask the learners how well they did in answering the questions. Find out how they remembered certain information to get the questions right. Find out why they misremembered or did not remember e.g. heard what they wanted to, made wrong associations between ideas.

How can listening skills be improved? (10 min)

Brainstorm the question above to discover the learners' ideas. Ensure the following are covered:

- take some notes about key points
- does it link with something you know about
- jot down what you agree/disagree with
- make a note of something not understood
- focus on what is being said, don't allow your mind to wander
- practice paying attention
- listen to what is said not what you want to hear

Questioning (10 min)

Brainstorm the question:

> **How can questioning help learning?**

The learners may suggest:

- finding out information
- checking something has been understood
- getting an answer about something which is not clear
- finding out precisely how to do something
- finding out what others think
- testing out an idea

Open questions and closed questions (15 min)

Ask the learners if they know the difference between open and closed questions, ask for examples. Explain clearly what these questions are and check for understanding by asking the learners to identify if the following are open or closed. They will need to record their answers on paper.

1. How can I help you?
2. How do you feel today?
3. Do you watch sport on TV?
4. What did you do on Saturday?
5. Have you been to the theatre?
6. How often do you go to a library?
7. Can you tell me the way to the station?
8. Can you use a computer?
9. Do you exercise?
10. What do you think about the new motorway being built near here?

Ask why open questions are more useful to learners than closed questions.

Discussion skills

Ask the group how discussions can help learning. Record their ideas on the flipchart. Ideas may include:

- sharing ideas
- finding more solutions than on one's own
- exploring issues or problems
- seeing an issue from someone else's point of view
- testing out your ideas with someone else
- finding out how other people see the world
- picking up information
- hearing about examples from other people's lives
- finding out things which were not known or not understood

How do you feel about discussions? (20 min)

Ask the learners to work alone for five minutes to complete the handout LS20. Then spend 15 minutes on group discussion.

Ask the learners to indicate:

- whether they enjoy discussion
- if they think discussions are a waste of time
- what they feel it is necessary to have in order to have good discussions
- what skills they may need to have as learners, to have better discussions

Ask for examples of evidence to support their answers. Explore some of the rules for running good discussions.

In small groups (10 min)

Ask the learners to get into groups of four and to spend about ten minutes talking about discussion activities. Ask them to address two questions:

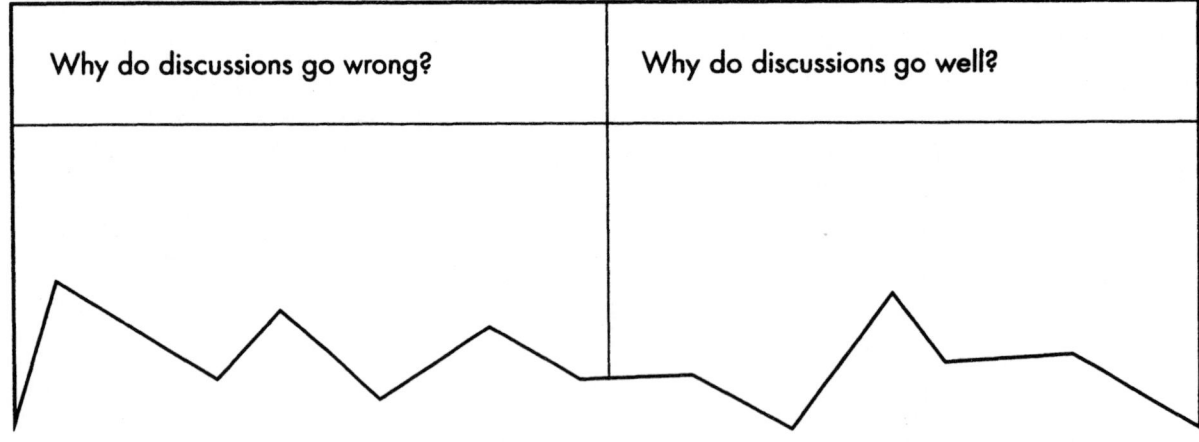

Why do discussions go wrong?	Why do discussions go well?

Draw this table out on flipchart paper so that the groups know what they should be focusing on. Tell the groups they will need to record their answers to feed them back to the whole group. Tell them they have ten minutes to come up with their ideas. Check everyone understands what is to be done. The table can be completed with various suggestions during the group feedback session.

Do not go round the group helping them to get on with the task. If any group needs explanations or some help give it briefly. Do not join in or stimulate ideas.

After ten minutes just stop the groups. Do not warn them that they are running out of time.

Group feedback (20 min)

Ask the groups to report back one by one offering reasons why discussion works well or badly. Gather as many reasons as possible and ask for examples to illustrate points.

Then, ask the group to think about the exercise they have done and about the whole group feedback. Ask them not to make personal comments or attacks but to consider:

- did anyone dominate either session and to what effect did this have on others and the discussion?
- did the small groups concentrate on the task or drift off?
- did the small groups use all the time to think of reasons or just be content with a few ideas and then drift off?
- how were alternative points of view expressed?
- did anyone not speak? Why? What effect did this have on the other learners?

Add these ideas to the list of reasons why discussions work well and badly.

Your lack of intervention as a trainer in policing the groups should have made it possible for them to drift onto other topics if they chose to do so. One point to draw out is that for those who insist that discussion is a waste of time, that they need to be aware they have to take responsibility to make discussions work.

Final brainstorm (10 min)

Ask the group to brainstorm:

> **What skills do learners need to have effective discussions?**

Discussion and observation (1 hour)

Set the group into a goldfish bowl arrangement. Have three to four observers in the outer circle and the rest as discussants in the centre.

Give everyone LS21 and ask each person to work alone for ten minutes to:
a. Read the extract on handout **LS21**.
b. Then decide and write down the order of importance of the 18 items for their survival.

The inner group has 20 minutes to reach agreement on the items in order by priority. The observers need **LS22**.

Time the discussion and remind them of time pressure. At the close of the discussion ask them to answer the following questions for the whole group:

- how did they feel they performed as a group?
- what went particularly well or badly?
- was it easy to reach agreement and why?
- was anyone unhappy with the final list or with the way the discussion had gone?
- as a group how would they rate their skills:
  - as listeners?
  - in asking questions?
  - in encouraging each other to talk?

Now ask the observers for their views on the discussion. Use a combination of questions from the observation sheet and some from the list used with the discussion group. Try to stop personal comments and attacks although it is useful for group members to know how they are seen by others e.g. as a good listener or as someone who does not give others a chance.

Drawing the session together (10 min)

Ask each learner to offer one thing which they have thought about or experienced during the session which they had previously not considered.

Session Six: Some study skills

 Trainer's notes

This session may be of particular use to learners who are taking more formal education programmes. However, there are many ideas useful to all types of client. It is broken into five parts:

a. self-assessment as a learner

b. reading faster

c. reading with a purpose

d. taking notes

e. getting organised and planning time

a. Self-assessment as a learner (30 min)

Ask the learners to complete LS23 and LS24. Check on individual progress and on the learners' abilities to identify learning strengths and needs. These completed questions should be the basis of a learning skills and experiences programme completed on a one-to-one basis.

b. Reading faster

The activities are for readers with a range of reading abilities who want to improve the ways they approach reading for study and leisure purposes. It will encourage:

- faster reading and

- create greater confidence.

This session is not for those who need help with developing more basic reading skills.

Introductory activities (15 min)

Brainstorm these questions:

1. Why do people read? How might this affect reading speed?

2. What makes some people better readers than others?

Reading speeds (30 min)

1. Ask if anyone has a sense of how fast they read and what influences their reading speeds.

2. Set the learners to read for three minutes. Time the group.

   Then ask each person to calculate their reading speed.

   $$\text{Speed} = \frac{\text{No. of words read}}{\text{time taken}}$$

   Write speeds up on the flipchart.

3. Ask students to work in pairs. A reads for four minutes while B observes how the reader's eyes move from left to right. B needs to check:
   a. How many times do the eyes stop in one line?
   b. Do the eyes go back over words?

   The pair then swap activities.

   Go round the group finding out about eye movements, regression, stopping etc. How do the learners think that eye movements affect reading speeds?

Improving speed (30 min)

1. Work through with the group some of the reasons why people read slowly. Use **LS25**. Discuss what each point means and ask who thinks they do it.

2. Using **LS26** go through some of the ways to improve reading skills.

3. Now ask the group members to practise trying to read faster for five minutes. Suggest that they:
   - Use a finger or pencil under the words
   - Try to read more words at each glance
   - Do not look back or re-read
   - Keep on reading whatever the quality of sense being made.

4. Again, time the readers for three minutes and ask them to calculate their reading speeds. Record these new scores on the flipchart. Have there been any differences?

5. Ask the learners which suggestions for faster reading they tried and how they felt.

c. Reading with a purpose

This work builds on from reading faster. It looks at developing as a purposeful reader. Having a purpose for reading is one reason why people read more quickly. It is also a reason for remembering what has been read. **This session needs to take place in the library.**

Opening questions (15 min)

Ask the learners:
   - what they read?
   - why they read?
   - what they want to gain from reading?
   - how they select their reading material?

Put these ideas on the flipchart.

Selecting and using reading material (30 min)

1. The learners need access to a library or selection of non-fiction books. Ask them to select an item which looks of interest. Having selected their reading material ask them how they would usually go about reading it.

   Record these ideas on the flipchart.

2. Work through the points on **LS27**. Check that the points make sense and ask how the learners would apply them.

3. Ask the learners to work through the points on **LS27** in relation to the book they have selected.

Considering the benefits (10 min)

Finally having tried out the points discuss how the learners think it would help them get more from their reading.

Compare these responses with those recorded on the flipchart earlier.

d. Taking notes

This session encourages understanding of note-taking from books and talks and suggests some ways to improve note taking.

Brainstorm (10 min)

Discuss the following questions:

> **Why take notes?**
>
> **How do you take notes?**

Taking notes (10 min)

Work through handout LS28 with the learners. Ask them for comments on what makes sense and what does not. Ask them what they could imagine themselves trying.

Taking notes from speech (30 min)

1. Read out the following text and ask the students to take notes. Recap before you begin reading on the value of:
   - headings
   - keywords
   - being concise and not writing out all that is said

A description of Uncle Ernest by Alan Sillitoe

A middle aged man wearing a dirty raincoat, who badly needed a shave and looked as though he hadn't shaved for a month, came out of a public lavatory with a cloth bag of tools folded beneath his arm. Standing for a moment on the edge of the pavement to adjust his cap – the cleanest thing about him – he looked casually to the left and right and when the traffic flow had eased off, crossed the road. His name and his trade were always spoken of in one breath: Ernest Brown the upholsterer. Every night before returning to this lodgings he left the bag of tools for safety with a man who looked after the public lavatory near the town centre, for he felt there was a risk of them being lost or stolen should he take them back to his room, and if such a thing were to happen his living would be gone.

---

2. Ask the learners to compare their notes. What differences are there? Discuss this as a group. Emphasise that taking notes is an individual activity and there is no right or wrong way.

3. Ask the following five questions to check accuracy. What was:
   a. The man's name?
   b. His job?
   c. The cleanest piece of clothing?
   d. What was it he left?
   e. The author's name?

4. Discuss how taking notes helped them to gain the right answers and why some learners may not have recorded the information for the questions.

5. Discuss with the learners any areas of difficulty which they are having.

Getting organised and planning time

This session briefly considers two key aspects of managing study, personal organisation and time planning. The activities should alert learners to any problems they have in these areas. The module *Managing time and goal setting* may be of help along with the work on action planning.

Why organise? (10 min)

Brainstorm:

> ### What does being organised mean?

Write responses on flipchart. These may include:
- being tidy
- managing time
- knowing where things are
- saving time

The responses may include:
- organising wastes time
- organising is boring – it's better to get on

How organised are you? (30 min)

1. Ask for **LS29** to be completed.

2. **Discuss:** How many learners consider themselves to be organised? How many feel they are not organised? What are the advantages and disadvantages of each way of being? Record the answers.

3. Ask the group to identify some reasons why it is sometimes hard to get organised. Put responses on the flipchart. Try to encourage broad thinking.

Responses may include:
- not knowing what to do
- not knowing the right order of events
- not doing what is more important first
- don't like planning
- didn't have all the necessary tools
- not interested in being organised

Try to prompt discussion on these areas.

Getting organised (20 min)

This section looks at one aspect of getting organised: knowing how to plan what needs to be done.

1. Ask the group to look at **LS30**. Talk through each of the steps to check on understanding.

2. Ask the learners to work in pairs and apply the process to one of the following problems.
- planning a holiday
- arranging a complicated journey using timetable
- finding a job
- tackling a personal problem
- tuying a car

Feedback (10 min)

Ask the group to report back how they found using the planning stages. Did they help them?

Managing your time (10 min)

Introduce the three key ideas of this session:

- timetabling
- priorities
- target setting

Ask the group what each word means to them and write answers on flipchart and leave visible for the whole session.

Thinking about time (20 min)

Hand out **LS31** and ask the learners to complete it. Allow ten minutes. Spend some time asking about how the learners scored themselves and what they have discovered about themselves. Generate a list of any issues about time management which need to be addressed. Offer the learners a weekly timetable **LS32**, which they can use to record their use of time and to plan their time for study tasks.

Session Seven: Review

Review: pair work and feedback (40 min)

Ask the learners to work in pairs to decide on six points which they think were key ones for them from the learning skills module. They should be prepared to present these with their reasons for their choice.

Record each pair's key points and reasons.

As trainer add any points which you consider to have been vital.

Action plan (20 min)

Working alone ask the learners to take stock of what they have learned by completing the learning plan **LS33**.

Review the completion of this with the learners and consider how best needs may be met.

LS2: Best and worst learning experiences

Describe your best learning experience	Who taught you?
How did you feel?	Why did you want to learn this?

Describe your worst learning experience	Who taught you?
How did you feel?	Why did you want to learn this?

LS1: Things I have learned

Think back over your life so far and pick six things you have learned. Write down how you learned them

Things I have learned	How I learned them
1.	
2.	
3.	
4.	
5.	
6.	

LS4: Learners' questionnaire

Please tick the statements which describe what you do.
Then complete the question at the bottom of the page

Statement	✓
I like reading and finding things out from books	
I prefer just to get on with something rather than waste time thinking and planning	
I like to think about problems and get all the facts	
I like to come up with several ways of doing something then test them out to find the best way	
I like working to deadlines	
I tend to practise until I get something right	
I have high standards for myself	
I am not so bothered about how well it is done, just so long as it is done	
I like working on something on my own	
I like to find out how to do something	
I prefer discussion to doing practical things	
I like to work with others	
I like to work with ideas	
Once I know how to do something I like to just get on with that	
I prefer to be told how to do something	
I like writing about things	
I like to learn practical things	
I prefer to be told what to do next	
I like working at my own pace	
I think learning new things is interesting	

Look back at the things you have ticked –
what does this tell you about yourself in a learning situation?

LS3: Things learned recently

Jot down some skills, facts, things you have learned about or learned to do recently

Things learned recently

Pick a couple of things/skills and decide how you learned about them, e.g. asked someone, read about it, followed a diagram, had a lesson, got someone to show you

Were you pleased with how you learned this?   Yes/No

Were you pleased with how you learned this?   Yes/No

LS6: Problem solving activity

Read the following case study below. The notes describe the behaviour, attitudes and wants of Robbie Bannister, a 14 year old.

Your team has been appointed to the case and has been asked to decide what should be done to assist Robbie in the immediate term and what should be in place to support him for the next two years.

Your team has been asked to work out his main problems, the action steps towards addressing those problems and how to do this.

Your team has also been asked to provide some support for Pat and Jane. What would you recommend?

WHAT NEXT?

Robbie is now 14. His parents separated when he was seven and his sister nine. His father just hasn't wanted to know about him, his sister or his mother for the past seven years. When he was at home he was out, drunk or in a foul mood.

Today Robbie has been taken from his family home after police again visited the house. Robbie has beaten up his mother again and trashed the house. This is the sixth or seventh time he's beaten his mother. It's the fourth time the police have been called.

He hates his mother, wants to go into foster care and this time he looks like he has succeeded. His foster carer is herself a single mother, is keen to have the £150 a week and doesn't mind her other foster children drinking or smoking. She is not often in the house to check on their behaviour.

Robbie's mother Pat and sister Jane are shocked by his violence to their home and his violence to his mother. This time they think they are going to let him go, but they are concerned:

- about his attitude to women
- that he needs help
- that Social Services do not seem to know what to do
- about what may happen to him in the future and what he may do if he does not get help
- about the foster mother and some of Robbie's new friends.

Robbie could not care less about Pat and Jane's concerns.

LS5: Confronting a problem

Think about the nature of the problem:
What are the real facts?
What are side issues?
What are misleading facts?
What are symptoms of other problems?
What might be other people's interpretations of the problem rather than your own?
How might thinking about it as they see it help you?

↓

What could be a desired outcome?

↓

How might that be reached?

↓

What other outcomes might be acceptable?

↓

How could these be reached?

↓

Collect information about the problem or issue and possible solutions

↓

Consider the issue/problem in parts or as a whole

↓

Consider the various ways to tackle the problem/issue and the consequences of these

↓

Discuss ideas with others. What ideas do they have?

↓

Should the problem/issue be tackled in whole or parts?

↓

Having weighed options consider the plan of action

↓

Allow sufficient time; order the actions;
define success criteria and who may help. Set a review date

LS8: Problems and solutions 1

Read the following situation and write down your solution to the problem of Juliet's death

Situation: Juliet is lying dead in the middle of the room.
                There is water and broken glass all around.
                Romeo is sitting on the chair looking down on the scene.

Problem: How did Juliet die?

Your solution:

LS7: What do you see?

Look at each picture and decide what you think it is

1.

2.

3.

4.

5.

What is going on?

1.

2.

3.

4.

5.

LS10: Problems and solutions 3

Without taking your pen from the paper or retracing your path join all 9 circles with 4 straight lines

Now try the same puzzle but using 3 straight lines

LS9: Problems and solutions 2

How many alternative ways are there to get from A to B
*You can only go through any other letter **once***

Your solutions:

LS12: Steps to collecting and using information

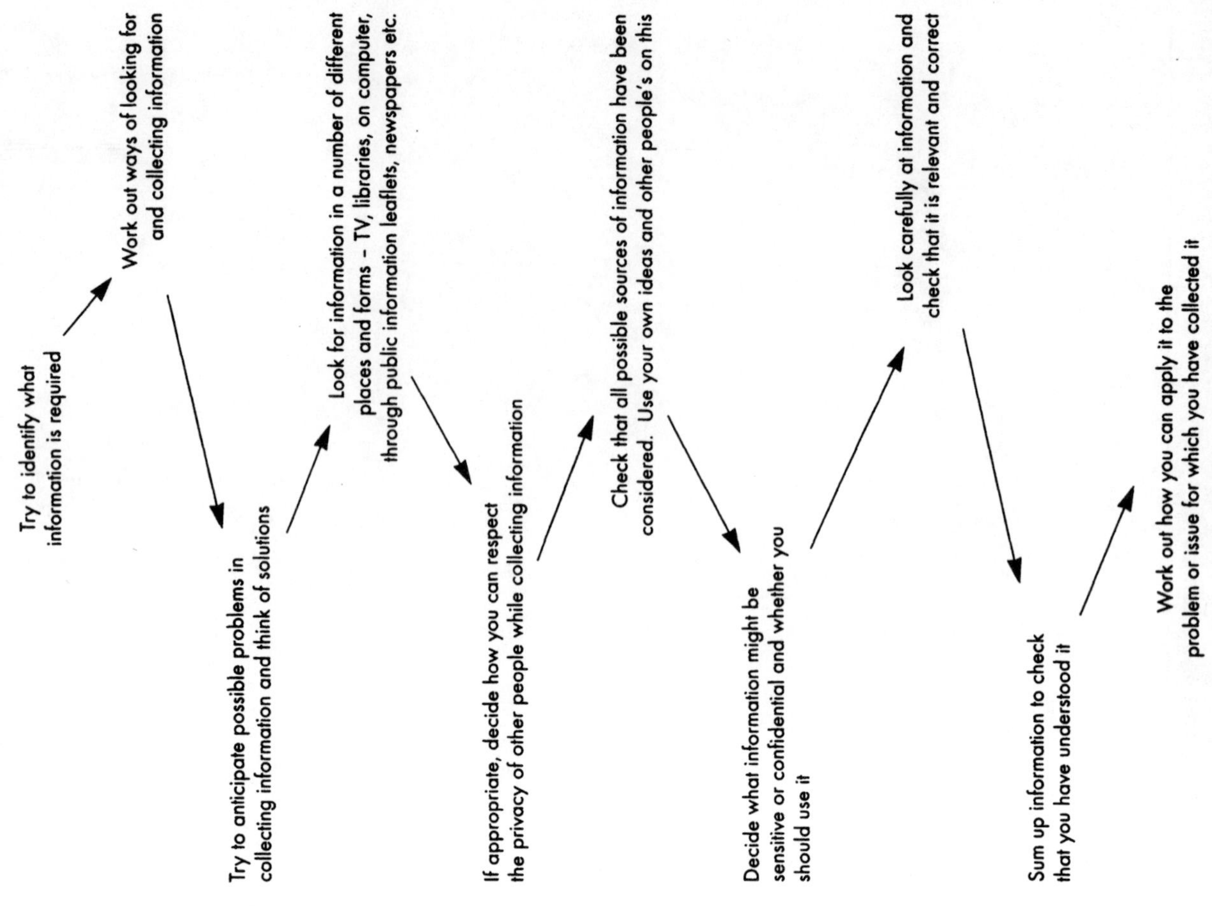

Try to identify what information is required

Work out ways of looking for and collecting information

Try to anticipate possible problems in collecting information and think of solutions

Look for information in a number of different places and forms – TV, libraries, on computer, through public information leaflets, newspapers etc.

If appropriate, decide how you can respect the privacy of other people while collecting information

Check that all possible sources of information have been considered. Use your own ideas and other people's on this

Decide what information might be sensitive or confidential and whether you should use it

Look carefully at information and check that it is relevant and correct

Sum up information to check that you have understood it

Work out how you can apply it to the problem or issue for which you have collected it

---

LS11: Mapping the consequences of possible decisions

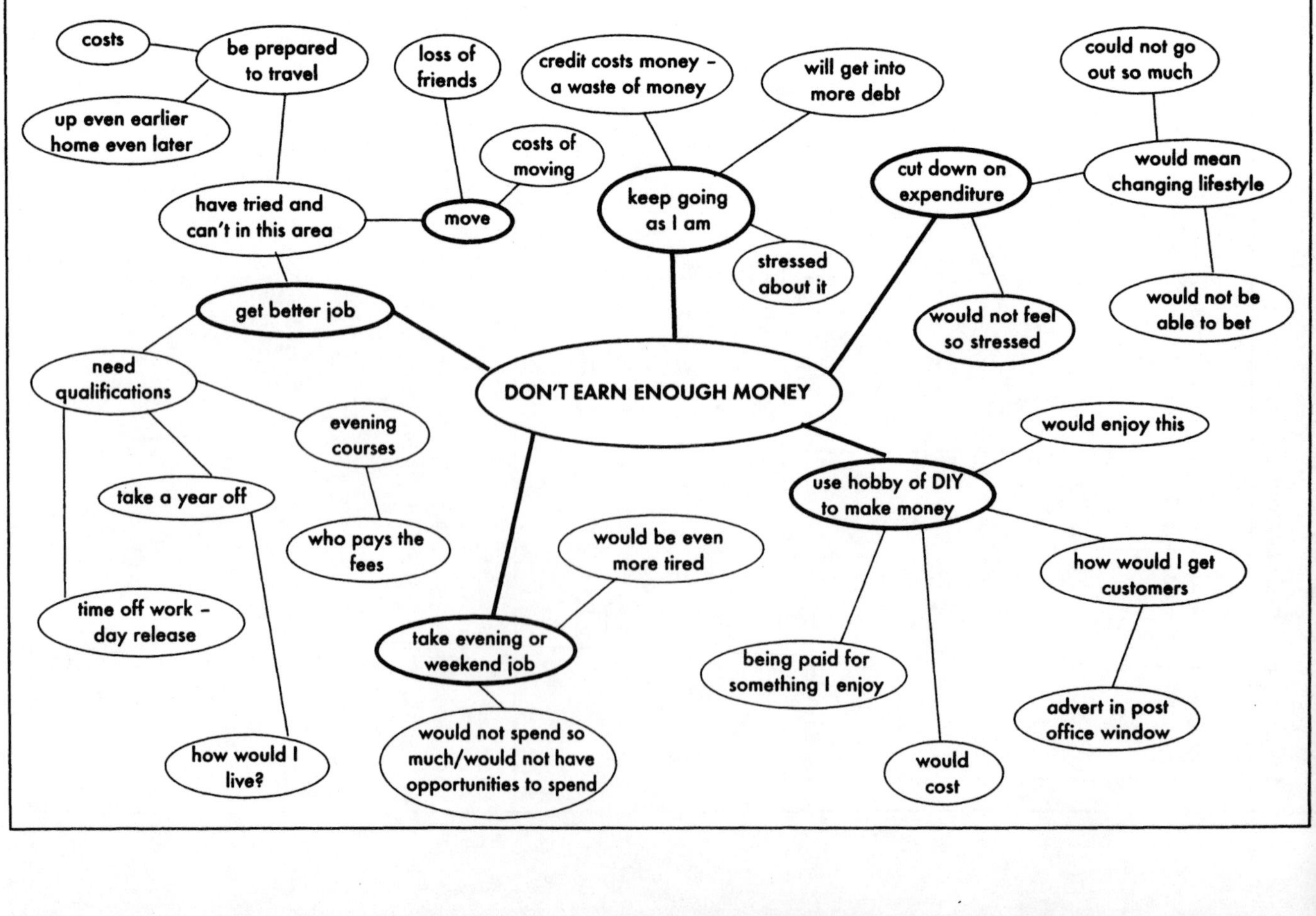

costs — be prepared to travel

up even earlier home even later

loss of friends

credit costs money – a waste of money

will get into more debt

could not go out so much

would mean changing lifestyle

cut down on expenditure

costs of moving

have tried and can't in this area — move

keep going as I am

stressed about it

would not feel so stressed

would not be able to bet

get better job

need qualifications

evening courses

DON'T EARN ENOUGH MONEY

would enjoy this

take a year off

who pays the fees

use hobby of DIY to make money

would be even more tired

how would I get customers

time off work – day release

being paid for something I enjoy

advert in post office window

how would I live?

take evening or weekend job

would not spend so much/would not have opportunities to spend

would cost

LS14: Action planning means

Action planning means I ask myself:

- What do I want to do?

- What does this mean to me?

- Why do I want to do it?

- Where am I now?

- How far am I from my goals?

- How can I get to where I want to be?

- What do I need to achieve my aim?

- Who else can help me to do this?

- By when do I want to achieve my aim?

- What smaller action steps do I need to take?

LS13: The value of action plans

Action planning helps me to:

- have a clear understanding of what I want and how to get it. This saves me time by avoiding unnecessary things

- think about alternative goals and what they would involve. I can select the best ones for me

- have a clearer idea about myself and what is important to me

- decide how to reach my goal and what I have to do or to give up to achieve it

- increase my chance of succeeding

- be able to measure my progress and success

- know why something is not working and what to do about it

- consider any potential problems before I face them and have some ideas about what to do just in case they are needed. This saves me time and stops me getting so frustrated

- have more control over my future

Not planning may mean not having a clear idea of what I want to achieve

Not planning may mean not having a clear goal and the route towards it

Not planning may reduce the possibility of dealing with problems

Not planning may mean failing

Not planning may mean wasting my time

LS16: Action plan

Goal:

Reasons for goal:

Action steps:

Date for completion

Resources or other needs:

I will measure success by:

Review date:

LS15: Action steps

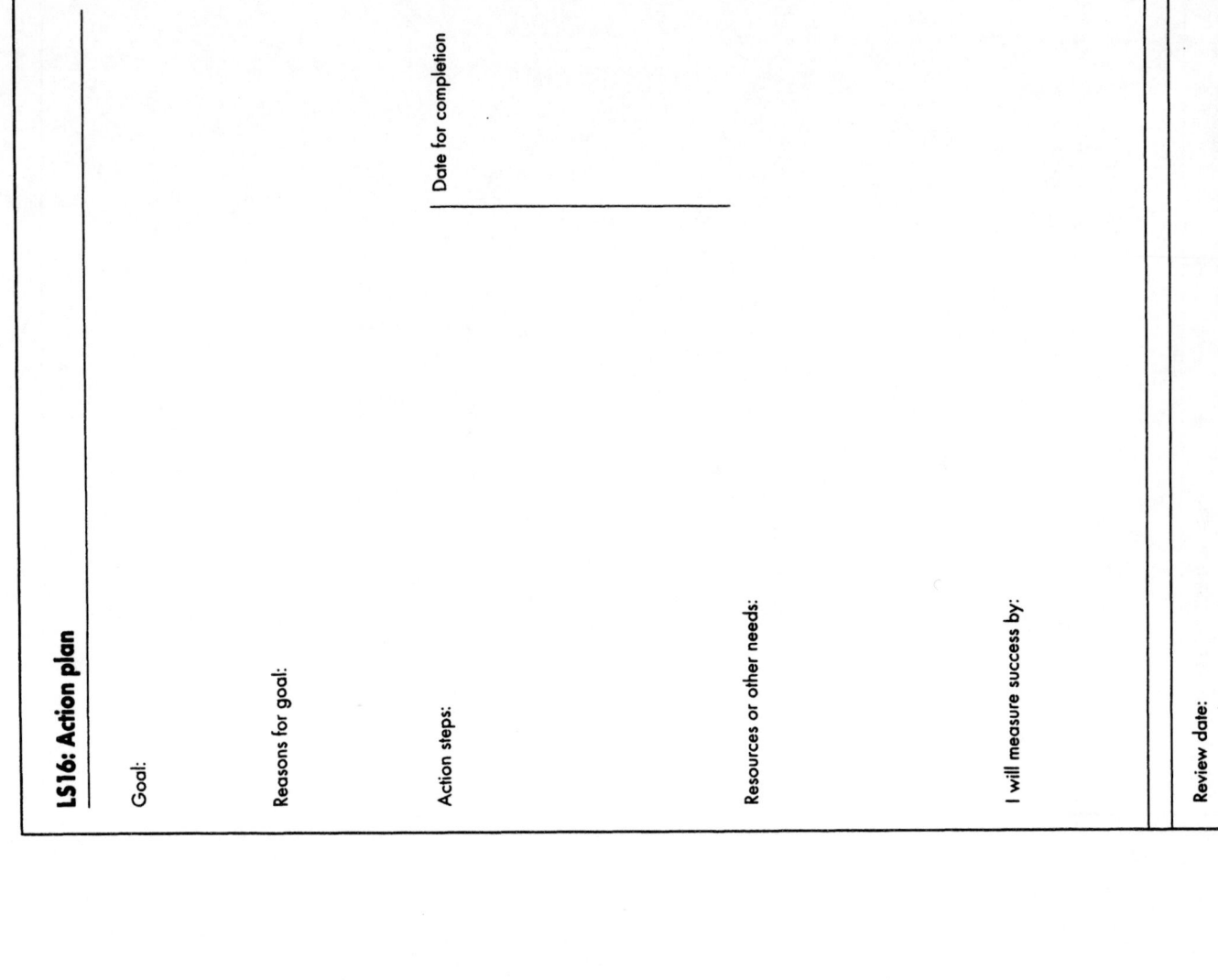

GOAL REACHED

Fill in each box with the small action steps or targets which you need to take so that you can reach your goal. You will need to think carefully about putting the action steps in the right order. Don't forget to put the date by when each step will be completed.

Handout LS18: Positive and negative feedback

POSITIVE FEEDBACK

Example	Who gave it	What was it like	What effect did it have on your learning?

NEGATIVE FEEDBACK

Example	Who gave it	What was it like	What effect did it have on your learning?

LS17: Questions to check on progress

What was I setting out to do?

How much have I done so far?

How does this compare with what I had expected to achieve by now?

What helped me to achieve?

What held me back?

Have I used more, less or other resources than I expected to use?

What are the effects of what I have done on myself and others around me?

What have I learned from what I have done?

Do I still want to continue with my plan? Why or why not?

What fresh targets do I want to set myself?

Do I need to change my timescale?

Handout LS20: How do I feel about discussions?

Tick any box when you feel you agree with the statement beside it

1. I'm afraid I won't have anything to say ☐

2. I think I might talk too much ☐

3. People might think I am stupid ☐

4. I might say the wrong things and people might laugh ☐

5. I feel it's too hard to join in discussions ☐

6. I don't want to tell other people things about me or my experiences ☐

7. Other people don't really understand me or my point of view ☐

8. Noone really listens properly ☐

9. I like talking to other people ☐

10. I think I have an opinion on most things ☐

11. I'm always ready for a good debate about something ☐

12. I like finding out about other people and what they think ☐

13. I'm not often stuck for an answer for anything ☐

14. Discussion's a good way to get things into the open ☐

15. Discussion teaches you to listen to others ☐

16. Discussion's a good way to share ideas ☐

17. Discussion is a waste of time ☐

18. You don't find out anything new through discussion sessions ☐

19. Now put down any other thoughts which you may have about discussions:

LS19: Problem situations

Read through the following situations and decide in pairs what questions would best help the person to find out how to improve or to discover what is going wrong

1. Barry couldn't do a thing right as far as Judy was concerned. Most things he said or did ended in some sort of sarcastic comment, bickering or even worse a row.

2. "This is the third time I've had to speak to you about your work. You've got to get it right by tomorrow or you'll have to go."

3. Ricky had spent four hours on an assignment over the weekend. He got it back with some strange green lines in the margin, some spelling mistakes circled and a comment, 'This would have been better if you have spent more than five minutes on it'.

4. Jo had been seeing a volunteer counsellor for the past four weeks to help her to sort out her problems. Each week they talked about the same things. Jo's debts, Jo's poor relationship with her child and the fear Jo had that Eric was going to dump her. Jo knew that this week they would talk about the same three things.

Handout LS21: Problem solving

You have just gained a job as a driver for an archaeological team exploring a ruined city deep in the jungle – ten days' drive by Land Rover from the nearest village, following rough jungle tracks.

Halfway along your very first journey, bringing equipment and a new member to join the expedition, you find the track flooded and take an alternative route. Several hours later you realise you are lost.

You try to find you way back but the Land Rover becomes stuck in swampy ground and slowly starts to sink in the mud. If the Land Rover sinks much more, you will be stranded, without supplies in the middle of a vast uninhabited jungle area.

You will not be missed for at least five or six days, and organising a search operation will take some time, with perhaps another five or six days before you are located – if at all!

Which of the following items would you take from the Land Rover (in whole or part) to help you survive?

List them in order of importance:

1. for the most important;
2. for the next important;
   and so on up to 18 for the least important.

THE ITEMS YOU MAY WANT

- 4 x 4.5 gallon cans of petrol
- 2 maps of the area (not necessarily 100% accurate, as produced by aerial survey only)
- 2 rucksacks
- a medical kit
- 4 large cases of composite rations (mainly in tins)
- 2 Calor Gas stoves
- 3 machetes
- 1 flare pistol
- snakebite serum
- 2 compasses
- 2 spades
- 6 x 4.5 gallon cans of water
- 1 hunting rifle
- mosquito netting
- insect-repellent cream
- a 12 foot length of nylon rope
- 6 mess tins
- 10 packets of salt tablets.

Handout LS22: Observers sheet

Watch the group discussing which are the survival items which are needed.

Watch and decide:

- Who speaks most?

- Does any one person dominate the group?

- Do some people not join in? Why?

- Does the discussion look at all the items or just decide on a few?

- Did anyone seem uncomfortable and why?

- Was anyone talked over or interrupted? What effect did this have?

- Did anyone ask anyone else questions or explain why they thought one item more important than another? How was this done?

LS24: Learners' questions

Complete the four boxes below

I think I learn best when:

My strengths as a learner are:

I think that my main concerns about learning are:

I would like help to work on:

LS23: Learners' questionnaire

Read through the following statements and ✔ the column which applies to you

	Good	Needs practice	Can't do
Using a computer to wordprocess			
Listening to feedback about my work			
Using a dictionary			
Knowing what information I need to find			
Using numbers			
Writing down my ideas			
Working to a deadline			
Using spreadsheets			
Completing longer pieces of writing			
Using a calculator			
Finding key points in a piece of writing			
Participating in discussions			
Using computers to find information			
Working with others			
Using libraries			
Working alone			
Taking notes			
Being able to hold my own in discussion			
Listening to others			
Concentrating on what I am doing			
Finding evidence to support my points			
Helping others			

LS26: Improving your reading

1. Have fewer eye movements each line – read in larger blocks of words.

2. Use a pencil or finger to underline the words and make your eyes move fast to keep up.

3. Do not re-read looking for sense.

4. Force yourself to read faster for a definite period of time and then take a break.

5. Decide why you are going to read something and what you hope to gain from it.

6. Undertake your reading in chunks so it is manageable; e.g. a chapter, a section etc.

7. Read in blocks of words – this will stop you trying to read words out loud or silently to yourself.

8. Minimise interruptions, your own and other people's. Read for an agreed period of time.

LS25: Reasons for slower reading

1. Reading small groups of words or even reading a word at a time.

2. Reading each word out loud or even silently to yourself.

3. Re-reading something you have read because you do not know a word, forgot what you read or did not understand.

4. Your concentration breaks so you re-read.

5. Getting stressed by having to read something or having a lot to read.

6. Not knowing why you are reading something.

LS28: Taking notes

Notes

- help you focus on relevant points
- are very concise
- help you to see key points and link between
- are good as memory joggers
- help you to organise ideas before writing or speaking, e.g.:
  - a letter
  - doing a talk
  - preparing an assignment
  - making a phone call.

Making notes:

- Helps you to learn as you see the words as well as hear them and you "feel" them as your hand writes them
- Helps you to make sure you understand the information because you organise it yourself, write things down, highlight the things you want and use your own words
- Just copying from books means you use someone else's words, don't extract the key ideas and don't make sense of things for yourself

1. Use key words – try to sum up whole paragraphs and long speeches in a few words.

2. Underline and highlight the key points and headings.

3. Take your notes in a way to make them memorable.

4. Use abbreviations: e.g.:

eg	for example	&	and
etc	and so on	=	equals
info	information	≠	does not equal
20	twentieth century	%	percentage
wd	would	∴	therefore
shd	should	∵	because
cd	could	min	minutes
v	very	h	hours
@	about		

LS27: Reading with more purpose

1. Look at the selected book or article and ask yourself:
   - how does it add to what you know about the subject?
   - does it contain the information you need?

2. Check the index of the book or its contents page to make sure it has what you want.

3. Before you begin reading:
   - jot down some things you want to know about the topic
   - jot down some things you already know about the topic.

4. Select a section that looks useful to meet your needs.

5. As you read be active:
   - ask questions about what you read
   - make notes
   - if it is your book highlight key points
   - ask yourself, do you agree with the writer or not?

6. When you have completed a section:
   - summarise what you have read
   - make notes on the material you want to use.

LS30: Stages in planning

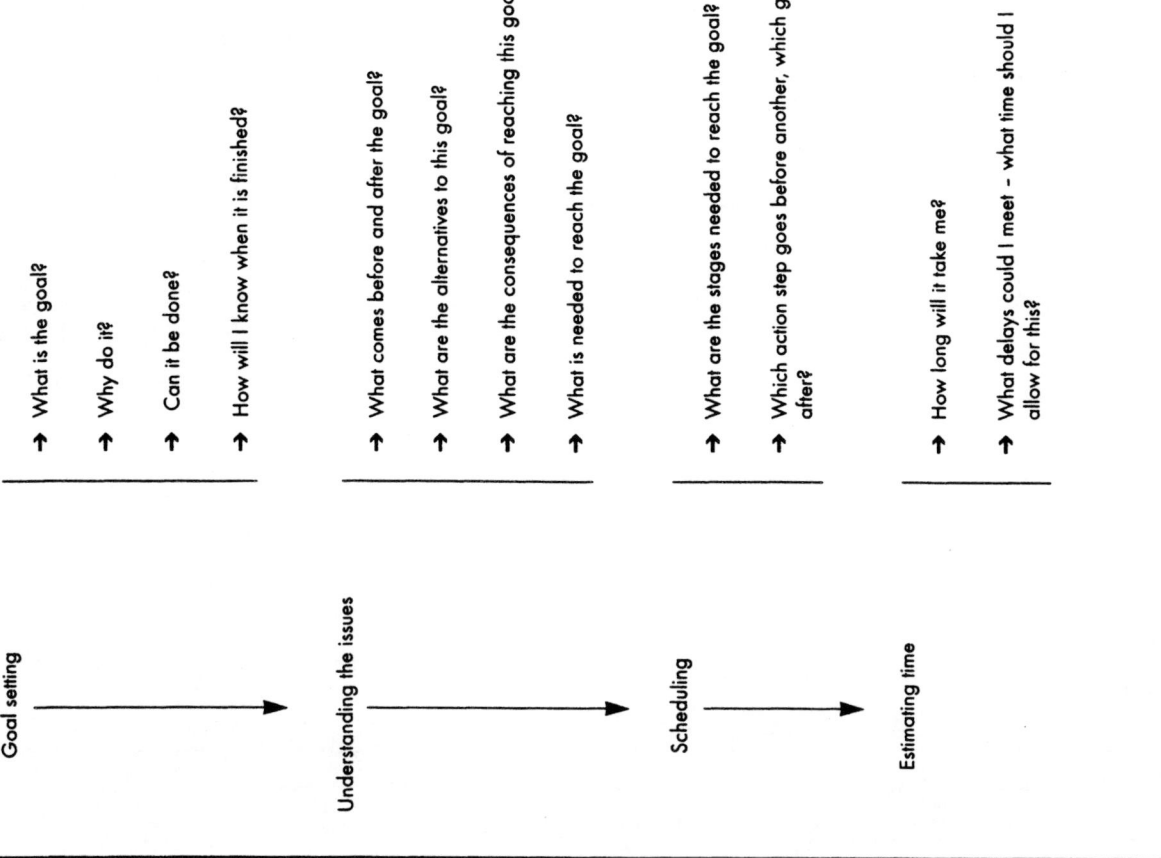

Goal setting →
- → What is the goal?
- → Why do it?
- → Can it be done?
- → How will I know when it is finished?

Understanding the issues →
- → What comes before and after the goal?
- → What are the alternatives to this goal?
- → What are the consequences of reaching this goal?
- → What is needed to reach the goal?

Scheduling →
- → What are the stages needed to reach the goal?
- → Which action step goes before another, which goes after?

Estimating time
- → How long will it take me?
- → What delays could I meet – what time should I allow for this?

LS29: Checking your organisation

For each question put a tick by the most appropriate answer

1. How much do you plan your time on average?

   Not at all   A bit   Quite a lot   Always

2. Do you use a diary to plan?

   Not at all   A bit   Quite a lot   Always

3. If you are going to undertake a task, do you set aside the time to do this and finish it?

   Not at all   Occasionally   If possible   Always

4. Do you plan out what you need to do and how you do it?

   Not at all   A bit   Quite a lot   Always

5. Do you get everything ready before you start the task?

   Not at all   A bit   Quite a lot   Always

6. Do you put things away when you have finished using them?

   Not at all   A bit   Quite a lot   Always

7. Do you have particular places for certain activities; e.g. woodwork or art area, a place where you always do paperwork?

   Not at all   A bit   Quite a lot   Always

8. If you need something, can you find it easily?

   Not at all   A bit   Quite a lot   Always

Using the answers to these questions can you say whether you regard yourself as: (tick one)

   Very organised   Average   Not organised

LS32: Weekly time plan

Week beginning _____

Targets _____

		MONDAY	TUESDAY	WEDNESDAY	THURSDAY	FRIDAY	SATURDAY	SUNDAY
MORNING	aim							
	actual							
AFTERNOON	aim							
	actual							
EVENING	aim							
	actual							

Review: _____   Next week: _____

_____   _____

LS31: Time

Your time

Tick the column which seems closest to your answer to each question.

	Often	Some-times	Rarely
1. Do you write daily to-do lists?			
2. Do you prioritise your to-do lists?			
3 Do you finish all the items on your to-do lists?			
4. Do you think you deal effectively with interruptions?			
5. Do you allow yourself to complete a task?			
6. Do you have short-term goals?			
7. Do you put things off until the last minute?			
8. Do you focus on preventing problems before they arise rather than solving them after they happen?			

	Often	Some-times	Rarely
9. Do you meet deadlines with time to spare?			
10. Are you on time to events?			
11. Do you have long-term goals?			
12. Do you waste time?			
13. Do you try to avoid getting on with things?			
14. Does your mind wander?			
15. Do you plan what you need to do to complete a job?			
16. Do you begin and finish things on time?			

Give yourself 4 points for every Often you ticked, 2 points for every Sometimes, and 0 points for every Rarely. Add up your score and compare it with the scale below.

Your time scoring	
45-64	You seem to manage your time very well.
33-44	You manage your time well some of the time.
21-32	You could benefit from better time management.
0-20	OK, so your time management is not too good at the moment.

PLANNING → **DOING** → **REVIEWING** → **CONCLUDING** → **PLANNING**

DOING

REVIEWING

CONCLUDING

PLANNING

Handout LS33: A learning action plan

Three learning skills I should like to develop:

1.

2.

3.

The reasons for developing these are so as to:

1.

2.

3.

Action steps

Area to work on	Action	Date

Review date:

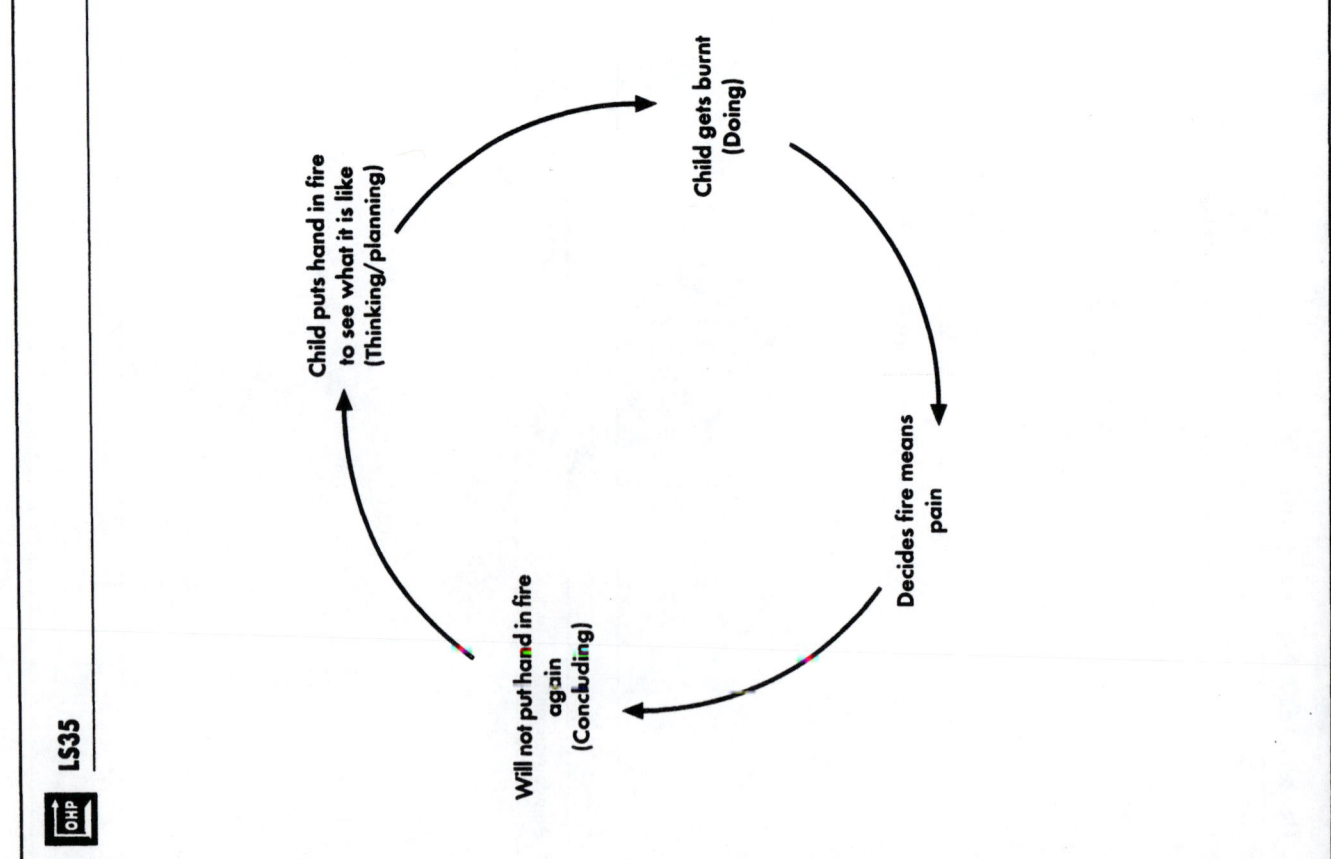

Child puts hand in fire
to see what it is like
(Thinking/planning)

Child gets burnt
(Doing)

Decides fire means
pain

Will not put hand in fire
again
(Concluding)

GOD

SAVE THE

THE QUEEN

Developing an understanding of the workplace and workplace skills

 This module is divided into five sessions:

1. Understandings and experiences of work and the workplace (1 hour)
2. Features of the workplace (5 hours)
3. Entry to the workplace and gaining acceptance (7 hours)
4. Managing working life (4 hours 40 min)
5. Creating a programme summary (1 hour)

 This module links with others in the *Developing Life Skills* manual. These include:

- Identifying personal and transferable skills
- DIY: improving your chances

It would be of value encouraging learners to also consider some of the self-management modules:

- Identifying and managing stress
- Managing time
- Managing money
- Food and nutrition
- Exercise and well-being

Many of these aspects of self-management will help the learner to be more effective in the workplace by managing life outside the workplace with greater success. Some strategies, for example dealing with stress can be used in the workplace.

A range of communication skills, the management of emotions and assertiveness skills are explored in the manual *Developing Social Skills*. Again, work on these areas will help the learner to be more effective in the workplace.

 The module uses the training and learning activities of:

- small and whole group discussions
- self-assessment
- brainstorming
- role-plays
- action planning
- group problem solving

 ## Trainer's notes

This module encourages learners to:

- develop an awareness of the ways in which the workplace is structured
- think about some of the qualities which are valued by employers and fellow workers
- consider how closely they can match such qualities
- consider their own work career and the ways in which it may be managed
- cultivate skills, qualities and understandings to fit themselves for the workplace

Why consider the workplace?

An understanding of and preparation for the workplace is important for people who have not previously been employed, who may have been in a residential setting and who may carry with them into the workplace such labels of ex-offenders, forensic or other psychiatric patient.

Rehearsal of expectations, rights, responsibilities and roles, and the management of self in the workplace may increase individuals' opportunities for successfully negotiating the workplace.

The importance of work in people's lives needs little underlining. It is often a way people add shape to their lives, find routine and structure, find or extend social activities and extend their skills and experiences. Work is often a way in which people define themselves, their roles and relationships to others. Work provides opportunities for growth and a sense of self-worth. Work provides access through the income it generates to various types of lifestyle, leisure activities and to socio-economic status.

Work can help ex-offenders and others from residential settings to create structures and social contacts to embed themselves back into a community. It can help provide purpose and some sense of personal direction. Gaining employment and further vocational training has been shown to decrease the likelihood of re-offending, of re-admittance to residential settings and of relapse.

Rehearsal of some of the benefits of thinking about preparation for and management of the workplace will be of value with the learners.

The centrality of work in terms of sense of purpose, as a way to define self and for the income it generates can make discussion of working life a difficult one. This module aims to raise awareness and to encourage a broad discussion about expectations of work, the functioning of the workplace and negotiating entry. It is not a module particularly designed to suit the needs of the long-term unemployed or for those with significantly negative attitudes towards employment. Although material in the module can be used with these two groups.

Session One: Understandings and experiences of work and the workplace

Introductory activity: brainstorm (20 min)
Brainstorm with the group what work means to them.

Encourage the learners to consider paid, unpaid and voluntary work, work undertaken to maintain a home or work for hobbies. Some learners may not engage with a module on work if they think it is just about paid employment. They may have little interest in or no experience of paid employment and may therefore not realise that they have many skills and experiences of working. This initial brainstorm should be an opportunity to introduce the diversity of experiences of work amongst the group members and to explore the meaning of work.

Encourage the brainstorm to range widely over feelings about work, experiences of work, expectations about work and places where work may take place. An example of a brainstorm follows overleaf.

An in-depth brainstorm will give the learners a chance to explore a number of feelings about the nature of work.

Experiences of work (30 min)
Working in pairs ask the learners to tell each other some stories about their experiences of work, paid or unpaid, in a workplace or at home. From the exchange of past experiences ask the pairs to be able to present to the group some ideas about:

> **why working is important to people and what they gain from it**

Ask each pair to contribute ideas to the whole group during a feedback session. Record these ideas on the flipchart. As a whole group consider the suggestions and add any more which result from the discussion.

Work may be defined in many ways by the learners.
Ask for examples of statements and for them to elaborate on their statements

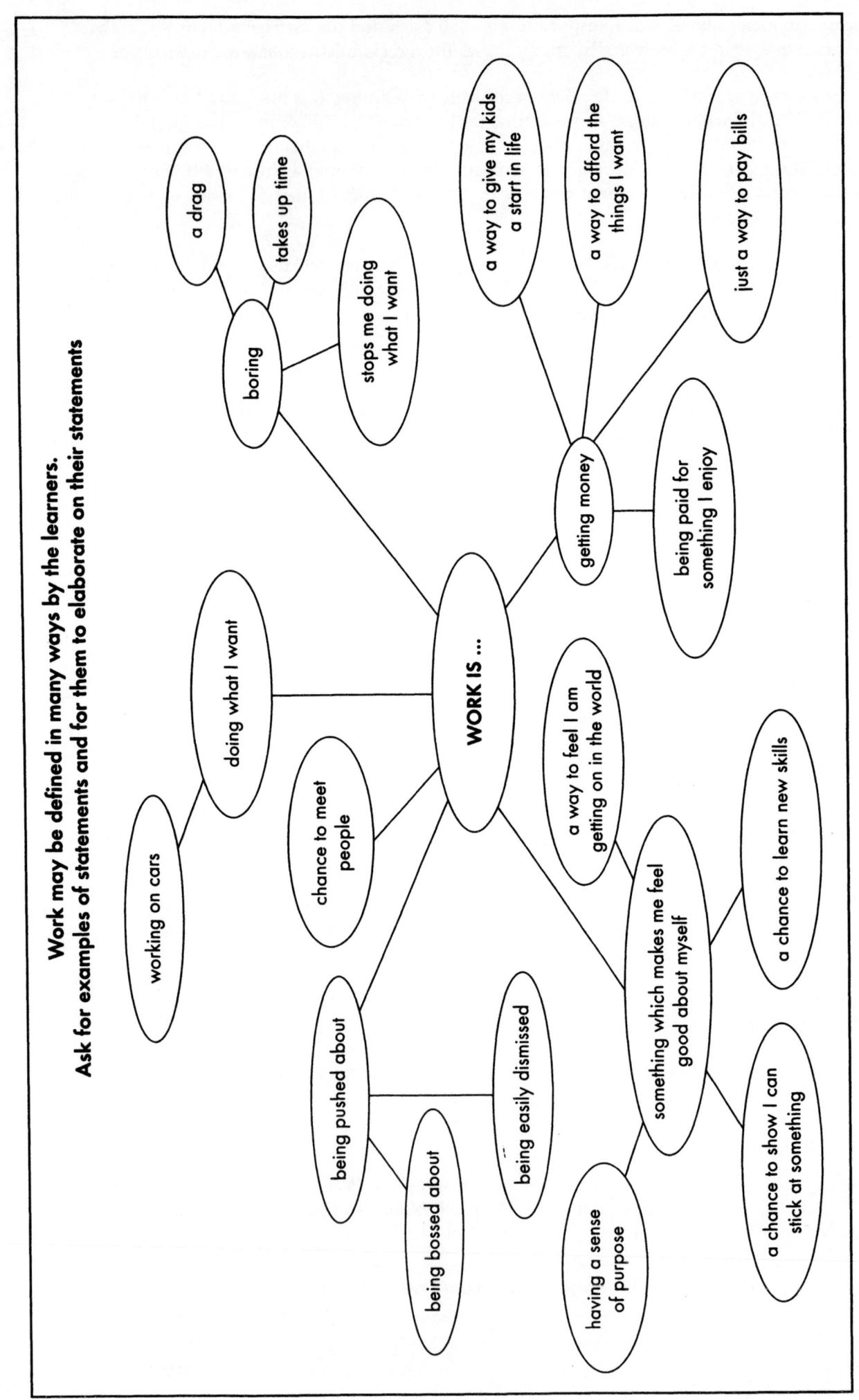

The importance of work (10 min)

After these two brainstorm and discussion activities, explore with the group the importance of work, of being prepared for work and understanding the workplace. Consider some of the points raised in the Trainer's notes about the value of work for encouraging self-esteem, structure and direction in life.

Outline the areas to be covered by the module such as expectations of employers and colleagues; understanding the workplace; understanding what individuals have to offer in the workplace; increasing chances of success in the workplace and planning how to make work-related changes.

Check that the group understands what these areas mean and why they are to be considered.

Session Two: Features of the workplace

This session considers three aspects of the workplace:
- A. expectations of employers
- B. expectations of colleagues and team working
- C. the changing workplace

A. Expectations of employers

What do employers want?

Working alone (10 min)
Ask the learners to work on their own reading through the statement cards (WP1). The learners should select the top 12 features which they think an employer looks for in an employee and be willing to explain why they have made such a selection.

Working in pairs (10 min)
In pairs the learners should compare their top 12 features, and through discussion select eight cards which they both feel an employer would look for in an employee.

As a small group (10 min)
Then ask the pair to work with another pair and to reach a decision on the top six features. These groups need a spokesperson to feedback to the whole group.

Feedback and review (30 min)
Each spokesperson will need to clearly justify why the six have been selected. The rest of the group may like to ask why a particular feature was rejected or was not part of their top six. In order to effectively manage the feedback ask each group to justify features which have not come up before or to add to earlier explanations. Do not just allow a group to repeat what another group has already said.

The whole group needs to reach some agreement on the top six attributes they think an employer would look for. Record these on a flipchart. Ask the group members if they feel that they have these attributes and how they could evidence having them. Record this evidence on the flipchart. (The learners may like to keep a record for their CVs or interviews.) Take note of any attributes which the learners feel they do not have or do not have the evidence to support.

Ask the learners to consider all the statements and the discussion and to complete four positive statements about themselves on worksheet WP2.

Role-plays (40 min)
Having discussed what employers want from employees, ask the learners to work in groups of four to role-play the situations on WP3. Give each group a different situation. The role-plays

should encourage the learners to see why employers expect certain behaviours and qualities from their employees and the consequences if these behaviours or skills are not present. Give the group ten minutes to prepare their role-plays.

Each group should present their role-play and then the whole group should explore the situation through thorough questioning before moving to the next role-play. The audience should be encouraged to help question the characters. The following questions may help:

To the employer/foreman/manager:
How did you feel about what was being done?
Did it feel personal?
What did you think was in their mind?
What were your concerns about their actions?
What were your fears about what they were doing?
What did you want to achieve by challenging them?
Did you feel pleased with the way you handled the situation? Why/why not?
Did you get the outcome you wanted?
What would you have done differently?

To the employee(s):
What motivated you to act in this way?
What were you hoping to gain from it?
How do you think the employer felt about what you were doing?
Why would they feel like this?
What did you feel when you were confronted?
Were you pleased with the outcome of the situation? Why?
What would you have done differently and why?

Ask anyone else in the audience what they felt about what was going on. Did they take sides? Whose and why?

Group discussion (15 min)
At the close of all the role-plays ask the whole group to offer any examples of things which they had not considered before or had thought about differently.

B. Expectations of colleagues and team working

 Trainer's notes

Just as employers have expectations about workers and ideas about what they want from a worker, so people who work in the same workplace have expectations of each other. If a group does not work well together then the workplace:
- may not function well and work may not get done
- may be a place of little trust between workers
- may feel and be hostile or tense and not a pleasant place to be in
- may have a workplace bully or a practical joker who upsets others
- may have some people who are excluded and made to feel bad
- may see some people blamed for things going wrong
- may not lead to a fair division of work

Depending on the type of work done, a group which does not work well as a team may create a dangerous workplace. For example, if someone cuts corners or does not think about the health and safety of others.

Learners are asked to consider:
- colleagues' expectations

- what makes an effective team
- what may lead to problems at work

Through these exercises the learners are to rate themselves as an effective colleague and to make a personal checklist of things to consider when they go into the workplace to work with others.

Colleagues' expectations

Brainstorm and story telling (40 min)

Ask the whole group to brainstorm what expectations workers may have of each other. If the group has had little work experience or finds the idea hard then give some examples of groups of workers in different working environments, e.g. working on a building site, working in a busy factory meeting an end of the week deadline or working as part of a new small or family business.

The group should be generating ideas such as:

- working as a team
- not making the workplace unsafe for others
- not preventing others working, e.g. disturbing them, taking all the necessary resources
- helping each other
- not bullying
- not grassing to managers
- not putting one another down
- covering for each other
- swapping shifts

Ask for a couple of volunteers to talk to the whole group about times when their expectations of their fellow workers were met and then they were not met.

Once they have told a story ask:

- how they felt about it and why?
- what happened to the work which was being done?
- what could have happened if the opposite had been the case?

Small groups (20 min)

Ask the learners to take ten minutes to decide on a list of their top five expectations of colleagues at work. Then run a ten minute group feedback to see how much consensus there is between the lists. Several learners should have stressed the importance of working as a team.

Team working

Pair work (10 minutes including group feedback)

In pairs, ask the learners to think of and tell each other a couple of stories about times when they worked well in a team or well with another person. The examples can come from any activity, not just paid work.

Once they have thought of and recounted the stories ask the pairs to decide and then write on a flipchart answers to the following questions.

1. What makes for good team/pair working?
2. What are the advantages of good team/pair working?
3. How does the experience of good team/pair working make you feel?

Ask for some feedback from each small group to the whole group and draw up a list of qualities/attributes of good team working and benefits of good team working.

Problem solving activity (40 min)

1. Randomly divide the whole group into teams of four. Encourage the learners to work with new people. The groups will need to have space in which to work without being overheard or disturbed. They will need to have free choice from a number of batons or balls which are the objects to be used in the game to be devised by the group.

2. Each team needs to work together to:
   a. decide what object(s) are to be passed by another team from one side of the room to the other
   b. decide on how the object should be passed and create simple and clear rules for the other team
   c. decide who is their team's representative to explain the rules to the other team

   The teams need at this stage to:
   • work well under pressure
   • to share ideas and to work with the best ideas
   • to work together to create clear rules
   • to work together to select the best representative

3. The teams should take it in turn to explain to another team their version of the game of passing the object(s).

   At this stage the team passing the object needs:
   • to support each other to ensure that everyone understands what is to be done
   • to work well passing the object, not blaming or making another person nervous
   • to work together to cope with pressure

4. At the close of the exercise ask each team to describe how they worked together as a team and what they might have done differently or improve upon.

   As a trainer you will need to manage the account of teamworking, steer the learners away from blaming particular group members and remind the group that teams work best when there is a sharing of tasks and use of strengths.

5. Check on the learning points.

Closing exercise (10 min)

Ask the whole group to offer some learning points about why teams work well and why they may fail. Compare these with the ideas from the first pairwork session. Thank the learners for their work on this exercise.

Why might problems occur between work colleagues? (1 hour)

Brainstorm (20 min)

Ask the group to work in pairs or threes to brainstorm a list of problems which can occur between people at work. Some may have personal experience to draw on and will have stories to tell, others may have no experience and will have to imagine possible problems. Ask the group members to think of real or imagined examples to illustrate their list of possible problems.

To manage the feedback to the whole group ask each pair or three to have five examples or ideas to offer to the whole group. Allow the small groups time to decide which they want to offer in the feedback session.

Feedback (10 min)

Take the examples offered from each group, ask for some illustration of the suggestions and record these on the flipchart. Once the group list is completed, work with the group to try to put the problems and the causes of the problems in categories. Most frequent causes of problems will be:

- poor communication – not listening, not giving instructions properly, failing to explain changes in the workplace
- feeling someone has been rude or abusive
- feeling someone has assumed a job will be done
- people not wanting to work as a team
- not talking about communication or relationship problems

1. Work out with the group how many problems come back to poor communications between workers in the workplace.

2. Work out with the group how poor communications could be improved. Try to generate a list for example:
   - telling each other clearly what needs to be done not guessing or assuming
   - giving full instructions
   - listening to each other
   - being friendly to the new person/the little liked person to make them part of the team
   - making an effort to be polite
   - asking if something is not understood
   - checking that you understand what is wanted

Working with colleagues: guidance notes (20 min)
Ask the group to work in small groups and to decide on a set of ideas or some guidance which they would offer new workers in a workplace to help them to get on successfully with others.

Ask the groups when they have agreed on their ideas or guidance notes to write them on an A1 sheet for display. Remind them to cover:
- good communications
- team working
- meeting colleagues' reasonable expectations
- how to manage situations which go wrong

Display feedback (10 min)
Display these notes and encourage each group to read the others' notes. If the group wants copies of these notes then arrange for this to be done.

C. The changing workplace

 Trainer's notes

The purpose of this session is to encourage the learners to think about:
- the ways in which workplaces change and have changed
- the changes in skills required to manage the workplace
- changes in expectations
- how workers may need to change to conform to the demands of the workplace
- why there are changes in the workplace

The success of the session will depend on the learners being able to identify changes which have occurred within their working lifetimes and using their imaginations to help them consider changes. Areas which should be covered are:
- changes in health and safety legislation, increased emphasis on working by such rules and the importance of so doing
- the increasing use of technology and the importance of computer skills
- the importance of not being afraid of technology

- the importance of being willing to try a range of different jobs and develop new skills
- the fact that there is 'no job for life' and that people will take on many new jobs and types of job in a single working life
- the importance of being accountable
- the importance of working within budgets, making good use of resources and being accountable for use of resources
- the importance of training and re-training to improve skills to tackle a job or to change jobs
- competition from foreign competitors
- the importance of identifying personal skills and strengths and being willing to develop these
- changes in national/international economy and therefore in demand for goods and services

This list is not exhaustive but it points the way. The trainer should be prepared to try to tease out similar points from the group and to ask the group to come up with examples to illustrate them.

Group activity (15 min)
Ask the group to think of ways in which the workplace has changed in their lifetimes or compare their working lives with their parents or grandparents. Thinking about the changing nature of employment may be a useful starting point, for example a move from manufacturing and light engineering to service-based industries or the rise of use in the information technology and so on.

Work with the ideas that the learners offer about the changing nature of work and the workplace. Try to tease out some of the points listed as Trainer's notes.

Pair work: identifying areas of need (20 min)
Once the group has exhausted what it can offer and you have no more suggestions to make then ask the groups to break into pairs to decide:
- how ready they feel for changes in the workplace
- on one or two areas they would like individually to work on developing. This should be recorded for future use (WP4).

Feedback (15 min)
Draw the group back together and ask for examples from the pair session. The areas which have been identified may be ones for which solutions can readily be found. Be sure to have some referrals ready which may help them, e.g.
- basic computing courses
- developing literacy and numeracy skills
- careers guidance facilities
- re-training programmes

There are a selection of leaflets available from Job Centres and Careers Centres about, for example, training and working abroad.

Final brainstorm (10 min)
Ask the group to brainstorm what changes they can imagine happening in the world of work over the next 20 years. Ask them to identify how these changes may call for further changes in their own skills and approaches to the workplace and working life. List these.

Give the learners a chance to note any changes identified thus which may be of use to them, use WP4.

Session Three: Entry to the workplace and gaining acceptance

This session is in four main sections, these are:

1. Looking for work
2. Applications and CVs
3. Job interviews
4. Making the right start

 Trainer's notes

Introduce the four areas covered by the session and explain to the group that it is important to realise how much effort goes into finding work and that having found work they need to be aware of how to best manage themselves in the workplace.

1. Looking for work
Looking for work (15 min)
Ask the group to brainstorm how they might go about finding work. The list should include such sources of help and information as:

- Job Centre
- local store noticeboards/corner shops
- newspapers – bought and free
- employment agencies
- shops/restaurant/pub windows
- asking family and friends
- writing speculative letters
- asking at any pubs or groups you visit frequently
- putting a card in a local shop
- leaflets through doors

Ask for examples of any ways in which the group members have found work. Find out if any of the learners got more permanent or other work by taking on a temporary job.

While looking for work (15 min)
Again, ask the group to consider, as a brainstorm exercise, the advice they would offer anyone who was looking for work about what to do while job searching. The suggestions should cover:

- staying fit and healthy
- keeping a routine in their day, so that going to work would not be such a shock
- taking an interest in the wider world, having ideas and conversation beyond being unemployed
- doing some voluntary or unpaid work to broaden experience and skills
- taking a free training course
- finding out about facilities offered locally for unemployed people to help assist them get jobs or re-skill
- finding out about facilities which are free or cheap for unemployed people, e.g. sport facilities
- making the best use of money, e.g. budgeting for food, ensuring that there is money for travel costs, that clothes can be repaired or replaced
- learning to do things for oneself and not paying others to do it
- swapping skills with others
- not giving up

Ask the learners to come up with reasons why they would offer such advice to people looking for work. They might consider their reasons in response to the following questions:

    a. How do these activities help get work?

    b. How do they help people prepare to manage work?

    c. What positive qualities would they show a potential employer?

Creating a checklist (20 min)

Ask the group to work in threes to create a 15 point checklist of essential things to do while looking for employment. Some things may be work-related, others may be about supporting the person while they are looking for work. Ask the groups to write down the reasons for each point on their checklist.

The groups need to write these out on A1 sheets for display.

Group sharing by display (10 min)

Give the learners time to read each group's checklists. If they feel that any checklists are very helpful then arrange to have these copied for the learners.

2. Applications and CVs

 Trainer's notes

This section considers the second hurdle to gaining entry to the workplace. It looks at making applications and preparing a CV or letter of application. You will need to stress how much time needs to be invested in job search activities and invested in applying for work before gaining work.

The activities in this session will require literacy skills and confidence in writing. You may find some of your learners have neither or need help. Be ready with suggestions of appropriate support and assistance. These exercises should not undermine the learners.

The previous section considered looking for work and maintaining oneself while looking for work. It emphasised investment of time, having a wide search strategy and resourcefulness in self-maintenance while looking for work. This section considers:

- reading job adverts
- making applications
- drawing up a CV or personal profile

Reading job adverts (25 min)

Ask the group to work in pairs.

To make the session realistic have a supply of job adverts ready and some examples of completed CVs and application letters. Give out several sheets of job adverts to each pair. Ask them to read through each advert and find a couple which are interesting. Ask them to use the checklist WP5 to decide:

- what information is in the advert?
- how they need to reply?
- what information they need to ask for?
- what information they need to offer?

Move round the pairs checking on their progress and helping with the answers to questions.

Group feedback (25 min)

Ask the group:

- What kinds of information was missing from the job adverts they read?

- What other information they might want to find out?
- How useful have they found it to work carefully through the job adverts in this way?

Ask for a volunteer to read out their advert and explain the key features of the job – check the group agrees. Note these on the flipchart.

Ask the group to decide on the key qualities and experiences which an employer would look for. Compare this list with the six points the learner was intending to make about why he or she would be good for that post.

 Trainer's notes

Stress that many employers screen out possible candidates by giving a telephone interview when they telephone for details. The learners should ensure they have thoroughly read an advert, considered the information offered, what they need to know and their reasons for applying before they telephone. Following **WP5** will help with this.

Completing a personal profile (30 min)

Building on from the six points which the learners identified in WP5 to offer in support of the job advert they read they will need to have gathered factual and other information about themselves. A way to prepare to successfully complete application forms and letters is to create a basic personal profile (see **WP6**).

Ask the learners to read through **WP6** and to ask about anything which they do not understand. Check on understanding by asking questions about one or two of the sections and asking for examples of what might be included in these sections.

Check on the completion of these forms. Ask the learners to keep these and to update them. Explain that these will be useful records to help for completion of application letters or forms.

 Trainer's notes

The completion of proformas which ask about employment, experience and qualifications are always hard. Sometimes it is hard to be brief and think of the key skills, sometimes it is hard because there is no experience or few formal qualifications. The learners need to be aware of the importance of making the best of what they have so:

- unpaid or voluntary work will have been experience and have been a useful source of skill creation
- taking a course but not the exam has still been valuable

Sensitivity and working with learners on these exercises will be essential. Change WP6 if it seems more appropriate to your situation.

Application forms and letters (30 min)

Hand out **WP7** a mock application form. Decide on a couple of jobs the learners may apply for at *Brown and Co.*, the skills needed and nature of the job. If possible, have to hand some adverts and job descriptions to help the learners to shape their answers.

Take ten minutes to work through the types of information wanted on the form and explain the various headings. Ask the learners to offer their ideas on what is wanted and then you can elaborate or correct them. Brainstorm with the learners how an application form may be completed. List their suggestions. They should include:

- sort out information needed on separate paper before beginning
- check dates, addresses and places
- make sure there are no gaps in time not accounted for

- write on the form in pencil first and then ink over
- check spellings before completing the form
- make use of profiles such as **WP6**

Ask the learners to work alone for a further 20 minutes completing the form reproduced as **WP7**.

Check each learner understands and is progressing well. Sit alongside and help any who are having difficulties. Encourage the learners to identify why and what their problems are.

At the close of the exercise ask the group to come back together and discuss what if anything they found difficult.

Application letters – talk to the group (10 min)
Explain that some employers like a form to be completed and a covering letter may be needed to accompany the form. This letter should:

- contain information about which post is applied for and why you are most suitable
- point to any particular strengths you have
- be brief

However employers may not always use an application form. This will mean that the learner has to get the same information across clearly and briefly but without the help of a form. It may be useful to have a CV prepared and to send this with a covering letter applying for the job. The letter will need to indicate:

- which job is being applied for
- what strengths and qualities the individual would bring to the company/job
- what makes them the special applicant
- any other features they have to offer the employer, e.g. reliablility, good health, loyalty etc.

Letters and CVs may also be used when no specific job has been advertised but when someone wants to find out if the company would have a vacancy.

Working alone (15 min)
Ask the learners to complete a CV. A sample is printed as **WP8**. It would be best if they could word process their CVs, so an arrangement for this if possible would be of greatest benefit. The CV should be kept for later use. The material already collated as part of the personal profile and application form will help in creating the CVs.

Covering letter (25 min)
Ask the learners to go back to the job adverts they selected and to write a letter of application applying for the job in which they have interest.

Before they write check on the key things they would put in a letter, with those on the flipchart as a reminder.

Remind them of letter layout by giving out handout **WP9** and explaining it to them.

3. Job interviews
Pair work and feedback (20 min)
Ask the learners to work in pairs to list as many things as possible which may make a job interview go badly. After five minutes check progress by asking for a couple of examples from each pair. After a further five minutes ask the pairs to give you a list of all the things which can make interviews go wrong. Record these on the flipchart. Only ask the pairs to add new ideas to the list.

You may have a brainstorm which covers:

- wearing the wrong clothes
- swearing in the interview, not being respectful
- not knowing details of the job or the firm
- not seeming interested in the job or the firm
- only asking questions about the benefits, e.g. pay, holiday, lunches
- not making an effort to talk about skills, qualities and why the job is wanted
- not having any sensible questions to ask about the job
- not really seeming keen about the job
- not offering ways in which they can develop in the job

Interview role-plays (40 min)

Ask the learners to again work in pairs. Explain that the role-play is a job interview and that one will need to be the interviewer and the other the interviewee. Each will need to have:

a. the job advert
b. the application letter

} these will need to have been invented by the trainer before the session and should reflect the type of jobs the group would be interested in having

Ask each learner to work alone spending ten minutes on their part. The interviewer needs to decide what questions to ask and inventing more details about the job. The interviewee needs to decide what might be asked, how questions will be answered and what further information will be needed from the interviewer.

Then, depending on the size of the group, ask for two or three pairs of volunteers to role-play their interviews for the whole group.

The whole group should analyse each interview once it is completed deciding:

- how realistic were the questions?
- what else could have been asked?
- how good were the answers and what else might they have added?
- what questions might they have asked the potential employer?

It is important that the group questions carefully, not upsetting either of the players. It has to be stressed it is a role-play and these people are in character. Interviews are a stressful and difficult situation and no learner will want to be reminded of a painful role-play in which they felt they had failed.

Ask each learner in character what it felt like to be the interviewer or interviewee, what was hard about the role and how each thought the other performed in their role.

Keep a running list of points made by the role-players and the group on a flipchart. Be clear about the learning points from the role-plays and then ask the rest of the group to undertake their role-plays in light of the observations.

Full group role-plays and observations (15 min)

Those who have already role-played can act as observers of the other pairs. They will need sheet WP10 to record their observations and to help give feedback to the role-play pair they are watching.

Feedback (25 min)

Draw together the role-play exercise. Ask for learning points from the observers and those doing the role-plays.

- what went well and why?
- what went badly and why?

Try to generate a group list of ten key things to do at an interview.

4. Making the right start

This section considers how to manage the first few days and weeks at work to create the best possible impression and to gain acceptance by colleagues and employers.

Opening brainstorm (10 min)

Ask the learners to consider what they need to think carefully about the first few days and weeks in a new job. Points might include:

- knowing exactly what is wanted
- not upsetting people
- not being thought an upstart
- doing the right thing
- not breaking any rules
- knowing the firm's policy on certain things
- creating the impression of someone reliable
- asking and not assuming
- not covering up mistakes
- checking before doing
- not thinking you are always right

Survival skills and actions (45 min)

Ask the group to work in pairs, with the points from the opening brainstorm to create two lists. One list should be evidence of ways in which the points selected from the brainstorm can be demonstrated, the other list, the skills or qualities which are needed to create the evidence.

So for example:

Creating the impression of someone reliable	
Indicator	Demonstration of a skill, quality or behaviour
• being on time for work • not phoning in sick • not asking for time off • not trying to get shifts covered or swapping with a colleague • doing what is asked rather than what I think • not wasting resources	• being punctual and having good time-keeping • organising things outside working hours, time management • listening carefully to what is wanted • thinking about the job before starting

Ask the pairs to write up their two lists on an A1 sheet of paper and have these sheets displayed on the walls.

Before allowing time for the pairs to look at each other's lists of survival ideas, skills and actions ask each pair to present a couple of their ideas to the group for the group to discuss.

Again if any in the group feels the lists are helpful, arrange to have them copied.

Self-assessment (20 min)

Ask each learner to consider how they rate themselves on some of the skills and qualities which will have been discussed in the previous exercise Survival skills and action. Use the checklist WP11 as a starting point and ask them to add any more skills and qualities on which they rate themselves.

Planning improvements (25 min)

The learners can work alone or in pairs as they wish to decide upon a plan for improving areas of skills or quality which they have identified as poor or as not yet accomplished during the self-assessment exercise. Use the action plan sheet WP12.

The trainer will need to work through the action plan with them, perhaps working an example of an area to improve. The trainer should draw up the action plan on the flipchart and ask for suggestions of concrete action, success criteria and who may help.

The learners may be more creative and thoughtful working in pairs or may gain more by comparing plans once they have completed their own plans. The trainer will need to check on progress and work with those who are presenting problems.

Session Four: Managing working life

 Trainer's notes

This session builds on the previous session on developing skills to manage the first few days and weeks in the workplace. It encourages learners to think how they should fit work into the rest of their lives successfully. It considers:

- managing stress
- dealing with communications and interpersonal relationships
- balancing work and home time
- developing and planning working life
- personal organisation

Once learners are in the workplace and have negotiated the first few days and weeks the habits to successfully sustain working life still need to be developed and to be reinforced. They need to be reminded that it is perhaps easy to create a good first impression but that it may become hard to sustain this. This session draws on individual learner's experiences and makes use of some information-giving sessions. There are handouts to accompany some of the issues covered in this session.

Many of the issues are covered in depth in other modules. For example, Communication Skills, Time Management and Stress Management.

Opening brainstorm (20 min)

Ask the learners to work in pairs or threes to generate a list of what can go wrong at work and in managing their work and home lives. The groups will work well with a mix of those with longer term experience and inexperience in the workplace. If groups flounder ask them to imagine problems or think of problems friends have told them about.

After ten minutes, have a feedback session with the whole group and explore some of the suggestions. You will cover some areas which this session tackles, for example:

- stress
- time management
- personal organisation
- boredom
- money worries
- loss of direction
- the job not living up to expectations

Stress and work

Brainstorming and small group solution seeking (15 min)
As a brainstorm decide:

> **What can be stressful about work?**

The suggestions may include:

- being on time
- not having enough money to manage on
- not worth going to work
- not having time to myself
- too many demands on time

- being bored
- not getting on with workplace colleagues
- always being in the wrong place
- getting picked on
- bullying in the workplace

The brainstorm will raise issues which will need exploring. The learners need to find out:

- why something happens
- what an individual could do to make it better
- who an individual could ask for help
- what an individual may do to change their reaction to it or their behaviour

Use these questions and explore a few examples with the whole group and then ask them to work in small groups to explore three or four stressors and try to come up with reasons for stress and solutions to these stressful situations.

Group feedback session (25 min)

Decide which of the solutions seem to be valuable ones. Remind the group of sources of help and things which they can do to help themselves. This could include:

- debt counsellors
- money management courses
- improving communication skills
- looking for other types of work
- getting training to make the job easier or to get on
- planning a personal timetable to fit in activities and cutting down on time-wasting activities or habits
- remembering assertiveness skills and being sure to ask for help or saying 'no' to additional demands
- basic stress management tips. These include:
    - identify the problem and talk about it to find a solution or to find a way to accept it
    - find something else to focus on to give you a break
    - take appropriate action to confront the problem once you know what it is
    - remove yourself from the situation if you cannot change the stressful situation
    - look after and don't abuse yourself, e.g. cut down on drinking, eat properly, get enough sleep

 Trainer's note

The following activities look at some of the main stressors about work in a little more detail.

Dealing with communication and interpersonal relations

Brainstorm as a group what can go wrong between people at work (20 min)

The list should identify a number of aspects of poor communication and demonstrate the importance to the learners of getting these skills right. The list might include:

- assuming people will do something rather than asking them
- not asking for help
- not being clear what is wanted or not asking for it to be clarified
- not listening properly to instructions
- not giving instructions properly
- being pushed about

Ask the group to identify those areas which are most problematic for them and then find appropriate communication exercises in the manual *Developing Social Skills* to meet these needs. There is a self-assessment exercising **WP13** which learners could use to help them highlight any areas of difficulty and help you to plan other learning activities (20 min).

Remind the group of the importance of being assertive within any relationship at work. Remind the group of the meaning of assertiveness. Trying to be assertive will give them the opportunity to clarify what is wanted of them and what it is reasonable to be expected to do. Assertiveness is dealt with in *Developing Social Skills*.

Balancing work time and home time (40 min)

Some learners may complain that work takes up too much time or that they are too tired to do anything else.

1. Remind the learners of the importance of having a range of activities in the day and changing activity to encourage a sense of energy and well-being. Recommend some exercise after work to change the nature of the activity which they have been doing and to encourage them to focus on something else and have the opportunity to feel better about themselves.

2. Encourage the learner to complete a time log to work out how they spend their time over a week and a week-end. An example is **WP14**. Ask them to divide it into:
   a. working/training time – committed time which is paid for by an employer, this will also include travel time
   b. maintenance time – time spent on sleeping, washing, feeding shopping, caring for others
   c. discretionary time – time they have free to watch TV, go to the pub, for hobbies or just to waste.

   Ask them to look at the way time is used and to consider how they may change the balance of their activities to release more time for something they want to do. Many people are surprised how they spend their time, how much of it is wasted or spent doing something they do not want to do.

3. Encourage the learners to look at different leisure activities which are available and which they might try. Cost, location of facilities, experience of leisure activities and self-confidence may all affect their choice and will all have an impact on choice of use of leisure activities and willingness to pursue it.

   Many people do not appreciate the value of leisure in promoting a sense of well-being, personal growth and in encouraging a change in focus of attention. Leisure activities teach new skills, may broaden the range of social contacts, may encourage good heath and self-esteem. The learners should be encouraged to consider how planned use of leisure time will have value for them.

4. Planning time and prioritising what is done with time will help the learners to find that work encroaches less on their lives and that it is a part of their lives. They will gain more by planning their time and from having allocated other activities into their lives.

Use **WP15** to encourage learners to think about possible activities.

Ask the learners to decide on a couple of activities which they would try out ask them to research how they would get involved e.g. what equipment, who would they go to for tuition, costs, location of the activity and what they would need to commit themselves.

Developing and planning working life (1 hour)

Some of the issues which may have come up may include boredom; not enough money; job taking up too much time; too far to travel or not a demanding enough job. The learners should be aware that they need to plan their working lives and so consider what they need to do to be successful.

This section asks the learners to make use of several self-assessment sheets to review their:

- skills
- work experience
- work interests

and to consider:

- their ideal job
- what they already have towards that job
- what they may have to do to be ready for such a job

The self-assessment sheets **WP16** and **WP17** are self-explanatory but review each sheet so the learners understand what is needed. There is an additional self-assessment worksheet **WP18** to use. The learners may want to refer back to **WP2** and **WP4** for thoughts about their strengths and areas which they would like to develop. Their CVs and personal profiles will also carry much useful information.

Once the learners are involved in thinking about ideal jobs and considering how they would plan what they want, draw the group together so that the group can become a solution finding resource for any learners who are unsure how to develop skills or seek out additional relevant experience.

In order to help the learners to think about their future working lives, a good resource base or access to careers guidance would be of value to help the learner to match identified interests and experiences, workplaces interests or skills which they would like to cultivate with opportunities which are available.

Personal organisation

The learners may identify areas of managing personal lives and working lives as presenting difficulties to them. In order to explore if this is the case for your group a brainstorm activity will help.

Brainstorm (15 min)

> **What aspects of life can become difficult while you are working?**

The list may include:

- managing time
- managing money
- personal appearance and clothing
- being tired
- keeping motivated
- keeping up with friends/hobbies
- staying well
- staying healthy or fit
- keeping calm or controlling anger when stressed

Finding solutions and feedback (40 min)

Ask the group to split into small groups or pairs and to pick up to six problems to which they need to find solutions. They will need to consider:

- is it one problem or several, how do they link together, what should be tackled first?
- what is involved?

- what is needed to be done?
- who might help?
- a plan of action

Bring the group back together and run a feedback to share these solutions.

Finally (5 min)

Take a note of particular areas with which the learners would like assistance with and ask them to record it in their files so that they can access other modules to assist them. You will also need to maintain a record to help in planning their individual learning routes.

Session Five: Creating a programme summary

The final session should serve as a review of the various learning activities to remind the learners of the number of tasks they have undertaken; learning points discovered; useful skills learned and documents which they have produced.

On the flipchart record the list of learning activities which have been undertaken as a series of headings, e.g.

- discussion of the value of work
- identification skills which can be used at work
- identification of strengths
- reading jobs adverts
- writing a CV
- writing a letter of application
- how to have a successful interview
- managing self etc.

The list will depend on what aspects were covered. Show the list to the whole group and ask for volunteers to suggest three or four key learning points from each activity. This group creation of a programme summary can then be reproduced for the learners' future reference.

The learners should be reminded of the documents which they have created and of the work they have undertaken on their own action plans to improve workplace skills.

A useful conclusion to the programme would be one-to- one reviews with each learner to create a final action plan **WP19**. This should then be reviewed at a later date.

Asking if an employee is not sure about something	Representing the firm in a good light	Trying to solve problems before asking for help
Being willing to try new jobs	Not knocking off before the end of the day	Wanting to do the best job possible
Thinking about a job and how to do it best	Being confident	Knowing when a job has been done badly
Paying attention to details	Not taking too many breaks	Being accurate
Being responsible	Taking work seriously	Not going on the sick

Photocopy onto thin card and cut out each of the cards

WP1: Employers' expectations

Use the following statements and select twelve which you think an employer looks for in an employee.

Being honest	Being able to write clearly	Using a skill learned on one job and applying it to another
Not cutting corners	Being able to use figures	Being well turned out
Being able to meet a deadline	Taking health and safety issues seriously	Making the best use of materials or resources and not wasting them
Putting in 100% effort	Knowing about computers	Remembering how jobs should be done and not always having to ask
Being able to do different jobs	Not stealing from the employer	Being able to give instructions

Photocopy onto thin card and cut out each of the cards

WP2: My positive attributes

Write down four statements about yourself and give some examples to support your statements.
For example:

In the workplace I can offer reliability. I know this because in my last job at Dunn's Dairies I was never late, and I was only away for two days with the flu. I worked there for three and a half years. I often worked on my own.

In the workplace I can offer …

1.

2.

3.

4.

WP1: Employers' expectations – continued

Coping with changes in what is wanted	Managing to work under pressure	Punctuality
Taking the initiative	Checking that the job is being done properly	Not covering up mistakes
Able to work alone	Being able to accept critical comments	Being able to work at different times
Getting on well with work colleagues	Taking an interest in what is to be done	Helping others at work
Being polite to colleagues, bosses and customers	Taking time to learn the job	Paying attention to instructions

Photocopy onto thin card and cut out each of the cards

WP4: Skill areas for the future

*Having thought about the changing workplace
make a list of some skills or qualities
which you may like to work on to help you in the future*

Skill area/quality	Reason for developing it

WP3: Role play situations

Situation one: lateness

Brian had been working at the King's Head for three weeks. He had been late for most of his shifts. The Manager wanted to see him to discuss this. What happens?

Situation two: respecting fellow workers

The Green Meadow housing estate was being built at great speed. As foreman you were taking on a number of labourers and not really checking their past experience. Two blokes had been taken on to help. They were good but were frequently breaking health and safety rules. You have to talk to them – what happens?

Situation three: theft

The Happy Fryer was your first fish and chip shop, one you had dreamed about owning. Last Friday and this you came in at eleven to find the staff giving out free food to their friends. What happens when you confront the workers?

WP6: Personal profile

Surname:	First names:

Address:

Telephone:	Date of birth:

Marital status:	Nationality:

Health record:

Secondary schools attended (addresses and dates):

Exams passed or other achievements at school and dates:

Name and address and dates of college or training programme attended:

Exams taken or qualifications passed and dates:

WP5: Reading and replying to job adverts

It is important to read job adverts carefully.
The following questions will help you to look for the key facts.

1. What is the job?

2. What hours are involved? Are they fixed hours? Are they regular hours?

3. What is the rate of pay? On what is it based e.g. half or a full-time job? Basic pay and bonus? Hourly rate?

4. Where is the job? Is it at a fixed location or can you be moved about?

5. How do you get more details?

6. How do you apply for the job?

7. When is the closing date?

> From the advert and what you know of the job so far, write down six points about **why** you would be good for the job or would like the job and what you have to offer the employer.

8. What other information do you need? e.g. start date

9. What qualifications are wanted?

10. What experience is wanted?

11. Are any qualifications or experience essential or desirable?

12. How closely do you match what they are looking for?

WP6: Personal profile – continued

List any skills or qualities which you would like to develop as part of working and why e.g. computer skills

---

WP6: Personal profile – continued

Employment history: List most recent first

Employer and address	Dates with employer. Type of work done, position and pay	Reason for leaving

List your interests, experiences, achievements and skills:

List any which may be useful to you at work and explain why this is so:

WP7: Application form – Brown and Co.

Post applied for:

Please complete in your own handwriting. Use a black pen.

PERSONAL DETAILS

Surname and title	First name
Previous surname (if applicable)	Marital status
Address	Date of birth
	Place of birth
Telephone	

SECONDARY EDUCATION

Name of school	Address	Dates from/to

FURTHER EDUCATION

Name of college etc.	Address	Course of study	Dates from/to

WP7: Application form – Brown & Co. – continued

EXAMINATIONS PASSED OR COURSES TAKEN

Name of course/qualifications	Date	Grade

Do you have computing skills?   yes/no

If yes, to what level?

EMPLOYMENT HISTORY

Please provide, in reverse chronological order, all details of your career, starting with your current or most recent employer.

Dates from/to	Name and address of employer	Nature of business	Position held, with brief details of duties and reason for leaving	Salary or grade at time of leaving

WP8: Curriculum vitae

Personal details:

Name -

Address -

Telephone number -

Date of birth -

Education and training:

Qualifications gained:

Employment history:

Other skills, and interests:

Referees:

WP7: Application form – Brown & Co. – continued

ADDITIONAL INFORMATION

Please write about any special skills, experience or qualities which you have and which would help you in the workplace.

Please write about your spare time activities.

What are your reasons for applying for this job?

REFEREES: Please give the names and addresses of two people who would supply a reference for you regarding your work experience and character.

Name

Address

| Name |
| Address |

HEALTH

Do you suffer from any serious illness or disability?   Yes/No

If so, give details

If you are a registered disabled person, state your registration number

Please re-read the form and then sign if you are able to declare that the information you have given on this form is true and accurate.

Signed: Date:

WP10: Observations of role plays on job interviews

1. How realistic were the interviewer's questions?

2. What else could have been asked?

3. What were particularly good about the answers?

4. What else might have been added?

5. What questions might the applicant have asked the potential employer?

6. Ask the two characters how each felt the other had performed their role?

7. Ask what it felt like to be an interviewer or an applicant?

8. What might they do differently if they had to do it again?

9. What have they learned from the role play which they can apply in a real situation?

WP9: Writing a letter to an employer

Your address

Their name and address

Reference no.:

Name of job interested in:

Date:

Dear Mr/Mrs/Sir

I am writing to apply for the post of — advertised in — (date).

1. My particular strengths, qualities, skills and qualifications are ...

2. Why I am most suitable for the post ...

3. In addition I would bring to the job e.g. loyalty etc. ...

4. Thank you for reading this letter and my enclosed curriculum vitae and considering me for this post.

Yours sincerely – if you know the name

Yours faithfully – if you don't know the name

Signature

Print your name

WP12: Skills/qualities I could develop

*Review your assessment sheet WP11
Consider the ✔ items Poor, OK and Never done and decide which ones you want to work on to improve. You might want to pick several which are the same and group them as one or two items to work on.*

List your goals:

1.

2.

What will will you do to improve these areas?

Write out the clear actions you will take and **when you will take them.**

Goal 1:		By when

Goal 2:		By when

WP11: My skills/qualities in the workplace

*Read through the following statements
and rate yourself as poor, OK, good or never done*

	✔ which applies to you			
	Poor	OK	Good	Never done
Being on time				
Organising myself to get to work				
Listening carefully to what is wanted				
Organising my life outside work				
Not asking for extra time off				
Being ready to learn new skills				
Asking if I am not sure about anything				
Admitting to making a mistake if I have				
Being smart in appearance				
Knowing how to speak to my manager/foreman				
Being ready to try new jobs				
Knowing the right things to say to customers				
Accepting advice, criticism and guidance and using it				
Being polite				
Knowing how to speak about the firm				
Being willing to work at different times				
Add any other skills or qualities				

WP13: Checking communication skills

Read through the following statements and tick which column applies to you

	I often do	I some-times do	I never do
I often interrupt people when they are talking			
Quite often I don't know what people want me to do			
Often I don't bother to listen to what people say			
People often interrupt me when I am talking			
I think noone really listens to me			
I don't like written instructions			
I have problems getting to the point I want to make			
I like people to explain clearly to me what I should do			
I am able to ask if I don't understand something			
Often I won't read any written instructions			
Often I know what people are going to say before they have said it			
When people don't understand me I shout rather than explain again			
I can't stand criticism or advice from others			
I let myself get pushed about and don't challenge what's said			
Jot down other things which might apply to you:			

WP12: Skills/Qualities I could develop – continued

Decide how you will know you have succeeded.

Success in Goal 1 means ...

Success in Goal 2 means ...

Who can help me?

Review date: _____

Review with: _____

WP15: Use of leisure time

Please answer the following questions and then tick the activities which you have tried

1. Have you ever had a hobby?
   What was it?
   Why did you stop?
   Would you do this again?

2. Do you know what sports facilities are available locally?
   Which have you tried?
   Which have you not tried?

3. Have you tried going to the theatre, cinema, art galleries or museums? (underline the ones you have) What did you enjoy about them?
   Why not?

4. Have you tried to learn an activity or gone to a course before?
   Why did you go?
   Why did you stop?
   Why haven't you tried?

Tick the column which would apply to you

Fitness/sports activities:	Happy to do	Tried out not again	Will have a go	Never
Swimming				
Fishing				
Gym				
Running				
Jogging				
Walking				
Climbing				
Aerobics				
Cycling				

WP14: Time log

	Morning						Afternoon					
	12-2	2-4	4-6	6-8	8-10	10-12	12-2	2-4	4-6	6-8	8-10	10-12
Mon.												
Tues.												
Wed.												
Thurs.												
Fri.												
Sat.												
Sun.												

WP16: Stocktake

Complete the *three* boxes below

From my work experience so far I can show I have the following skills:

The things I have liked most about work so far have been:

In the future I would like my job to involve:

WP15: Use of leisure time – continued

Tick the column which would apply to you

	Happy to do	Tried out not again	Will have a go	Never
Social:				
Pub				
Darts				
Bingo				
Dancing				
Meetings				
Playing in a band/singing				
Outdoor:				
Gardening				
Walking				
Picnics				
Birdwatching				
Indoor:				
Reading				
TV				
Listening to music				
Jigsaws/puzzles				
Modelmaking				
Making clothes				
Cooking				
Playing cards				
DIY				
Self expression:				
Painting				
Playing music				
Dance				
Photography				
Writing				
Acting				

WP18: Thinking about your work experiences

Think about aspects of jobs you have done and work out how you may give examples of the four types of activities for each aspect of your job

Task/job	Working with people	Using information	Working with technology/ equipment	Problem solving/thinking/ being creative

WP17: Looking ahead

Complete the four boxes below

My ideal job would be/involve:

Looking at the experience, skills and interests I have identified that I have so far, I have the following:

I think I need to develop the following skills/get experience in for my ideal job:

I will do this by:

WP19: My workplace action plan

Name: _____

Summary of areas to be given attention to improve workplace skills:

Task/job

Working with people

Select up to three learning points:

1.

2.

3.

Date

Using information

Action to be taken on the learning points:

Date of Review: _____

Review with: _____

WP18: Thinking about your work experience – continued

Look at the sheet you have completed about your experiences at work and rate yourself in terms of done or not done and whether you enjoyed or did not enjoy that activity.
Put a mark on the lines to show where you place your experience and your enjoyment. This will show you something about the types of job you may prefer to do in future.

Task/job

Have done a lot —————— Not done much

Enjoy a lot —————— Do not enjoy

Working with people

Have done a lot —————— Not done much

Enjoy a lot —————— Do not enjoy

Using information

Have done a lot —————— Not done much

Enjoy a lot —————— Do not enjoy

Working with technology/equipment

Have done a lot —————— Not done much

Enjoy a lot —————— Do not enjoy

Problem solving/thinking/being creative

Have done a lot —————— Not done much

Enjoy a lot —————— Do not enjoy

Developing communication skills

 The module is divided into eight sessions. These are:

1. Thinking about communication (3 hours 25 min)
2. Listening skills (1 hour 40 min)
3. Non-verbal communication (2 hours 30 min)
4. Discussion skills (1 hour)
5. Developing negotiation skills (2 hours)
6. Using the telephone (1 hour 10 min)
7. Giving and receiving instructions (2 hours 5 min)
8. Learning points and planning ahead (30 min)

 Within this module there are links with the modules:

- Identifying and managing stress
- Developing and maintaining positive attitudes
- DIY: improve your chances

 The module makes use of the learning and training activities of:

- self-assessment checklists
- role-play
- goldfish bowl
- small and large group discussions
- action planning
- collage work
- mime
- games
- continuum

 Trainer's notes

This module offers some practical activities and self-assessment exercises for learners to undertake to encourage them to understand the importance of developing their own communication skills and to encourage the self-identification of any areas of their communication skills where they find shortfalls.

This module can only be a partial introduction to the vast area of managing interpersonal relationships. Communication skills and a broader treatment of the management of relationships is the subject of the learning resources manual *Developing Social Skills*.

It is important that the trainer takes time with each learner to help identify individual learning needs and to consider what learning programme may best meet those needs. The activities and assessments in this area need to be managed skilfully so that learners experience them as signposts towards developing these crucial life and social skills and do not feel they have failed or that they have been undermined by the activities.

In residential settings it can become easy to lose communications skills, to not practice nor develop them. People can feel powerless and isolated, not able to express their needs and feelings and can be without the opportunities for so doing. Social worlds can become narrow and inward looking. Contacts with people outside may become tortured by the barriers set up by the residential setting, the constraints of time and the frequency of the importance of dealing with practical needs rather than holding other sorts of communications. A lack of communication, a poor letter or phone call can become imbued with meanings which were not intended.

Managing effective and successful social interactions brings quality, meaning and satisfaction to lives. It also helps to ensure social acceptability, integration and involvement with others.

The learners need to understand the value of communication skills in a residential, placement or training settings, within working lives, in dealing with those in authority, with friends, family, partners and workmates.

The module is designed to:

- encourage learners' awareness of the broad range of communication skills
- encourage awareness of the range of situations in which communication skills are used
- raise learners' awareness of the importance of developing appropriate communication skills for various types of situation
- encourage an appreciation of why social interactions may go wrong and where the fault may lie with poor communication skills
- encourage in the learners a realisation that their communication skills can be developed and improved upon
- encourage an awareness of the link between poor communication skills and stress, low self-esteem and poor interpersonal relationships
- encourage a sense of the richness in communication

Session One: Thinking about communication

Opening comments (5 min)

Ask the learners if they can think of one thing which is common to all types of relationships, relationships with people they know or do not know, and common to good and bad relationships.

A learner may have the answer – **communication**. If not, offer the answer and discuss why communication is so important. Without communications what would relationships between people be like? Would relationships be possible?

Move from this discussion to saying that the next activity will ask the learners to think about their own experiences of communications.

Reflecting on recent communications (30 min)

Ask the learners to work alone and think back over the past month. Ask them to remember three separate occasions of communicating with others and to complete the three sheets which make up CS1. Work through the questions on the activity sheet to check the learners' understanding before they work alone.

Group feedback (30 min)

Work through each type of encounter asking for some of the learners' answers to the questions. Five headings for the question areas to be discussed and to record information on the flipchart are listed below.

Draw out from the learners:

- the type of communication which took place i.e. phone, letter or face-to-face and the effects which this type may have on the success of the communication
- who it was with, i.e. how well known the person was
- who began it and what was wanted from it
- what it was about and how this may have affected the learner
- what made them unhappy, happy or satisfied with the communication. For example, was it because they felt they were walked over, were listened to, were respected, or were not listened to and so on

Emphasise that they do not have to disclose anything they do not want but that they should try to draw out any key points to help their learning. For example, if the learner did not want the communication and was not comfortable with the topic of the communication it is not surprising they did not feel happy with it or that it went wrong in their view.

Generate a list of ideas for each of these five headings. Record the answers on the flipchart and discuss whether there are any patterns or points which can be drawn out.

Three brainstorms (30 min)

Having collected a number of ideas and experiences ask the learners to focus on three questions about communication.

> ### Why is communication important?

The learners may suggest:
- so people know what the other person is thinking, feeling or wants and does not just guess
- so people can give instructions
- so people can share information or ideas
- it makes life interesting
- it is a way of finding out more things
- it is a way to test if ideas are true
- it is an opportunity to get to know someone
- it stops muddles and assumptions
- it allows people to express themselves and not bottle up feelings

> ### What creates good communication?

Ideas might include:
- being honest about feelings, thoughts or wants
- having equality between people
- being willing to listen to someone else
- accepting someone has a right to their view
- listening properly
- reaching a shared point of view
- having time for someone
- being interested in what they say

> ### What creates bad communication?

The group may suggest:
- not listening
- being distracted
- not having time for someone
- not being interested
- not caring what is said
- having a fixed view despite what is said
- power imbalances and not needing to listen

Small groups (15 min)

Following the brainstorms ask the learners to work in fours and to decide on their top three priorities for each of the brainstorm questions. These should be written down. They must have no more than 15 minutes. Remind them when they have seven, five, three etc. minutes to go.

Group feedback (15 min)

Ask the pairs to quickly offer one of their lists of three priorities until all the brainstorm areas have been covered. Then spend time discussing how the groups worked together:

- did they take it in turns to talk?
- did one person dominate?
- was there listening?
- what was the effect of the time pressure?
- did they feel they worked well together and why?

Record these comments on the flipchart.

Brainstorm: How do you feel when communication has been good and when communication has been bad (25 min)

As a final introductory activity ask the group to think back to the first activity about recent communications and to think about the recent brainstorms. Ask for a volunteer to recount how it felt when an act of communication went well. Use this as a stimulus for a brainstorm.

> **When communication works** it leaves me with feelings of ...

Repeat the same procedure for a brainstorm on:

> **When communication does not work** it leaves me with feelings of ...

Taking stock of current levels of communication skills – explanations and checklists
Explanation: learning and unlearning (15 min)
Explain to the learners that:

- communication skills of all kinds have had to have been learned by them
- just as poor communication skills can be learned so they can be unlearned and replaced with good communication skills
- where certain communication skills may not have been learned earlier on in life they can be learned now

An anecdote of some communication skills which the trainer has learned or improved upon would help to illustrate the point. It would help the learners understand what is possible and that needing to unlearn or needing to improve upon skills is nothing they should be ashamed about.

Ask the learners if from the brainstorms and exercises they have done so far they can think of any skills which they could learn or unlearn. Record these on the flipchart.

Communications checklist (20 min)

Ask the learners to work alone for 20 minutes and to complete checklist **CS2** on their current levels of communication skills. Explain that the checklist is to help them to think about the skills they have and need to have, and to help you to devise the best programme to meet those needs.

Check that the learners understand the checklist before they start. Work with any who are unsure. Check on the progress of completing the checklists.

Note:

The checklist should be reviewed by trainer and learner on a one-to-one basis early on in the module. It can be used to help set individual learning goals (CS3) and an individual learning programme. This may well involve more than the completion of this single module. It will probably draw on relevant modules in the manual *Developing Social Skills*.

The checklist and identified learning goals should periodically be reviewed to chart progress and to determine further learning needs.

Group expectation (20 min)

Ask the learners why a module on communication skills might be of value to them. Record these answers on the flipchart.

Ask the learners what they would like to gain from a module on communication skills. Record these answers on the flipchart.

Thank the learners for their contributions to the session.

 Trainer's notes

So far the activities will have:

- raised awareness of the importance of communication for effective relationships
- helped identify particular learning needs
- helped identify that there are various aspects to communication skills

The following sessions can all be worked through to give an overview of a number of aspects of the role played by communication and communication skills or you can select from the sessions to meet group needs.

Session Two: Listening skills

Opening activity: counting to ten (10 min)

Ask the learners to form a circle, explain that as a group you will count to ten. Each person should offer a number, listening carefully to what has been said and trying to listen to who else in the group may speak.

The learners will quickly become attuned to listening to the silences and anticipating whether someone will speak or not. The group will eventually reach the successful count of ten, be more attuned with each other and have exercised great concentration.

Introduction to listening skills (15 min)

Brainstorm with the group:

Why is it important to listen?

The group might suggest:

- to know how people feel
- to hear instructions properly
- to know what people want
- to understand better
- to find out what people think of ideas
- not to impose on others

If the group does not begin on a brainstorm route of what happens if you do not listen then undertake this as a separate exercise.

By the close of 15 minutes the group should have an impressive list of the value of good listening and consequences of poor listening.

How good a listener are you? (15 min)

On a continuum from excellent to poor, ask the group members to rank themselves according to how good they feel they are as listeners. Once the group members are in place ask a few learners to explain why they have placed themselves at those points. Ask for some examples to evidence their statements.

Give the group an opportunity to change places after discussion. Check why any have changed their places.

Pair work (15 min)

Ask the learners to think about something they find interesting. Divide the group into pairs. Call one A and the other B. Then ask the As to talk to their partner for about five minutes. B should help the person speaking but not do more than that.

As five minutes approaches stop the pairs. Ask the Bs to tell the As what they were talking about. Then, go round the group asking the As how well they thought the Bs had listened by giving a mark out of ten and an example. Record this on the flipchart.

What makes a good listener? (15 min)

Ask the group in what ways it is possible to show good listening skills besides just repeating back the main points of what was said. Record the suggestions.

 Trainer's notes

Use the following notes to add to learners' thoughts.

Good listening skills include:

- establishing a rapport with the speaker
- clarifying – checking understanding of an issue and share understanding, helping speaker to separate fact and opinion
- encouraging – enabling the speaker to expand upon and explore an issue however tentatively
- summarising – drawing together key themes and issues
- reinforcing – supporting, where appropriate, the speaker's understandings, perceptions and concerns once they have been explored
- focusing – helping the speaker to determine what are the key concerns and aims and the strategies for dealing with or meeting them

- accepting silence. this seems much longer to the listener than the speaker who may well need time to collect his thoughts
- showing understanding – using "mms", nods etc.
- adopting a relaxed and interested body position
- arriving at some conclusion, even if only to state the problem clearly, separating fact from opinion and offering some suggestions

How can you tell a bad listener? 15 min)

Brainstorm the question above and make use of the notes below to help add to the learners' suggestions. Poor listening skills may include:

- interrupting the speaker
- jumping to conclusions
- not checking what was heard
- finishing sentences for the person talking
- not concentrating on what is said
- trying to hurry them along
- telling the person what to do
- looking at watch/appearing bored

- no eye contact
- making judgements
- leading the person
- blocking/belittling what is said
- disputing what the speaker is saying
- adopting a superior 'know all' attitude
- bullying the speaker

In pairs again (15 min)

Reform the pairs. Tell the Bs it is now their turn to talk and the As to listen. Stop the pairs after five minutes. Go round the room asking the As what it felt like to be a listener. Ask the Bs of what they were aware. Both As and Bs should have been very conscious of what a good and bad listener should have done. The talking probably felt forced. Ask if either the As or Bs were aware of a particular thing the listener did, it may have been positive or negative. Again, repeat that skills can be learned and that they will have been thinking about listening skills and will be more conscious of how to be a good listener as a result of the session. Remind the group of the value of listening, i.e. making fewer mistakes, being more sensitive to others, learning about others' thoughts and reactions to you and your ideas.

Thank the learners for their effort in the session.

Session Three: Non-verbal communication

 Trainer's notes and introduction (10 min)

Remind the learners that one of the ways in which they were able to demonstrate good or poor listening was by their non-verbal communication:

- the way they held their bodies
- the way they looked at or away from the speaker
- nodding or shaking their head and so on

Body language is also important as a speaker, it shows interest in what is being said, commitment to what is said, a sense of urgency or importance about what is said, a desire to help the listener to understand and a liking for the listener or the opposite of any these things.

Introduce the session as focusing on non-verbal communication and offer some opening comments. Non-verbal communication says more than spoken communication. It gives clues about real feelings and thoughts. It gives many clues about a person's current emotional state and what they are thinking and feeling which may be nothing to do with what is being said or the situation the speaker and listener are in.

Non-verbal communication can help emphasise what is being said. Being aware of non-verbal communication helps spoken communications to go more smoothly. For example, if a person was showing irritation or anger it would not be a good time to ask for help or a favour.

Collage work (30 min)
Ask the learners to create a collage of various non-verbal communications from magazine or newspaper pictures. The learners should find a range of facial expressions and body postures and so on, group them and label them. They can work alone, in pairs or threes as best suits the learners.

Group feedback (10 min)
The learners will have been successful in identifying a range of non-verbal messages. Ask them to explain what clues they looked for and found and how they were able to tell how people in the pictures felt or what they were saying.

Record their answers on the flipchart. They should cover:
- position of head
- use of shoulders
- use of gestures
- position in relation to other people
- eyes – downcast, open and looking ahead
- use of mouth – smiling, thin-lipped
- use of eyebrows – surprise, frowning

Three activities to look at non-verbal communication
1. Observations of others (20 min)
Using pre-recorded video materials with the sound off, the learners should:
   a. decide what is taking place
   b. record what gives them the clues about what is happening

The sound can be restored and the learners can then record how non-verbal communications reinforces or does not support what is said.

The learners will need an activity sheet to work on. The following questions could be used:

Observing non-verbal communication

What is taking place?
What gives you clues about this?
How does the non-verbal communication support or not support what is said?

Re-run the video material and discuss the learners' findings:
- Was there agreement amongst the learners?
- What was not observed and why?
- Was anyone offering different answers? If anyone was, this should be discussed with the individual learner.

2. Representing moods and emotions (20 min)

Give the learners a card with a mood or emotion printed on it, e.g. sad, sulking, angry, happy, not interested etc. Ask all the learners to sit except for one learner who leaves the room. This learner comes into the room behaving according to the mood or emotion on the card. The learner should not speak. The rest of the group should guess what mood or emotion the person is representing.

If the group has problems guessing then stop the learner from miming so long that they become embarrassed.

3. Pair work (20 min)

Ask the learners to work in pairs. Ask for one of each pair to volunteer to tell a story they enjoy telling from their past. But before they begin, seat the pairs back to back and then ask for the story to begin. Allow five minutes then stop the pairs and question:

- how did it feel to tell the story and why?
- how did it compare with previous re-tellings and why?
- what did they miss from the hearer?
- what was it like to listen and why?
- what would the listener have liked to have done?
- how much encouragement was it possible to give the speaker?

List some of the ingredients of telling and hearing a good story. These will include a number of non-verbal communications.

Summing up (10 min)

Pull together the main learning points from these three activities and from the collage work.

Appropriate body language

 ### Trainer's notes

While use of gestures, nodding, eye contact are important for encouraging effective communications some body language can be inappropriate. For example, looking too long at someone, standing too close to them or touching them:

- eye contact should be regular but not prolonged. Intense staring could be seen as confrontational or impolite
- too much facial expression, e.g. smiling could be seen as not taking something seriously or not being sincere

Non-verbal communication needs to match verbal communication and the situation in which and about which communication is taking place.

Brainstorm (20 min)

Introduce the idea of appropriate non-verbal communication. Ask them in pairs to list some types of non-verbal communication and to describe some occasions when it may be inappropriate. Work through one or two examples on sheet CS04 with the group so they understand. Check on the pairs' progress.

Group feedback (10 min)

Use the headings from the activity sheet CS4 for the feedback session. Ask for some examples from each pair.

When the feedback is complete discuss with the group whether gender, age and culture have an effect on what is and is not appropriate non-verbal communication. You should collect some examples of the role and types of non-verbal communications in other cultures.

Session Four: Discussion skills

This session considers the particular skills which the learners will need to develop to enable them to communicate without conflict or tension with others.

Brainstorms (20 min)

1. Ask the group to consider what can be gained by discussion, between a pair, a few people or a larger group of people.

   Record the answers on the flipchart. They should suggest ideas such as:

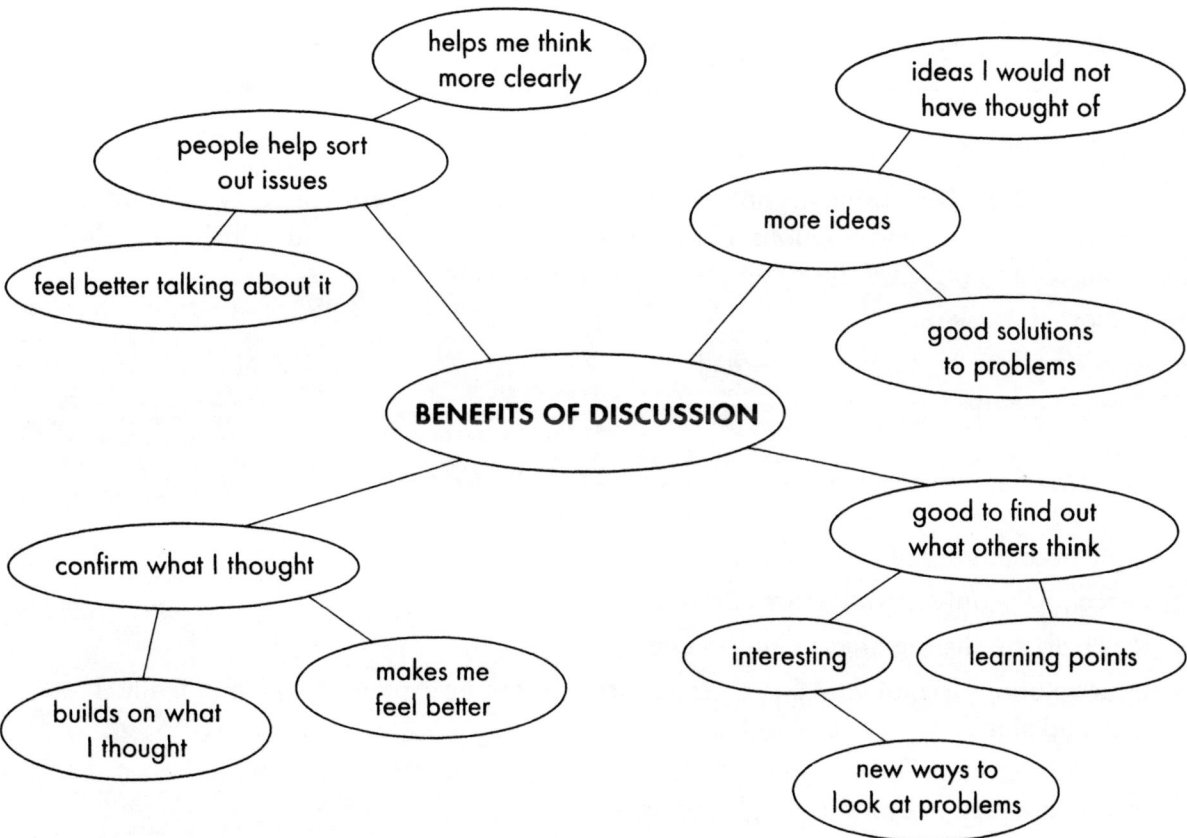

2. Ask the group to suggest what communication skills are needed for good discussions and list these on the flipchart.

3. Now ask the learners to individually give themselves a mark out of ten for how well they think they do in a discussion. They should write this down.

Discussion activity (20 min)

Explain the purpose of the goldfish bowl room layout and ask for three or four to volunteer to be observers. The rest of the group should be involved in the discussion exercise. The participants in the discussion need CS5 and the observers CS5 and CS6. Allow observers and the discussants to read through CS5 and the observers CS6 as well. Check the observers know what they have to do. Allow the discussion to run for 15 minutes.

At the close of 15 minutes ask the discussants the questions on CS6 and record their answers. Then ask the observers to give their observations according to their completed sheets. Again record the answers.

Group feedback and discussion (20 min)

Ask the group as a whole:

- what are the main differences between the people involved in the discussion and the observers' viewpoints?
- why are there differences in points of view?
- what surprises or learning points are there from the exercise?

Record these answers. Ensure that there are not personal attacks being made. Show the learners their earlier list of the skills needed for discussions. Ask if there are any more they would like to add. Ask the learners to again consider their mark out of ten as a person who participates well in discussions and ask them to write down one or two skills they might like to develop.

Session Five: Developing negotiation skills

 Trainer's notes

The learners will have been using negotiation skills in the discussion exercise. They will have been exploring problems and solutions and trying to agree on a solution with which they felt comfortable. Some people will have compromised their views in order:

- to move the task on
- for the team to continue to work well
- to avoid conflict

Some may have felt bullied and some may not have contributed to the discussion.

Developing negotiation skills are useful because:

- they allow people to work more effectively together
- they help the sharing of ideas and solutions
- more solutions to problems and their implications can be explored than an individual may find alone
- a shared solution is likely to be stronger than a single person's imposed solution because it will be agreed to by more people and they will try to make it work
- more people feel they have been involved in the discussion and considered. This makes people feel better

Work on developing negotiation skills links with work on assertiveness, working in teams and developing effective relationships.

Introduction (10 min)

Introduce the session drawing on the notes above.

Opening activity (20 min)

In pairs ask the learners to think back over their experiences of successful and unsuccessful negotiations. Offer some examples to stimulate their thinking. These could include negotiations:

- with friends to get some help
- to buy something new or second hand
- to get some work done, e.g. repairs to their home

- to share work or to swap jobs or rota duties
- to get a child to do something

Ask the learners to tell each other some tales about their negotiations and to draw out the key points about:

> ## What is involved in successful negotiating?

Feedback and discussion (15 min)

Ask the pairs to offer some of their ideas about what is involved in successful negotiations. Their suggestions may include:

- listening to what someone else wants
- being prepared to compromise
- looking for other solutions

If the group gets stuck then ask why negotiations do not work and draw from these suggestions why something should work.

Ask the group what the difference is between a successful negotiation and getting one's own way. The group should suggest:

- compromise
- both parties feeling involved
- feeling listened to
- not necessarily having your own way but knowing the solution adopted will work
- not feeling that you have imposed something on someone else
- a win–win situation

Role-plays (45 min)

Ask for six volunteers to undertake a role-play. Divide the six into three pairs. Offer a different role-play to each pair (CS7). Give the pair a couple of minutes to prepare, check they understand what is wanted and ask them to perform the negotiation in front of the whole group.

The trainer and group should question the characters after each role-play situation:

- Did the character feel what they did was realistic?
- Why had the negotiation gone the way it did?
- Did the characters really find out what each other wanted?
- Had they got what they wanted from the negotiation? Why or why not? What else would they have wanted?
- What could have been done to avoid conflict?

Ask the whole group if they can think of other ways to have managed the negotiation. Ask the characters what they think of the suggestions.

Record the key learning points on the flipchart.

Points for negotiation (20 min)

Go through with the learners some key rules for managing negotiation. These are listed below and should be copied for the learners.

Points for successful negotiations

- Decide what you would like as an outcome

- Decide what you would settle for

- Decide the important points over which you would not want to compromise

- Decide what you could trade or compromise over

- Think about the other person/people, what their concerns may be and what they might like from the situation

- Be calm before and during the discussions

- Be ready to listen and acknowledge if a point is good, reasonable or fair

- Agree where you can

- Accept others' points of view if they are useful or valuable

- Remain assertive, not bullying nor giving in

- Work through each point step by step

- Check you have understood by summing up what has been said

Check the learners understand what each point means and ask the learners for examples.

Summary (10 min)

Ask the learners to each offer a key point they would like to practice. List these on the flipchart. Have copies for the learners if they would like them.

Session Six: Using the telephone

 Trainer's notes

There are many occasions when learners will need to use the telephone. It is important that the learners are aware of the possible pitfalls associated with its use and the need to think carefully about the various situations in which they may use it.

The telephone relies mainly on the words said and the listener does not have all the clues of non-verbal communications. There will however be clues from tone of voice, speed of speech, volume and types of words used. Both listeners and speakers need to be aware of what they may disclose or gain from these clues.

Developing such sensitivity is important as much may hinge on a telephone call. Continued amicable contact with family and friends, an initial screening interview for employment, trying to gain information about benefits or other entitlements or trying to present a case clearly to support a claim or complaint.

The telephone can create frustrations and tensions for some learners. They may feel confronted by faceless bureaucrats, they may feel frustrated at being passed from department to department and they may get angered by wasting time waiting to be connected to the right department.

The frustrations associated with the phone can make learners less effective communicators than they should be.

Introduction (10 min)

Introduce the session making use of the notes and asking for learners' experiences.

Opening brainstorm (15 min)

Ask the group to brainstorm:

> **What can go wrong using the telephone?**

The suggestions may include:
- having the wrong tone of voice
- not thinking before speaking
- not knowing how the other person is responding because no non-verbal communication
- being caught unprepared for the call – they rang you
- having your mind elsewhere or being distracted
- not having thought what you want to say and not having documents ready
- they do not want to talk to you
- you forget to ask if someone has time to speak
- you forget to ask them how they are and are just too concerned with getting to the point

Pair work (15 min)

Ask the group to then work in pairs to list out some of the situations when they use the phone and to list particular problems with those situations. They should also suggest ways to prevent problems (CS8).

Feedback and brainstorm (10 min)

Ask the pairs to share some of their problems and suggestions with the whole group.

Ask the group to suggest situations when using the phone has advantages over other means of communication. The brainstorm may help learners to see the potential of the phone:
- especially for gaining support and guidance anonymously
- when they have concerns about being in control of a situation
- when a face-to-face encounter seems daunting
- to save travel costs
- to gain access to people who may not be available for a face-to-face meeting
- to save time

Phone rules (10 min)

Ask the pairs to devise ten rules for most effectively using the telephone. The rules should be in priority order, written out and ready for display.

Group sharing by display (10 min)

Allow time for the groups to read each others rules and copy sets of rules for the learners if these are thought to be useful.

Session Seven: Giving and receiving instructions

🍎 *Trainer's notes*

There are many ways in which this area of communication can be difficult for learners. Often learners do not stop to listen or they may selectively listen. This causes frustration when things do not then go well. Likewise learners may have problems in thinking clearly through all the stages and steps when they give instructions. Again this may cause difficulties and frustrations. The session encourages learners to become more aware of some of the difficulties and problems in this area of communication.

Opening activity (10 min)

Ask the learners to brainstorm why receiving and giving clear instructions is important. The learners can be encouraged to think about some of the consequences of giving or receiving poor instructions. Some may perhaps have had such experiences.

Record their ideas on a flipchart and supplement from the notes above.

Giving and receiving instructions (20 min)

Ask students to work in pairs and to write simple instructions for various tasks , for example.

- hanging a car tyre
- making a cup of tea
- putting up a piece of wallpaper
- making a sandwich

Once these are written ask the students to work with another pair. One person in a pair reads the instructions very slowly while one in the other pair mimes the activity. The remaining two learners observe what happens. Were basic instructions left out? For example, putting water in the kettle, plugging in kettle. Were assumptions made e.g. that the person reading the instructions knew that the air pump could be found in a garage where petrol is bought?

Feedback (20 min)

Ask the group to re-form. Ask for the two observers in each group of four to say what worked well and why or what may have gone wrong and why. These points should be recorded on the flipchart.

Writing poor instructions	Writing good instructions

Stress that the importance of writing clear instructions is to assume that the person who is to read and follow them is absolutely ignorant of the matter in hand, but by no means stupid. Stress the need to use simple language and short sentences, making these active. Words to look for are *Firstly, Go, Do, Put,* etc.

Instruction giving and feedback on Activity two (20 min)

Suggest the pair which has not yet offered its instructions takes a few minutes to check its work. Then repeat the exercise, again with two learners observing. Re-form the group and ask if there has been any improvement on the first exercise and why this may have been so.

Pattern making (25 min)

Ask the learners to again work in pairs. They need CS9 and to *listen carefully* to the trainer's instructions.

Ask the learners to cut out the shapes on CS9. Once this is done they need to decide who will give instructions (person A) and who will receive them (person B). The two learners then sit back to back.

Once back to back, person A arranges the shapes in any patterns of their choosing. Once this is completed the pattern is described to person B who has to interpret what has been said and to move their shapes as seems to make best sense. Person B must not ask questions, nor ask for clarification. Neither A nor B may turn around. Once A feels that they have described the pattern sufficiently well then the two need to compare their versions of the pattern.
Allow about 15 minutes for this.

The two should address the questions which are on CS10. Allow about ten minutes.

Feedback and discussion (30 min)

Bring the group back together to analyse the activity and the learning. Use the flipchart and record what worked well and what badly and what may have accounted for this.

Find out how the As and Bs felt doing this exercise, for example:

- Were there similar feelings?
- Was blame attributed?
- What feelings did the exercise generate?

It is important to remember that part of the problem may have arisen because of B's ways of receiving the instructions. B may not have listened to the whole instruction; B may have thought they knew better and ignored things; B may have seen a pattern and pursued it despite the evidence of their own ears.

Try to find some general guidelines for giving instructions from this exercise. These might include such things as:

- use familiar language
- make sure that you can be heard; speak more slowly
- try to find other ways of expressing things using everyday images
- set boundaries around the activity

Record these group generated rules for successful instruction giving and receiving. Copies of these should be available for learners if they would like them.

The learners may like to compare these rules with their initial brainstorm to see the ways in which their understanding of this area has deepened.

Session Eight: Learning points and planning ahead

🍎 *Trainer's notes*

During Session One, the learners completed CS2, a checklist about how they rated their communication skills. During the module they will have explored several areas of communication in some detail. During the final session they should:

- look at their starting points and note improvements
- be aware of further work which they need to do
- be aware of particular areas which they need to practice

The learners should also be able to evaluate what they have gained from the module.

Group review (20 min)

As a round, ask each learner to offer something which they found interesting from the Communications skills session. Record these.

Run a second round, where the learners each offer something they have learned. Record these.

Run a third round where each offers something they would like to know more about. These may not necessarily be areas covered in the sessions. Record these.

In the final round, ask each learner to offer something they will work on. Record these.

Review the four lists and compare them with the earlier brainstorms in which the learners noted what they would like to gain from the communications sessions. How well were the learners' needs met?

Planning ahead (10 min)

Ask each learner to use CS11. They should write out their gains, the points they should individually remember and the ways in which they intend to do so.

Check on the learners' progress in completing the plans and offer suggestions as appropriate.

Activity CS1: Recent communications with member of family or partner

Who was it?

What type of communication:

telephone   letter   face-to-face

What was it about?

Did you want the communication?

What did you want from the communication?

Did it go:

Why?

How did you feel about it:

Why?

Activity CS1 (contd.): Recent communications with friend/workmate

Who was it?

What type of communication:

telephone   letter   face-to-face

What was it about?

Did you want the communication?

What did you want from the communication?

Did it go:

Why?

How did you feel about it:

Why?

Activity CS1 (contd.): Recent communications with official person

Who was it?

What type of communication:

telephone   letter   face-to-face

What was it about?

Did you want the communication?

What did you want from the communication?

Did it go: ☹   🙂   🙂

Why?

How did you feel about it: ☹   🙂   🙂

Why?

Activity CS2: Checking your communication skills

Read through the statements which are printed below and decide about each one whether you:

- Yes, can do well 🙂
- OK 😐
- No, need help ☹

Circle the symbol on each line which applies to you

Do you feel happy to talk to people you don't know?	🙂	😐	☹
Can you get your ideas across to someone without difficulty?	🙂	😐	☹
Can you talk easily over the telephone to people you don't know?	🙂	😐	☹
Can you easily make yourself understood?	🙂	😐	☹
If you have to complain about something can you do so without it becoming an argument?	🙂	😐	☹
Can you easily talk to people in authority?	🙂	😐	☹
Are you happy about using the phone?	🙂	😐	☹
Could you take a telephone message and leave a message for someone without problems?	🙂	😐	☹
Can you follow instructions which someone tells you?	🙂	😐	☹
Can you give instructions e.g. how to get somewhere or how to do something?	🙂	😐	☹
Can you read the newspapers and magazines you want without difficulty?	🙂	😐	☹
Can you read any books you want to?	🙂	😐	☹
Can you use TV and entertainment guides without problems?	🙂	😐	☹
Can you understand most forms you are sent?	🙂	😐	☹
Can you complete any forms you need to?	🙂	😐	☹
Can you read written instructions on items?	🙂	😐	☹
Can you use telephone directories?	🙂	😐	☹
Do you feel you can write letters well if you need to?	🙂	😐	☹
Can you make use of maps?	🙂	😐	☹
Can you follow instructions on diagrams?	🙂	😐	☹

CS4: Times when non-verbal communication may not be appropriate

Type of non-verbal communication Examples 1-9 and spaces 10-15 for your examples	List the situations in which and reasons why the non-verbal communication is not appropriate
1. No eye contact	
2. Looking at someone for a long time	
3. Smiling a lot	
4. Not smiling	
5. No expression	
6. Using gestures e.g. nods, moving hands and arms	
7. Touching someone e.g. handshake, pat on shoulder	
8. Standing close to someone	
9. Having a relaxed posture	
10.	
11.	
12.	
13.	
14.	
15.	

CS3: Communication skills goals

Assessment of current strengths and areas for development:

Key learning goals:

Action to meet learning goals. Note specific learning programmes and activities, start dates, expected completion dates:

Date:
Review date:

Signed & name:

CS6: Observers' sheet

*As an observer you need to watch the group carefully
as they decide on the occupations which are most important*

Try to answer the following questions and keep notes.

Did one person dominate?

Did anyone put anyone else down?

Did all participate? Who hung back, why?

Was there much agreement?

Was the group supportive or argumentative?

Were some people more concerned with finishing the task, e.g. checking on the time left?

Did some people help others, encourage and listen to them?

Were some people more concerned to hear themselves speak and not listen to others?

CS5: Discussion activity

Survivors

It is the year after World War Three and most of the world's population is dead. The survivors live in nuclear shelters underground where they must remain until it is safe to return to the surface.

You are members of a committee set up to decide how the survivors should be trained or retrained to be of maximum usefulness (a) during the long period underground, and (b) when they return to the surface.

As a committee you must decide on, and make a list of, the order of importance of the following occupations for training the surviving people:

Nurse	Farmer
Telecommunications engineer	Soldier
Dentist	Carpenter
Musician	Blacksmith
Teacher	Waste disposal expert
Tailor	Fisherman
Actor	Doctor
Miner	

CS8: Using the telephone

Situations in which the phone may be used	What can go wrong	What can be done to prevent this

CS7: Role plays

Situation one:

Both people are keen to reach an agreement.

Two friends.
One wants help with decorating the outside of his house. He cannot afford to pay anyone.

The other friend will help but only if his motorbike/car can be repaired in return.

Situation two:

The manager needs the worker's special skills. A changed shift pattern or payrise can be agreed, but the manager does not want to give in too easily.

A manager. They need the worker.
A worker. The worker wants to change shift patterns/have a pay rise. The worker knows their particular skills are essential to completing a new contract.

Situation three:

Neither parent nor child want to give in to the other.

Parent wants teenager to stop hanging round with a particular group of friends and to come home at a reasonable time.

Teenager does not want to be told what to do and to have freedom of decision-making limited.

CS10: Analysing the exercise

How easy or difficult was it to give instructions – why?

How easy or difficult was it to receive the instructions – why?

How did the speaker assist you to understand the pattern which was formed?

How could the speaker have made it more easy for you to visualise the pattern?

Did the listener feel that the speaker was trying to help? Why was this so?

How did your sitting positions help or hinder you in this task?

CS9: Giving and receiving instructions

Making patterns

A and B each need a sheet of the shapes below. Both should cut around the shapes. Then carefully follow the instructions offered by the trainer.

CS11: Planning ahead

I feel that I have the following communication skills:

I should like to work on the following skills:

I will do this by:

Managing time and goal setting

The module is divided into six sessions:

1. Why think about time? (1 hour 20 min)
2. What do you do with your time now? (2 hours 15 min)
3. Planning and goal setting (4 hours)
4. Translating goals into action (1 hour – but allowance needs to be made for one-to-one work)
5. Getting things done (55 min)
6. Concluding the module (15 min)

 Work on taking control over time has links with many other areas of work:

- Identifying and managing stress
- Assertiveness
- Planning
- Decision-making
- Managing time and goal setting
- Developing an understanding of the workplace and workplace skills

A number of these areas will be mentioned in this module. Modules in this and the companion manual *Developing Social Skills* can usefully be linked to the work on time management and planning.

 The module makes use of the training and learning activities of

- brainstorm
- pair and small group work
- drawing and charting
- small group presentations
- individual self-assessments
- whole group discussion
- lecturettes
- action planning

Trainer's notes

This module will help you to work with your learners to:

- emphasise the importance of managing the very precious personal resource of time
- think about the ways in which they currently use their time – or indeed have time used for them
- think about planning life goals and to relate these to the management of time on a day-to-day basis
- think about ways to get more in control of themselves and of their days by considering time management tools and goal setting
- encourage feelings of self-motivation, personal progress, a sense of achievement, a sense of self-esteem and a sense of purpose in daily life

Time management is a phrase often heard and used in working life and in organisational contexts. It is often associated with busy working people who deal with many demands and are under pressure. Quite sensibly such people need time management skills. However, all types of people without employment, acting as full-time parents or as carers, or those who are living in residential settings all need effective skills to manage their time, to put boundaries around various activities and to timetable in productive leisure time.

Time is a personal and precious resource. Tomorrow will not happen again for anyone, irrespective of a person's job, status or role in life. If everyone's time and life are of value then everyone needs to know how to manage their own personal supply of time. Nobody wants to arrive at the age of 70 with a list of regrets about things which were not done, decisions which were not taken and having pursued a course of life which was accidentally followed because someone else made decisions about it.

As a trainer you will need to be clear about the value of managing time, able to rehearse the various advantages of time management and its tools and be able to explain such reasons and values to your learners. Some of whom, if unemployed or in a residential or prison setting with many restrictions or rules to follow, may be doubtful, or even think that looking at time management and goal setting is a joke or an insult.

Managing one's own time, having the skills and tactics to do so, helps create structures in life, a sense of purpose, ways to value time, one's life and oneself.

The module has activities on:
- individuals' lives and life planning – the value of thinking about time
- individuals' current use of time and the importance of tracking time
- getting value from time
- planning – short-term lists
- planning – long-term goals
- getting things done

Session One: Why think about time?

 Trainer's notes

Asking people to think about time and its management can seem rather abstract. It is a difficult resource to consider because many people do not feel that they have much control over it or say about its use. One way to make time seem more tangible is to ask people to think carefully about their own lives so far and the extent to which they have valued their time. They can reflect on what has been enjoyed and been satisfying, on how many occasions they have taken control over making decisions about the ways they made use of their time especially in relation to events which were satisfying or enjoyable.

Life so far (20 min)

As an introductory activity ask the learners to work on a large, A1 sheet of paper with various coloured pens to draw out their life to date. They need to work alone and to know they have 20 minutes for this activity. Whatever they do can be confidential. They do not have to show it to others but they will need to use it to reach some conclusions from their work.

Ask the learners to draw a line, any shape, size or thickness going from left to right on the page to cover the period from their birth to date. The larger the line the easier it will be for them to mark on key events.

Ask the learners to consider putting in all the highs and lows in their lives, to use different colours if they want to show periods which were particularly happy or when life was just neutral. The learners should use words or symbols to show particularly important events.

Organise serious and quiet time for completing this activity and space so the learners can work away from others.

Thoughts about life so far (20 min)

Once the learners have completed their lifeline, ask them to think about and make some notes on these questions in relation to their lives to date.

- What have been the best times of your life so far and why?
- What have been the worst and why?
- Who was important in making them best and worst?
- How central were you in making those times best and worst?
- Did you make decisions about what you did?
- Did someone else?
- Did things just happen?
- Did you plan things?
- Looking at your life so far, overall are you pleased with the way you have spent you time?
- What changes would you make and why?
- If you are going to live your life again, what advice would you offer yourself?

These questions are difficult and may ask the learners to address some personally difficult or distressing material. They may need help in working through the questions. The questions will need to be produced on a handout and may need to be carefully explained. It is important that thorough, full and honest answers are given. If the learners do not work carefully and thoughtfully through this exercise then they may fail to gain sense of the importance of:

- having spent time in positive and negative ways
- their role in playing a part in how that time was spent, for example by making decisions or opting not to
- time passing and that a significant chunk of time has already passed for them

You will need to work with the learners from the starting points:

- that there is the possibility of control
- that time has already passed
- that they are on a continuum from birth to death

This work on the lifeline and the answers from these questions are also useful for a number of other modules in this manual *Developing Life Skills* (for example, Managing Change, Developing Positive Attitudes. This work will be used again in this module).

Sharing thoughts on life so far (20 min)

The learners may now have spent 40 minutes working on their lifeline activity. They will want some break from solitary work. Bring the group back together and begin the feedback session moving from general to more specific questions.

- How did the learners find the exercise?
- Was it enjoyable, difficult or interesting?
- What surprised them most?
- How many learners felt that they were taking a key part in making decisions about their own lives?
- How many learners felt they allowed others to make decisions or just let things happen? *Ask for some examples*
- What are the consequences of being in charge of making decisions or not being in charge of how your time is spent?
- Overall how many feel they could have spent their time differently? *Again ask for some examples*
- How many would like to have spent their time so far differently? *Again ask for some examples*

Brainstorm (10 min)

As a final brainstorm activity explore the two following questions:

> **What do you think are the links between looking at life so far and looking at managing your time?**
>
> **What would you like to find out about managing your time?**

Drawing the threads together (10 min)

The answers to the second question will help the trainer to think about which parts of the module to tackle. However, many learners do not know what they may need to know or have to learn so an outline of the programme needs to be offered. Spend a final ten minutes summarising the learning points so far, e.g. importance of making decisions; time as a precious and finite resource; value of taking control of life and outline the materials the module covers. Use OHP MT13.

Session Two: What do you do with your time now?

As a group (10 min)

Ask the group members to suggest the activities in which they are involved which take up a twenty-four hour period. There may need to be two different lists to cover weekdays and weekends.

You may want to start them off by suggesting some simple activities, so that the group understands they are thinking about all sorts of everyday activities so:

- sleeping
- washing
- dressing
- shopping
- walking children to school
- going to work
- going to a training course
- walking the dog
- going to the pub
- washing clothes

Individual work (20 min)

Ask each group member to work individually and to estimate how much of their time is spent on any activity during an average day. Ask them to guess the percentage of time. You may need to explain percentages simply and emphasise that they are guessing.

Ask each group member to draw a pie chart or bar chart of their time use. The principles behind these charts may need to be explained and an example worked on the flipchart.

Out of session work

Ask the learners to keep a list of the ways in which they spend time over the course of week. Give everyone enough copies of the MT1: Time spent, to cover the period and ask the learners to bring these back to the next session.

Review activity (35 min)

Ask each learner to review their week's sheets of time spent, and to complete the seven questions on MT2. Firstly alone for ten minutes and then to compare their answers with one or two others for 15 minutes. In discussing them they may get more ideas about things they would prefer to do with their time or they may become more aware of wasted time. The tutor will need to go to each of these small groups helping them to focus on the task.

Ask for group feedback on the Time Spent Activity for 10-15 minutes. You may want to use the following questions to help structure the feedback and discussion.

- What activities were in the waste of time category and why?

- How many found their estimates of time spent were accurate?

- What things did people feel were a valuable use of time?

- What things have to be done?

- Are there any ways to do these faster?

- What activities would people prefer to do with their time?

- What is a valuable use of time? Ask the group to define what it means by value

Explanation and discussion

Types of time (30 min)

At the end of the feedback introduce the idea of different types of time:

1. **Sold time** – time which is spent on employment, on courses or is committed in some way.

2. **Maintenance time** – things which have to be done, e.g. house cleaning, shopping for food, budgeting, eating, sleeping.

3. **Personal or discretionary time** – time which each person has in which they can do things they want to do.

Ask the group for examples of each type of time and put these on the flipchart under the appropriate heading.

Ask the group which of the types of time can they control?

Ask the group to work alone on their time spent sheets to work out what time they spend falls into each of these categories. They can work alone or in small groups, whichever is the most helpful, to get the idea of different types of time.

Habits and changing use of time (40 min)

Ask the learners to complete the MT3 and MT4. They may want to work with a partner to help them think of ways to replace habits or to change what they do with time.

At the end of this individual or pair work ask the learners to feedback some of their findings to the group. Take ten minutes for this.

 Trainer's notes

The next part of the exercise on spending time will be to encourage the learners to consider taking greater control over the ways in which they spend their time.

They should have:
- identified time they feel they waste
- identified activities which have little value to them
- identified activities which they do not want to do, which fall not in sold time or even maintenance time, but which they do, perhaps out of habit, perhaps because they cannot think of anything else to do or perhaps just to go along with other people

- identified an amount of personal time which they can use to do things which make their lives more satisfying
- identified a list of maintenance activities. They may want to consider if these things can be done in a different way to free up time for something they would like to do.

The success of any exercise in thinking about re-arranging time usage depends on the learners:
- having ideas about activities they prefer to do or would like to do more of
- having some goals and a sense that they can begin to take control over their own lives to release time to work on their goals
- feeling they are able to make changes and to take control over habits or patterns of spending time
- feeling that they want to do something different

It needs to be noted that many learners have little idea about use of leisure time and ways in which they can extend what they do. Information and ideas should be readily available to the learners.

MT3 Identifying habits and MT4 Making changes can be used to help in the process of identifying what to change. However work on changing how time is spent needs to be linked to the next section on Planning long-term goals. Without a longer-term sense of what should or could be done there is little reason or motivation for changing current time usage.

The section on short-term time planning supports realising long-term goals and making changes in how time is spent.

The section on getting things done has some useful tips on getting started. You will need to draw out the parts of each section which are useful to your learners. You will need to make links and to go over the ideas and the skills which they have already explored to reinforce the learning.

Session Three: Planning and goal setting

 Trainer's notes

Work on the area of longer-term planning requires the learner to:
- work again on their lifeline, projecting their life into the future and so thinking about what changes they want in their lives so life can be, in their terms, happy and successful
- identify what is personally important, that is to be clear about what each individual values
- learn how to set goals and to manage the process of achieving them

As a group (10 min)
Introduce the aims of the session and the areas of work to be covered. Clarify any lack of understanding and address learners' questions.

Completing the lifeline (40 min)
Ask the learners to go back to the work they undertook in the opening session. Ask them to continue drawing their lifeline. They will need coloured pens and may need more paper. Ask them to imagine that they can take full control over their lives and steer it in any way that they wish. Ask them to complete their lifelines putting in all the things they would like for themselves between now and the close of their lives.

Before they start they may want some time to brainstorm ideas about their possible future lives either as a group or alone, provide either the brainstorm chart, MT5, or begin an exercise on the flipchart to consider such areas of future life as:

- relationships with children, spouse, friends, parents. How would these be in an ideal situation?
- work – what would they like to do and why?
- money or wealth – what is their ideal situation and why?
- realising ambitions – what ambitions do they have?
- what type of home and its location would they like?
- what future lifestyle would they like?
- what would make them feel their lives had been of value?

Feedback (15 min)

Once everyone has completed their lifeline, they can discuss in pairs or offer to the group some things which they would like in their future lives. The extent of self-disclosure will depend on how well the group functions.

You may want to encourage the group to reflect by asking questions such as:

- Did anything surprise you about the future life you have drawn? If so, what?
- How much different is their future life from their life to date? What makes it different?
- What have you found out about yourself from drawing your future lifeline?

The last question should help lead the group to the next section, working on personal values.

Personal values

Trainer's notes

A key to effective living, to valued use of time and to planning goals to which there is real and full, rather than partial, commitment is to fully understand and realise personal values. Often people do things or say they want things out of habit because they have not thought about such things or because others around them want such goals for them. This exercise asks the learner to think carefully and honestly about what is currently important to them.

The activity below asks the learners to clarify and to prioritise their values. With this information the learners will be able to review their lifeline, to see if it is in line with their values and to shape their future goals by bringing them into line with their values. People who are more in balance with their values are more likely to be successful and feel fulfilled. Personal values should underpin all areas of their lives.

Brainstorm (15 min)

Ask the learners to work on a group brainstorm on:

What are personal values?

Why are they important?

This process will allow you to clarify with the group the meaning of personal values. You will need to be ready with some ideas to support why the exercise is important and to help with definitions. This should support not pre-empt the brainstorm. Encourage the group to come up with a wide list of suggestions. These may include such as:

- having money
- having a family
- being happy
- having fun
- having a sense of purpose
- making someone else happy
- being employed

- working hard
- feeling useful
- being able to get the best for my kids
- having people notice me
- having a good relationship with my partner
- doing good for others
- God

You may want to prompt the group to come up with suggestions for various areas of life if they fix on only one area. The activity is fairly demanding as learners will be disclosing things about themselves. Ensure that no learner criticises another for the personal values which they contribute to the group brainstorm.

Individual work on values (30 min)

Ask the group to think about these pooled ideas but to identify their own personal values. The learners will need **MT6** and **MT7** for this.

Feedback (10 min)

The individual work on values can be shared in pairs or with the group members if such disclosure is possible. Where disclosure needs to be limited the tutor can ask questions which can be discussed at a more general level. These include things such as:

- How useful was the exercise?
- In how many areas of life could the learners identify clear values?
- Did their values tend to be spread throughout all aspects of life or was the emphasis on one or two areas?
- Where there is an imbalance do learners know why this is the case?
- How many learners are living according to their values?
- How many are actually working against their values?
- How does this feel to work against values or to work with them?
- What strategies are there for getting life and values in greater harmony?

Values and the lifeline (30 min)

Ask the learners to find their future lifeline and values list and to compare the two. They need to ask themselves:

How good is the match between the values list and the future lifeline?

The same values symbols ✓, –, X could be used to mark various events and points on the projected lifeline. Ask the learners to consider the following questions:

- Does mis-match cause the learner concern? Why or why not?
- What could the learner suggest to deal with mismatches?

The learners could look at their past lifeline and the values list and again consider

- if their values fit
- if there is a values mismatch
- are there any occasions of good fit or very great mismatch?
- have these occasions led to particular happiness or distress for the learner?

Ask the learners to keep their work on values safely.

Other exercises to support thinking about values can be found in *Becoming An Effective Trainer*, however the brainstorming work with the group should help stimulate thinking about values which give meaning to individual lives.

Setting longer term goals

 Trainer's notes

Goals are very specific ways of thinking about channelling time and life-energy. In determining goals the three points below should be taken into account. Goals should:

- be realistic for the individual
- fit with the values of the individual
- be something to which the learner feels commitment

There is further explanation and other activities to support goal setting in *Becoming an Effective Trainer*, and this material may be used to support the activities and notes below.

By the close of the session learners will have:

- been made aware of the value of goal setting
- been exposed to the seven step process of goal setting and the key principles for setting goals
- undertaken several activities which will help them to set goals

As a group (10 min)

Set up the expectation that the group will consider goal setting by asking it to brainstorm the question

> **Why set goals in life?**

Collect a list of suggestions then ask the learners to volunteer any experiences which they have had in setting goals or working towards goals and how they felt about it.

You may need to allow some time to counter opposition to goal setting and to explain what goal setting is about. You may need to deal with comments such as:

- it is a waste of time
- nothing works out in reality
- you cannot control other people or events
- why plan for things, no-one gives people like me a break
- I cannot afford/have not got the qualifications/experience/physical health to achieve my goal

Goal setting is meant to be motivational, offering learners something clear to work towards. It is also meant to be something which is achievable within the constraints of the individual learner's physical and emotional resources and abilities. The issue of constraints will need to be confronted. You will have to stress the importance of being realistic, of setting goals which enable the individual learners to achieve them and of not including in their goals checks on other people's actions.

You can emphasise that goal setting focuses the individual by helping to plan what needs to be done to reach the goal and to make decisions about use of time rather than using the limited resource of time without thinking.

Setting achievable goals (20 min)

Take the group through the following seven steps for successful goal setting and planning. This will take the form of a lecturette. OHTs **MT14** and **MT15** will assist your explanation. The key messages are that goals need to be:

- specific
- based on realising what is important to the individual, i.e. values based
- broken down into easily attacked action steps
- timebound

The seven steps are as follows:

1. *Take stock of yourself:*
   Where are you now?
   What are your values?
   What values are important to you but are ones which you are ignoring?

2. *What could my future be like?*
   What is important to me?
   What range of options do I have for my future?
   How do these options relate to my values?

3. *Reviewing options:*
   What of all the possibilities I have, do I really want to pursue?
   What is realistic in terms of my current levels of achievement, finances, lifestyle and the things I would be prepared to trade or sacrifice?
   What is a real goal, i.e. something to pursue now?
   What is a gleam in my eye, i.e. something I might do, something which might be nice to do in the future but to which I cannot fully commit myself now?

   A goal may seem unlikely at first glance. For example it may take a long time to realise, but it does not matter if it is a long way off, so long as there is the commitment to keep working towards it. This will be more difficult and will involve great self-discipline and many action steps but it remains possible. A goal may seem unlikely because the learner may have to undertake a number of steps before the goal can be started. Again, so long as the learner realises that this is the case and has the motivation to continue with a long-term plan then the ultimate goal can be reached.

   Where goals are long-term or there are a number of pre-goals to be met before starting the learner needs to have many clear steps mapped out along the way. Each of which will be needed to structure the route to show progress and to generate a reward.

4. *Planning to reach your goal:*
   Set smaller steps to achieve the goal. These need to be **SMART**:

   Small
   Measurable
   Achievable
   Realistic
   Timebound

   If the action steps are not SMART then reaching the goal becomes unlikely because the learner could:
   - go off along the wrong track
   - waste time doing the wrong things
   - keep doing the same things and not progress
   - not take action in the right order and so waste time
   - not realise that progress is being made and so not feel motivated

5. *Take action:*
   Check that the actions are in line with the action steps and are leading to the overall goal.

6. *Review action:*
   What has been successful?
   What has proven to be hard?
   How much has been completed toward the goal?
   How might targets need to be re-written?

7. *Take further action:*
   Keep doing this until the action steps are completed and the goal is reached. Use the OHTs and ask the group to help sum up the key learning points.

Individual goal setting exercise (1 hour)

Learners will need to work alone for this exercise but may want the support of a planning partner or the tutor. Learners will need copies of:
- OHT MT15 as a handout
- MT8
- MT9
- MT10
- MT11
- some blank paper
- their work on their values
- their work on their extended lifeline

Ask the learners to review their extended lifeline and values sheets.

Ask all learners to work through MT8 Long-term goal setting completing the boxes as they go. They will want to use a copy of OHT MT15 as a guide.

The learners may be helped by using MT9 to help them sift through their ideas to decide what are gleams, real goals and others' imposed goals.

MT10 will help in deciding what needs to be done to reach a goal and MT11 can be given out once the double diamond chart has been completed to help the learner to order their action steps for their goal.

Session Four: Translating goals to actions

 Trainer's notes

This session moves from looking at and setting longer-term goals to being able to implement them. Three strategies are considered:

- an action plan
- weekly 'to do' lists
- daily 'to do' lists

All of which take larger tasks and break them into smaller steps.

Once this session is completed the learners will be familiar with:

- all three strategies for shorter-term time management
- the value of managing time in smaller chunks
- linking short-term time management to longer term goals

The session will take one hour to complete. There is an expectation that learners will complete some work out of session and review this at a later date with their trainer.

The final part of the session is the construction of an action plan. This may need to be done on a one-to-one basis and 20 minutes should be allowed for each group member.

Introductory talk (20 min)

Extract the key ideas from the following notes and present them as a short talk to the group. OHTs or handouts may be needed of the action plans and a 'to do' list.

Determining to use time effectively and to work to realising long-term goals can be helped by following an action plan. This is setting out shorter-term SMART targets, fixing a date for their completion and then reviewing what has been completed. Action plans formalise the process of setting goals, they are most effective if discussed with and reviewed with a trainer or planning partner.

There are examples of simple action plans which the learners may want to use overleaf. The learners can also devise their own action plans using blank paper.

Each learner has undertaken work on their future goals and current values and has seen the importance of managing the resource of time. The completion of action plans and making use of the work on goals and values should be undertaken. This will enable the practice of target setting and time management skills to be tested. The learners should relate their action plans to their weekly or daily 'to do' lists. These are discussed next.

Learners need to consider blocking time so they are always doing something towards their longer-term goal. They can make use of their action plans when planning their weeks and days.

So, having gone through a process and deciding upon a goal they should then be deciding upon action steps they need to undertake, on a week by week basis, to do something towards meeting those action steps. They then need to decide to do something each day wherever possible to meet part of an action step. Time management requires that time is used to specific ends, be it planned leisure and relaxation or other activities. Time management does not always mean doing but it does mean being in charge of one's own time.

Action Plan

Name: _____

My present situation:

Note: Skills, experience of work or training; personal qualities, achievements, current circumstances

What do I want to do?

How do I achieve this? (include timescales involved)

What help do I need?

Who:

What:

Who: Training organisations, employers, tutors, careers service, TEC
What: Transport, specialist equipment, education help, confidence building, counselling, supervision, development of personal skills

Additional action points/any other comments

Note: longer-term targets, other people to be in involved in the plan, links with current situation, etc.

Signed .... Date ....

Signed .... Date ....

Review date:

Action Plan

Learner's name: _____   Date:

Write your goals in the middle box and the action steps in the outer space. Include timescales; resources needed; people who may help and any issues you may need to consider for each action step.

Review date:

Action Plan

Starting points for action

Name .... Date ....

Personal details:

Summary of assessment:

Identification of issues: *(place these in order of priority for action)*

Action to be taken:

Actions steps *(write out in details, include options to deal with anticipated problems)*

Completion dates

Sources for help for plan's completion

Review date:

Action Plan

The broad goal is:

Break this goal into parts and list these parts:

Select one of these parts of your goal →

Break this into SMART targets →

List four targets below and complete the target steps

Target 1 is:	Target 2 is:	Target 3 is:	Target 4 is:
I will do this by:	I will do this by:	I will do this by:	I will do this by:
Who can help me?	Who can help me?	Who can help me?	Who can help me?
Date done by?	Date done by?	Date done by?	Date done by?

Review date:

Short-term weekly lists of tasks towards the action steps may mean the learner decides to draw up a list like this:

Week beginning 10th July	
Tasks	**Date**
Contact three colleges and get prospectuses	
Haircut	
Read book on *How To Go To Interviews*, pages 35-69	
Make dental appointment	
Dan's birthday – get present and card	
Book next driving lesson	
Pay Council Tax	

Some of the items on the weekly list will be parts of action steps (reading the pages in the Interview book) on the action plan or even whole action steps (contacting the colleges). The learner by doing something towards the action plan will always be seeing progress and will experience a sense of motivation.

The learner may have a daily 'to do' list. This can again have parts of action steps on it or even if time allows that day a whole action step.

Chunking time up into weekly and daily blocks encourages things to be done and prevents the learner becoming overwhelmed by the largeness of tasks, or paralysed by their own failure to take action and/or being simply afraid to get started.

Design task (20 min)

Having discussed some of these issues as a group and looked at the idea of a weekly list and a daily 'to do' list, ask the group to work in twos or threes to design weekly and daily lists which they would and could use. Before beginning the designs they will need to list out what information is needed on each type of list. They will need large sheets of paper and pens.

Feedback (20 min)

These ideas can be pooled in a group feedback session. Allow each group a maximum of five minutes to sell their design to other group members. They will need to do their presentations with A1 sized versions of their lists.

Individual work

Individuals will need to decide which lists they want to adopt. For a week they should try using the lists for their time management. They will need to relate activities to their action plans.

At the close of a week review issues or problems in trying to work in a more organised way. Group sessions are valuable but one-to-one review with learner and tutor would be most beneficial in diagnosing particular issues or difficulties.

Ongoing surgeries to support the learner to gain the habit of goal setting, action planning and short-term time management practices will be essential for these practices to become established with the learner.

Session Five: Getting things done

This session offers the group the opportunity to explore the reasons why tasks may never be completed or not be started.

Brainstorm (20 min)

Brainstorm with the group the question:

> **What stops people from getting things done?**

The group may come up with a range of suggestions such as:

- not knowing what to do
- not having the time
- not being sure what needs doing or how to do it
- fear of failing
- not having money or other resources
- not being organised
- being anxious about starting
- just putting it off
- not knowing where to start
- not wanting to do something
- not being able to make decisions

Once there are a number of suggestions, draw from the group what they mean by some suggestions and ask for some examples. Examples can come from any part of their life. If the group does not work too well together when it comes to disclosing things, then suggest that the group work in smaller groups and comes up with examples to be fed back to the whole group. Take a further five or ten minutes on this.

What stops people (15 min)

Now introduce some key ideas to the group about why people fail to get things done. These include:

- procrastination – putting things off, so that they get increasingly difficult to start or just get so large
- wanting to do everything so well and being a perfectionist so that things may not get started and many not get finished
- feeling overwhelmed by the size of the task because it is so important or so large and so not starting it
- feeling unequal to the task, not having skills, knowledge, resources or other necessary things to complete the task
- being unable to make a decision or questioning decisions once taken

Make use of **MT12** and talk though the suggestions for getting things done.

After working through each one, ensure the group understands what it means and ask how the suggestion could have been applied or could be applied to one of their tasks not yet done.

Preparation for individual activities outside the session (20 min)

Ask the group members to think of something they have not started but need to do and ask them to apply one of the following techniques from MT12 as a way to start.

1. *Devise a plan for the task.* Identify what needs to be done and in what order. For example, decide what resources are necessary. Determine when it will be begun and completed and how success can be rewarded.

2. What *associated task* could be completed which leads on to the main task.

3. *Construct a list of advantages and disadvantages* of completing the task and anticipate the feelings of having completed the task and then decide if it is worth doing.

Ask for some examples of the ways these techniques might be applied to tasks which have not yet been done. Check for learners' realism and the sufficiency of action steps.

Ask group members to apply any of these methods and to report back at the next appropriate session. Ensure that there is report back for the group members to hear how techniques were applied and tried. Have a group brainstorm their feelings about managing to start and complete tasks.

Session Six: Concluding the module

Managing a summing up session need not be seen as an opportunity to repeat everything which has been done to date. Rather it should be a brainstorming session where you draw out from the learners:

- key ideas which they have heard. This list will need to be fairly comprehensive if the exercise is to serve as revision. You may want to add some suggestions or prompt the group for more suggestions
- ideas which they will be using

An evaluation proforma could be used to conclude the module. There are examples of these in the Trainer's tools.

MT2: Estimated time and actual time spent

1. Were there any surprises about how much time you spent on certain activities? Which ones were these and why?

2. Were there any surprises about how little time you spent on certain activities? Which ones were they and why?

Compare the amounts of time you really spent with your pie chart or bar chart estimates.

3. How much time did you enjoy over the course of the week and why?

4. How much time did you spend doing things that you did not want to do? Why did you do these things?

5. How much time do you think you wasted over the course of a week?

6. What would you rather have done instead of doing things you do not like or wasting time? Why are these activities better?

7. What changes would you make in your week to make the time spent more satisfying?

MT1: Time spent

Keep a log of the way you spend time. Try to complete this sheet as often as you can in any one day

Time	Day	Date	Activity
7-8			
8-9			
9-10			
10-11			
11-12			
12-1			
1-2			
2-3			
3-4			
4-5			
5-6			
6-7			
7-8			
8-9			
9-10			
10-11			
11-12			
12-1			
1-6			

MT4: Making changes

The things which I would like to spend less of my time on are:

The things I would like to spend more of my time on are:

***I have identified that I can make changes in the way I spend my time by** (put down a list, e.g. not going to the shops every day; not putting off things and making excuses; not spending so much time in the pub or on watching TV etc.)*

MT3: Habits

Look again at your time spent sheets. Consider each activity and put an H by any which are habits, are things which you just do because you have always done them.

Some things like getting dressed are things you always do – but you have to. However you could consider your morning routine and find that the process of getting dressed takes much longer than it needs to, that you spend a few hours getting round to getting dressed.

List below any habits which you would like to change, reduce or get rid of.

Habit	Estimate how much time it takes weekly	Replace with or do instead

MT6: My values

Consider the question at the centre and think if there are any particular aspects of life which you value under each of the headings. Add more branches to the chart as you need them.

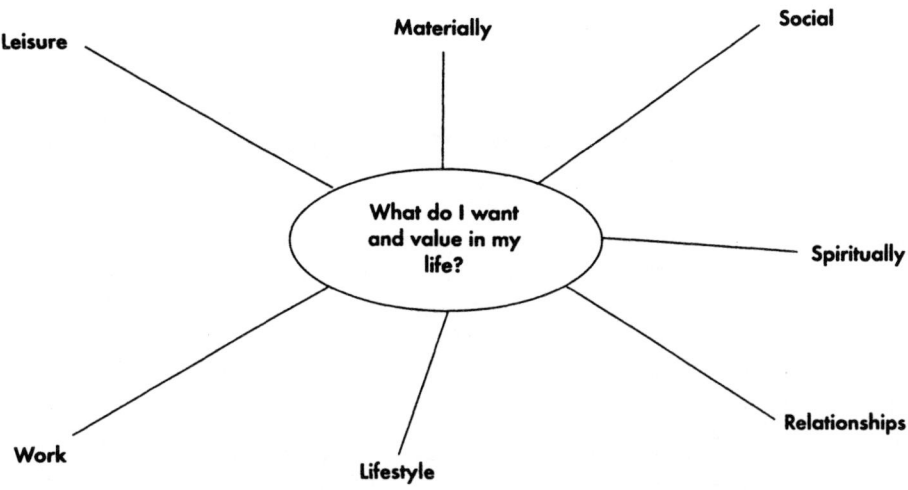

MT5: Aspects of my future

Complete the spider diagram putting your brainstorm ideas under each of the printed headings. Add more branches to the diagram about things you would like in the future.

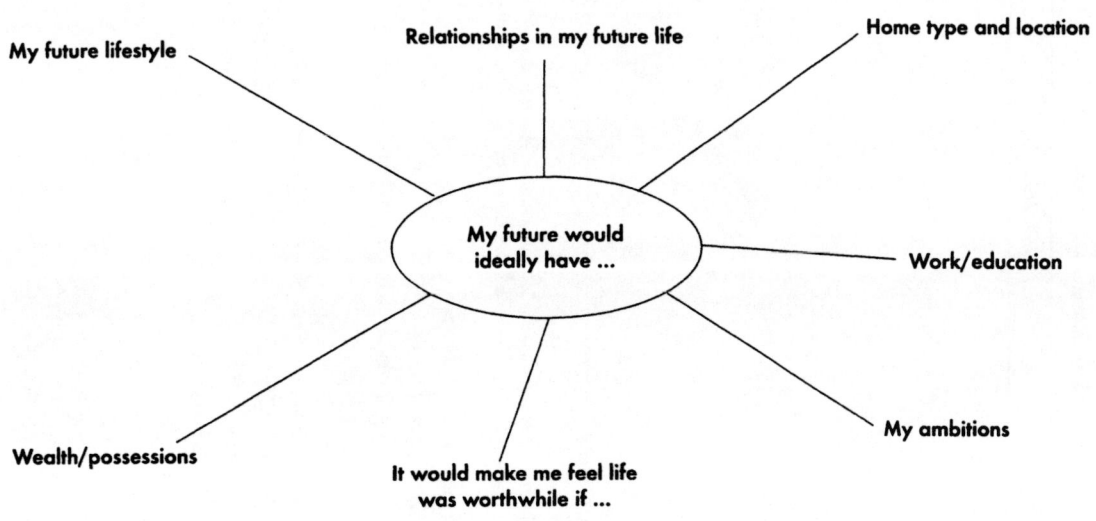

MT8: Long term goal setting

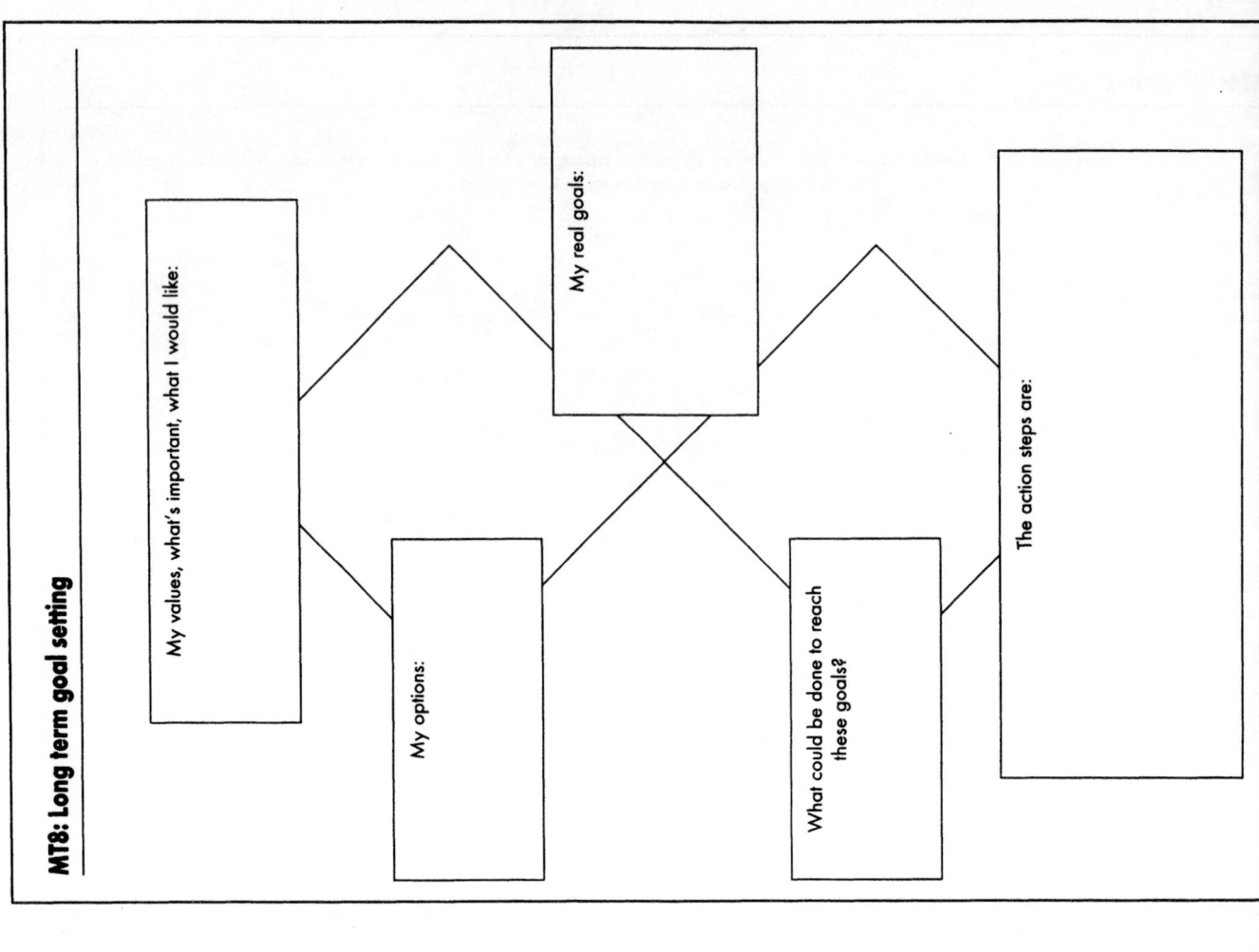

My values, what's important, what I would like:

My real goals:

My options:

What could be done to reach these goals?

The action steps are:

MT7: My values and my life

Having brainstormed your values or the aspects of life which are most important to you, think about each one and put the top six or eight in order of importance to you.

MY VALUES

-
-
-
-
-
-
-
-

Try to decide what each value means to you and how you would see it operating in your life – write down a few words. Try to write a little about why these values are important to you.

Now look at each value and consider:

Are you fulfilling it in your life?

Are you working against the value by the way you are living?

Are you neglecting it in your life?

Test each value against each of these three questions and mark it:

✓   if you are fulfilling it

X   if you work against it

–   if you are neglecting it

MT10: Brainstorm on meeting my goal

Think about your goal and jot down as many ideas as you can of the things which may need to be done so that you can achieve your goal. Later on you might find there are a number of things which you do not have to do. Your tutor will help you with this.

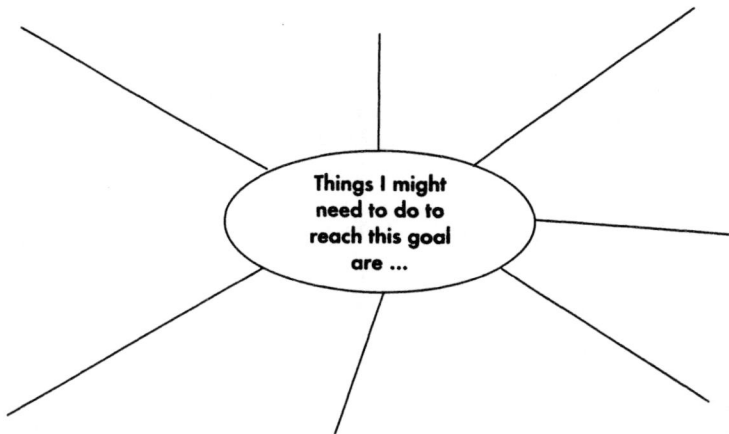

Things I might need to do to reach this goal are ...

MT9: Making some choices about my goals

Look at the ideas you have come up with about your future. Now try to find the ones you really want as your life goals. Ask yourself the following questions about each goal on your list of possible goals. Work through your whole list until you have a smaller list of the goals you really want to try.

Do I really think this is important to me?

What would I have to do to get it?

What else is involved in trying to get it?

How possible is this?

What would I be willing to do to get it?

Is this going to be enough to get it?

When will I start?

How does this affect anyone important to me?

Do I still want to do it?

Can I imagine myself getting there?

Can I imagine myself seeing it through?

MT12: Getting things done

1. Don't eat the elephant whole!

Tasks which seem very large either in size or importance are best tackled by dividing them into smaller, bite-sized pieces. Listing all of the small tasks means that after each is done it can be ticked off, progress can be seen and the same goal is being worked towards.

2. Imagine you're already started

Think hard about what you would do and have already done if you were actually doing the task now. Having begun to visualise what it's like to be doing the task, act as if you have begun and just get on with it.

3. Start anywhere

If a task seems so large or difficult just do a bit of it that can be done and keep on doing bits which can be done to make in roads into the whole.

4. Do a task which is associated

Do a task which is associated with the one you keep putting off but which helps you to get started.

5. Make a list of all the advantages and disadvantages

Make a list of all the advantages and disadvantages of getting on with the task and try to imagine how you will feel once it is done. Do the advantages outweigh the disadvantages.? Often they do and the positive feelings of having finished are often great, these factors should be a motivator.

6. Decide on a reward

Decide on a reward for actually getting started and the finishing the task. Make sure that you give yourself rewards.

7. Decide on a time

Decide on a time for which you will work at the task. Select your start time, your break and a completion time and then stick to it. If you can keep going for another block of time then do so.

MT11: Putting the action steps in the right order

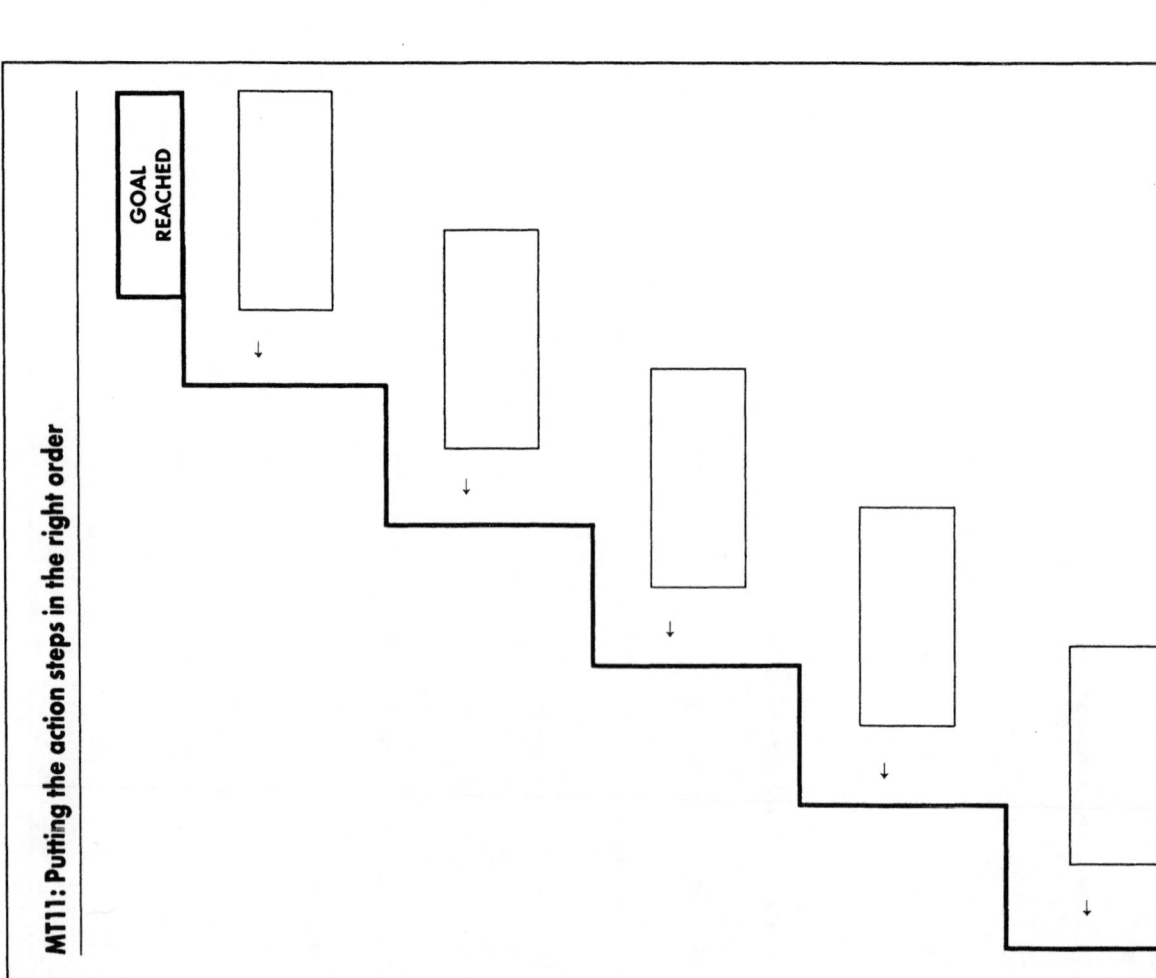

GOAL REACHED

Fill in each box with the small action steps or targets which you need to take so that you can reach your goal. You will need to think carefully about putting the action steps in the right order. Don't forget to put the date by when each step will be completed.

MT12: Getting things done – Continued

8. Start working at the task at the best time of your day

Start working at the task at the best time of your day for such activities. Some people are on their best form early in the morning, others late at night.

Decide when you are most likely to succeed when other people you need will be able to help you or when you will be left uninterrupted to get on. Then start the task. For example, there's no point in trying to get help with a housing application when you know the office is closed or the staff most likely to be busy.

9. Just get started

Often just getting on with the task is enough to keep you going working on the task.

10. Know what you need to do before you start

Know what you need to do before you start. Get organised, make a plan of the task, make a list of information or resources you need.

11. Allow yourself to succeed

Starting at the wrong time, without knowing what should be done or having the resource to do it will mean failure. This stops people trying again and completing a task.

12. The decision you make

The decision you make probably does not matter – but making it does.

Many people simply fail to make a decision because they do not know what decision to make. Making the decision and deciding to then get on rather than changing the decision or questioning it will save time and allow you to get on with life rather than putting part of it on hold.

 MT13: Managing time more effectively

This course will help you to:

- **find out about how you spend your time**

- **find out ways to better organise your time to spend more of it doing what you want**

- **identify your longer-term goals**

- **identify what is important to you – your values**

- **find out how to spend your time to help you to reach goals and to live in harmony with what's important to you**

- **learn about ways to get started to get things done, and to get the most from your days**

- **find out better ways to get in control of and get the most from your life**

OHP

MT15: Long term goal setting

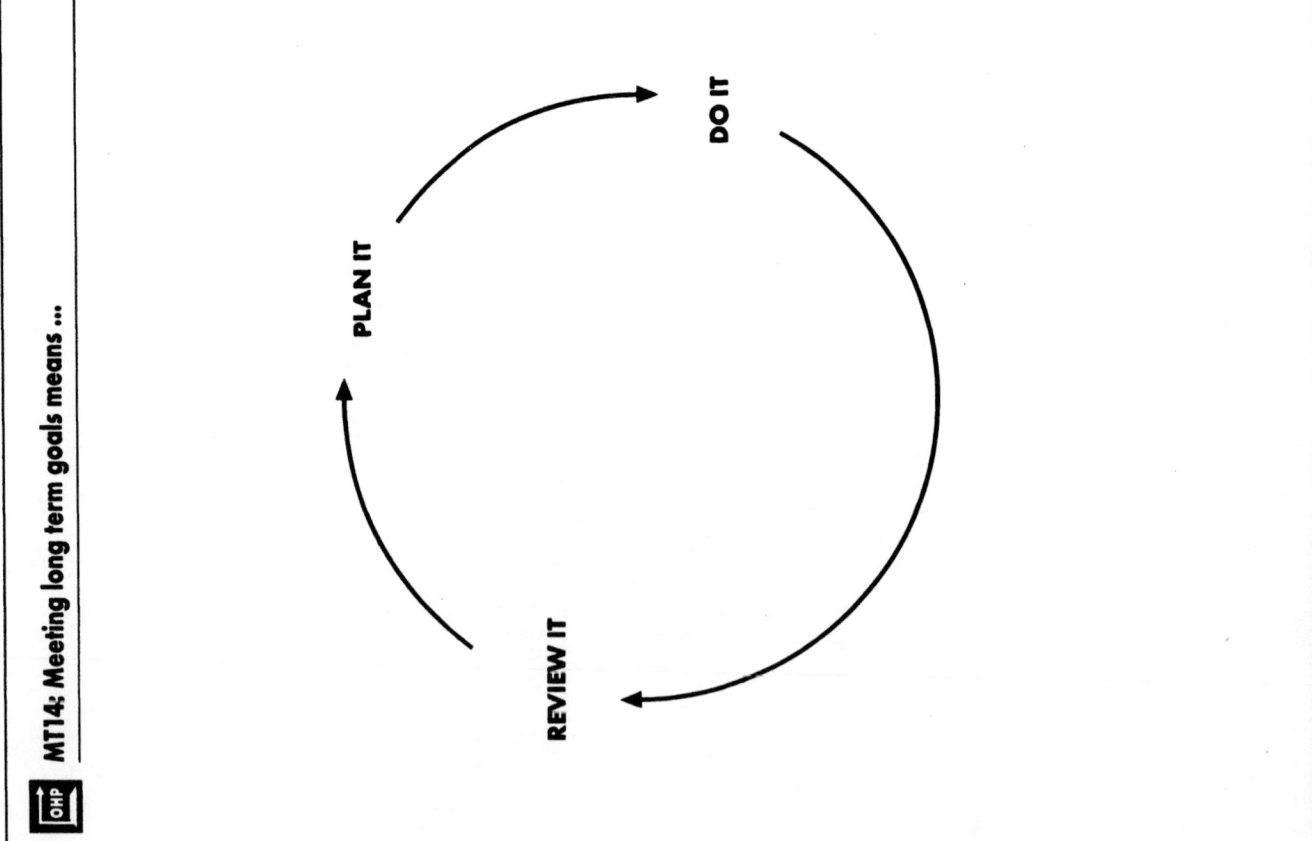

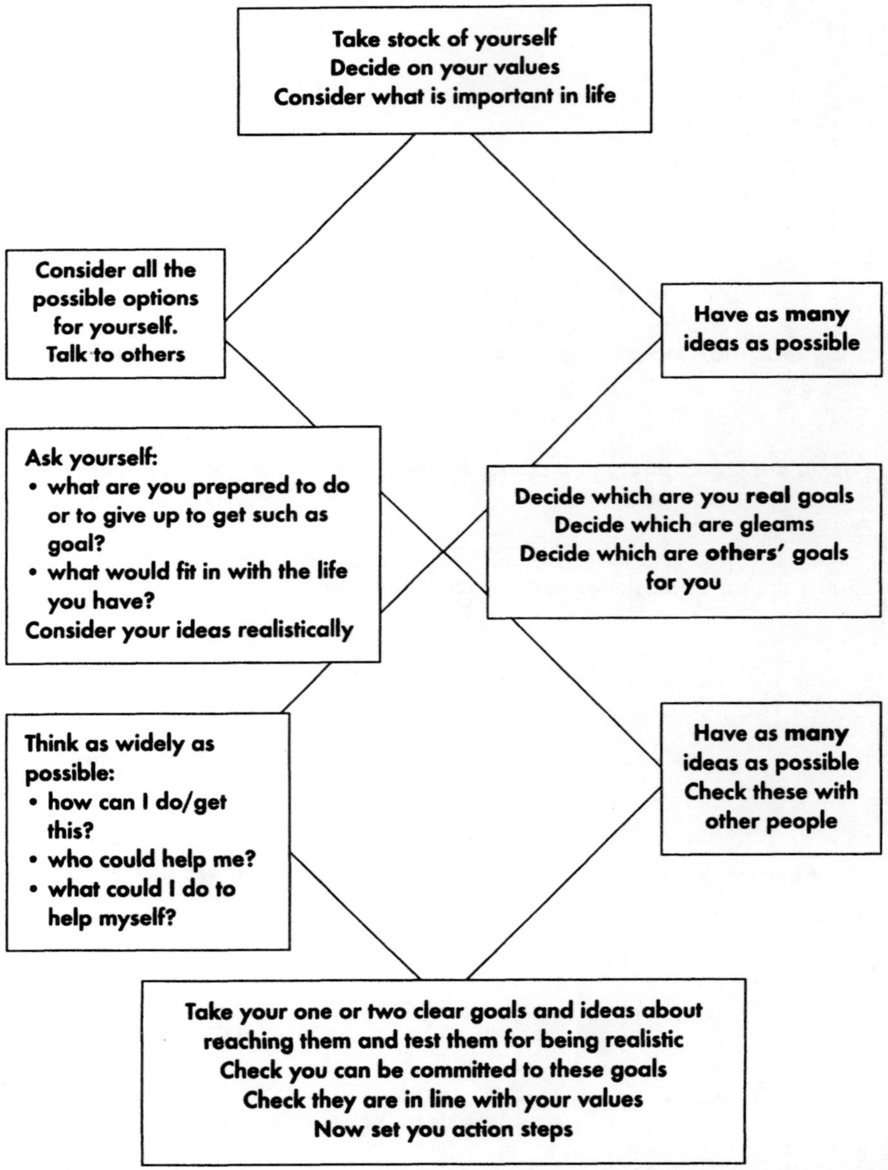

Take stock of yourself
Decide on your values
Consider what is important in life

Have as many ideas as possible

Decide which are you real goals
Decide which are gleams
Decide which are others' goals for you

Have as many ideas as possible
Check these with other people

Consider all the possible options for yourself.
Talk to others

Ask yourself:
• what are you prepared to do or to give up to get such as goal?
• what would fit in with the life you have?
Consider your ideas realistically

Think as widely as possible:
• how can I do/get this?
• who could help me?
• what could I do to help myself?

Take your one or two clear goals and ideas about reaching them and test them for being realistic
Check you can be committed to these goals
Check they are in line with your values
Now set you action steps

OHP

MT14: Meeting long term goals means ...

PLAN IT

DO IT

REVIEW IT

Managing money

 The module is divided into eight sessions. These are:

1. Raising awareness of money management (1 hour 25 min)
2. Spending and budgeting (3 hours 25 min)
3. Avoiding and managing debt (2 hours)
4. Problem solving financial problems (1 hour 35 min)
5. Calculate interest and work out percentages (1 hour)
6. Managing credit (1 hour 40 min)
7. Savings (50 min)
8. Drawing the threads together (30 min)

 The module makes use of the learning and training activities of:

- self-assessment checklists and statement writing
- continuum and other ranking exercises
- brainstorming
- discussion
- working alone
- role-play
- information giving and use of handouts

In addition the learners will:

- complete budgeting activities
- do simple calculations
- problem-solve

The learners may need calculators. Examples of savings, credit and other money adverts would be useful illustrative material.

 Trainer's notes

The aim of this module is to encourage learners to understand the value of and to develop some skills of financial literacy. Financial literacy means being able to make judgements and decisions about the use and management of money.

The past decade or so has seen many changes in people's financial and material expectations. There have been many more owner-occupiers of houses and many more mortgage defaults and repossessions. There has been a huge increase in the number of households and individuals in debt. This may be through recession and the rise of consumer credit which has encouraged too many to spend beyond their means.

Often people seek help with their financial situation once they are already in crisis and in need of specialist debt counselling. This module offers some basic principles of money management and highlights the importance of taking responsibility for managing personal money before debt and financial crisis.

This module encourages learners to:

- understand how they currently manage their money
- consider their attitudes towards money
- undertake a stock-take of their current financial position

- understand the principles of basic money management, e.g. budgeting and planning
- apply problem-solving skills and decision-making skills to money management
- be aware of some key calculations and terms used in money management
- be aware of further sources of help for better money management and advice
- think about money management and to appreciate it is something they can do

Session One: Raising awareness of money management

Brainstorming managing money (20 min)

Ask the group to consider as two separate brainstorm exercises:

> **Why should people learn to manage their money?**
>
> **What might it mean to manage personal money?**

Depending on the age of group members, their experiences and the amount of responsibility for and interest they have taken in their own money you will get more or less sophisticated and plentiful answers.

You might get responses like:

- to keep out of debt
- to make money grow
- to get the best/cheapest loan
- to make money go further
- to help you save for a rainy day

- having to learn how to do percentages
- having to find out what interest means
- having to think about hard things
- keeping a note of what is spent
- knowing what money is committed

Working alone: raising awareness of personal money management (30 min)

Ask the group members to complete the Money Management Activities MM1–3 to stimulate their thinking about their own money management habits. The final exercise asks for a summary of what the learners have found out about themselves.

Ensure that each exercise is thoroughly explained before it is started. Ensure that the trainer checks on individual learner progress, helping as necessary.

Continuum (15 min)

Having completed MM3 set up a continuum. Ask for those who are very good at money management to stand at one end and poor as money managers on the other. Ask the learners in light of the activity sheets they have completed to arrange themselves on the line.

Ask some of the learners to explain why they have taken the positions they have. Ask for examples to support their statements. Through the discussions and examples try to reach group agreement about what the group feels is good and poor money management.

Give the learners the opportunity to re-position themselves if they wish. Ask any who have changed position to explain why they have done so. Thank the learners for their participation.

Feedback and brainstorm (20 min)

Ask the group what they have found out about themselves as money managers.

- What has surprised them?
- What has pleased them?
- What has shocked them about their own money management?

Record the responses on the flipchart.

Brainstorm with the learners why a module on money management would be of value to them. Write up their hopes and expectations. Refer back to anything from the previous session.

Keep this list to refer back to at the close of the module. Take a note of any learners who feel they need help opening a bank account or who have particular needs. These should be addressed on a one-to-one basis.

Session Two: Spending and budgeting

Current spending habits (25 min)

Ask the learners to work alone on activity MM4: Your spending. Ensure the learners understand what they should do before they start. The learners *need only to guess* what percentage of each month's income they spend on particular items.

Note: Calculating percentages will be the subject of Session Five.

Feedback (20 min)

Ask the group to come back together.

- How many of the group felt confident that they really knew what they spent their money on?
- How many felt confident that they could estimate their outgoings?
- What surprised the learners about how they spent their money?

Record these answers on the flipchart. Then ask the learners:

- How many spent money on things they should?
- How many preferred to buy things other than those they should and why this was so?

You can expect a lively discussion about the word *should*; let this play itself out and ask the group to define should and the types of things which should be bought and why.

Ask for a list of things people *should* spend money on and *did* spend money on. Do not be critical of what they spend money on, just put up the lists.

Prefer to spend money on:	Should spend money on:
Gambling	Food to cook at home
Alcohol	Better housing
Drugs	Heating
Cigarettes	Dentist
Clothes	Children's clothes
Cars	
Take-aways	
Going out	

Ask the group what they think are the long-term consequences of spending money more on things they prefer than on things which they should?

Introducing budgeting (45 min)

The following exercises will be useful for learners with no experience of budgeting. After exploring the relationship between monthly income and expenditure it asks the learners to look at the case of John Williams.

As a group decide what are:

1. Reasonable weekly expenses and write these on the flipchart.

Item	Amount
e.g. Bus fares Food Rent Heating/light One-off expenses e.g. birthday present for son	

2. A reasonable weekly income and write this on the flipchart.

3. Then looking at income and possible expenses decide how money should be spent; prioritise what is important. Decide what may not be bought. Consider what may need to be saved for.

4. As a group, if there is money over from the weekly income decide how should it be used.

Now ask the group to work in pairs or threes to do some analysis of John Williams' weekly income and expenditure (MM5). Allow 25 minutes for the groups to work on the problem of John Williams. The group may need a calculator and will need pencils and paper. Before the group starts check that the learners understand the activity sheet and what is wanted. Stress that they have already done similar work in the whole group exercise on the flipchart.

The trainer will need to check each group understands what needs to be done and to check on each group's progress.

Note: The trainer may find some learners need significant help with the calculations and seem to have little awareness of the meaning of figures and relationship between them. While the general principles of income and expenditure can be explained the trainer should note the need for help with numeracy for particular learners and make appropriate referrals. It is important that learners do not feel exposed or feel inadequate because of any difficulties they may have with numeracy.

Feedback (15 min)

Go through the activity finding out what each group decided. Is there agreement between the groups or are there differences, if so why is this?

Find out if any groups had any particular problems with the exercise.

Working alone: individual budgeting (20 min)

An outline for a budget is printed on MM06. The learners should try to complete the budget for a week or a month whichever they find most useful. Before the learners begin, run a brainstorm to gather ideas about possible weekly/monthly expenses. Help with some calculations may be necessary. There is a space to record irregular expenses, e.g. vet bills, MOT, Christmas, water rates etc. Help may be needed with calculations to spread these over the year and with suggestions about managing irregular expenses – but see later exercise.

Group review (15 min)

Check on how the learners found the activity and ask how they could apply it to their everyday lives. Find out why some think it useful and others less so. Try to encourage the learners to think about the value of being more in control of their spending.

Encourage the learners to look at ways in which they can monitor their expenses for a week or month. Encourage the learners to think about ways to make sure that what they spend comes from their income and not from credit. Encourage thinking about saving any spare money. Ask the learners for concrete examples from their own lives to make these types of actions more realistic.

Longer-term commitments and planning

 Trainer's notes

MM7 is a twelve month calendar for planning expenditure and income. It can be used to record regular monthly commitments, one-off annual payments like TV licence, MOT costs, car tax, twice yearly demands such as sewage and water rates and so on. Any irregular income could also be recorded.

The learners should be encouraged to take a longer-term view to develop an awareness of the necessity of saving each month to cope with expected outgoings e.g. house insurance.

Two brainstorms (20 min)

Brainstorm one:
What are the advantages of planning finances over a longer period rather than just looking at a month at a time? Record the reasons. If learners cannot think of advantages encourage them to suggest problems which may occur from not planning ahead.

Brainstorm two:
The types of expenditure which may occur over a year. Record these.

Individual work (20 min)

Ask the learners to use MM7 a twelve-month income and expenditure sheet to record actual or imagined income and outgoings. Once learners have completed this ask them to work in pairs to review what they have done and add to their lists as a result of the pair discussions.

Group review (10 min)

Review the various expenses and their frequency. List these. Ask the learners to suggest ways in which they may manage more irregular expenses, e.g.

- monthly direct debit for gas
- buying TV licence stamps
- council tax monthly payment slips

Encourage learners to see the value of identifying expenses to help them with their basic financial planning and with debt avoidance.

 Trainer's notes

In creating weekly or monthly and annual records of expenditure and income, it may become clear that:

- the learners do not have a clear sense of the likely demands on their income
- they have neglected to pay for or do certain things, e.g. buy a TV licence, pay for house insurance

The trainer will need to assist learners by providing information about certain types of expenses and how they can be paid. The trainer may need to help with realistically costing some outgoings and exploring the pros and cons of not buying certain services or paying for certain licences, e.g. the cost of the fine for no TV licence versus the cost of buying one.

Building up a store of leaflets, e.g. on the council tax and devising lists of costs and penalties for not making certain payments may help make the exercise more realistic. Having some copies of irregular bills such as water rates or an application form for car tax will also help.

Trying to anticipate demands both regular and one-off will help encourage the learner to have a sense of being able to plan and to anticipate.

Review: what has been learned so far? (15 min)

Ask the learners to now reflect on what they have learned about their own spending habits, budgeting and money management. Use a learner's summary sheet (**MM8**).

Session Three: Avoiding and managing debt

Brainstorming activities about debt (30 min)

Ask the group to brainstorm:

> **What is debt?**

Write group responses on the flipchart. You may need to distinguish between long- and short-term debts; debts which many people regard as legitimate, e.g. a mortgage; debts which are planned for e.g. a loan for a car or for some furniture and which can be paid back and debts which are unplanned and just keep growing. The latter are the dangerous types of debt.

Ask the group to brainstorm:

> **Why do people get into debt?**

Encourage as many ideas as possible. They may suggest:
- unrealistic expectations
- easy credit
- too many credit or store cards
- not having the income to support wants
- moving loans from one company to another
- not paying off loans before getting more things
- not realising credit cards/credit arrangements are about creating debt
- feeling a need to have what others have
- needing to have designer label products
- children's wants and giving in to them
- loss of job
- loss of income
- changes in family e.g. new child, having to look after someone

- partner leaves
- partner loses jobs
- not having money set aside to pay for an emergency and having to borrow
- getting desperate and borrowing from expensive credit givers

Finally brainstorm:

> **Who is responsible for people getting into debt?**
> **Why are they responsible?**

Again, try to get as many ideas as possible. Answers may include:
- peer group pressure
- advertising
- shops offering you credit
- buying through catalogues and magazines
- easy terms
- the family
- children's demands

It is important that the learners realise that they as individuals have responsibility for their own actions. Discuss why people try to blame others and who they blame? How many people fail to realise that they need to take charge of the money they have?

The consequences of debt
Brainstorm (10 min)

Ask the group:

> **What are the consequences of getting into debt?**

Record the answers and leave these displayed as they will help the learners think about the role-play activity.

Joe Brown's debts: a role-play (50 min)
Preparation (10 min)
Ask the learners to work in groups of four. They will each need MM9 outlining Joe Brown's situation. The groups will need to use some ideas from the previous brainstorm to help them consider the characters in the role-play and to decide how they will solve Joe Brown's problems.

Presentations and questions
Ask each group to perform its view of Joe Brown's situation and its solution.

After each role-play ask and encourage the other learners watching to ask questions of those in role:
- How did it feel to be Joe Brown?
- What did he think might happen to him next?
- How did it feel to be asking for help?
- Was he surprised by the response people gave him?
- Did he expect someone to help him who in fact refused to? How did that feel?
- Was there anyone whom he did not want to ask for help?

Of those in the role-play:
- How did it feel to try to help Joe Brown?
- Did you feel sympathetic to him?
- What did you think about him and his situation?
- What do you think will happen to him in the long run?

Of all the characters ask:
- Did they think his situation and what he said was realistic?
- Would they have done the same?

Put up ideas on the flipchart. Try to tease out the differences and similarities between all the role-plays. Find out what the group had learned and what it felt like to be in that position.

How to avoid debt (30 min)

Make links with the material which came from the role-plays and ask the group to come up with suggestions for avoiding debt. Write these on the flipchart.

Suggestions could cover:
- planning for the longer-term
- saving before buying large items so not needing credit
- do not be impulsive
- do not look for quick finance
- do not be taken in by credit companies
- do not get under pressure to buy things because of adverts, buying through catalogues or on credit, to please friends, to have a big Christmas or birthday celebration
- do not just get trapped by wanting designer clothes
- having a clear idea of weekly and monthly commitments

Handout **MM10**: Tackling debt. This can be given out after the brainstorm. Work through the various points on the handout with the learners.

Use this session as a way to pull all the threads together about spending, longer-term planning and taking responsibility for spending.

Session Four: Problem solving financial problems

Group problem solving (40 min)

Divide the group into four smaller groups to deal with the situations which they will be given. Each situation is about a person who or household which is not managing very well. Each group should try to act as a group of advisers to the person /household in trouble. They should come up with as many options as possible with reasons and then try to come up with an action plan to manage the situation. Each group will need to present their problem and solution during a feedback session.

You will need to copy the cases written below. Each group will need one case. There will need to be sufficient copies for each group number.

1. *Harry is 27. He has been living in the same rented flat for two years. The rent has gone up at the same time that his company is stopping overtime. He has an HP arrangement on a drum kit. He is now struggling to cope. What should he do?*

2. *Jenny is a single parent. Jon is three years old. Jenny's rent is paid by housing benefit. She has very little income and has a regular HP commitment for a washing machine. She is having problems coping. What should she do?*

3. *David and Annie have been living together for three years. Annie is now pregnant and will be stopping work in five months. Dave's job as caretaker in a community centre has been cut to part-time. They have various financial commitments to HP companies and a £500 credit card debt for a recent holiday. They have been spending heavily on things for the new baby. They have no savings. What should they do?*

4. *A family of four, Jerry (eight) and Lisa (three) with both parents out of work are finding it increasingly hard to cope. Sandra and Jim are fighting about money most of the time. Jerry is getting more demanding about things he wants. They live in rented accommodation and get various benefits. What should they do?*

With all of these cases you will need to be on hand to help with questions to encourage the groups to think through as many options as possible. Given them the case study and the planning sheet **MM11** to structure their discussions. You will need to have up-to-date information on entitlements and benefits. Where the learners have questions you cannot answer make a note of these and bring the information back at a later date.

Preparation for presentations (10 min)

Allow ten minutes for the group to finalise their solutions for their problem situation. They may wish to draw out their action plan on a sheet of A1 to assist the presentation.

Feedback (45 min)

Give everyone **MM12**. This carries all four problem situations. The learners should read each case through.

Ask each group in turn to present their solutions. The rest of the group may want to question why one option was favoured over another or may have alternative solutions to suggest. Encourage discussion of the cases. Record any similarities and differences in approaches between the groups.

At the close of the feedback ask the learners what they gained from the exercise and what skills they used. Encourage the learners to consider how they may make use of the process of problem-solving in cases they worked on. Ask the group if there was any information they needed to know or anything about which they were unsure which came up as a result of discussing the cases. Record these. Try to supply some answers but better still arrange 'expert input'.

 Trainer's notes

It is likely that these cases will generate a number of questions and an outside expert from the Benefits Agency or Money Advice Centre to come into speak to the group would be a useful input into their Money management programme. The fact that they have been thinking through some issues and coming up with questions will also make the group more prepared for such a visitor.

Session Five: Calculate interest and work out percentages

 Trainer's notes

Two calculations which are commonly used in money management are percentages and interest. The following activities and explanations should help the learners to feel more confident with both of these calculations and what they mean.

Simple interest: explanation and examples (40 min)

Simple interest is the money which will be paid for money which is borrowed. Interest is paid if you invest money in, e.g. a building society. Interest is charged if you borrow money.

Example One
I invest £600 for 1 year @ 7% interest.
How much interest will I get at the **end** of the year?

Amount of interest	=	7% × 600
(7% = 7 ÷ 100)	=	0.07 × 600
	=	£42

Example Two
I borrow £4,000 for 3 years. If the rate of simple interest is 12%, find the amount of interest I have to pay.

Amount of interest for 1 year	=	12% × 4,000
(12% = 12 ÷ 100 = 0.12)	=	0.12 × 4,000
	=	£480

So amount of interest for 3 years = £480 × 3 = £1,440

The total amount which has to be repaid is the capital, the £4,000 and the interest, the £1,440 – £5,440 in all.

A formula for working out simple interest is

$$I = \frac{P \times T \times R}{100}$$

where

I	=	the amount of interest you will either receive or pay
P	=	amount you invest or borrow
T	=	time (always in years)
R	=	rate (i.e. the %)

Work through the following examples to show the learners how the formula can be applied and worked.

Example Three
Find the simple interest if £2,500 is invested for 5 years at 7% per annum.

$$P = 2,500 \quad T = 5 \quad R = 7$$
$$I = \frac{P \times T \times R}{100}$$

$$I = \frac{2,500 \times 5 \times 7}{100} = \frac{87500}{100} = £875$$

Example Four
Find the simple interest if £3,400 is borrowed for 2 years at 12% per annum

$$P = 3,400 \quad T = 2 \quad R = 12$$
$$I = \frac{P \times T \times R}{100}$$

$$I = \frac{3400 \times 2 \times 12}{100} = \frac{81600}{100} = £816$$

What is the total to be repaid?
$$£3,400 + £816 = £4,216$$

The learners can be encouraged to try out some other examples. There may be ones which can be taken from newspapers and other adverts which advertise money to be borrowed or saved.

Understanding simple interest will be sufficient for the learners to calculate the costs of borrowing and the gains from saving. The proper calculation is that based on compound interest but a building society or other organisation would do this calculation for the learner.

Percentages: explanation and examples (20 min)

A percentage is defined as a proportion of a hundred. Understanding percentages are necessary when, for example, working out VAT on an item, checking to see how much is coming off an item in a sale and finding out what percentage of income maybe committed to an HP agreement or something similar.

Example One
All items 10% off in the sale.
Pair of shoes £35 – 10%
So 10% of £35 is:

$$\frac{35\ (£) \times 10\ (\%)}{100} = £3.5$$

(always the denominator for percentages)

Shoes in the sale cost £35 – £3.5 = £31.50

Example Two
5% off for shop damage to goods
£47 item less 5%

$$\frac{47 \times 5}{100} = 2.35$$

£47 – £2.35 = £44.65

Example Three
Quote for repair to bathroom not inclusive of VAT

Tiles:	35
Fixative:	12
Labour:	25
	£72 plus VAT

$$\frac{72 \times 17.5\ (VAT)}{100}$$

£72 + £12.60 = £84.60 total for job

Finding out what percentage of something is as an amount is worked out as follows:

18% of all receipts are used to buy better equipment. Receipts total £50,000 every year. To find out what is spent on new equipment:

$$\frac{50,000 \times 18}{100} = 4,000$$

Again, the learners should be given some examples from real life in which calculations of percentages are needed.

Session Six: Managing credit

 ### Trainer's notes

This session looks at credit and what it means to buy on credit. Learners may need help to work out percentages, to understand terms such as Annual Percentage Rate (or APR) and to understand how an annual rate compares with a monthly rate of interest.

People often borrow or get into arrangements because they think they understand one option better than another or because one seems easier than another. This session should encourage the learners to feel more able to understand credit or to know what questions they should be asking.

Opening brainstorms (20 min)

Ask the learners to address the two following brainstorm questions:

What does credit mean?

What problems might there be with purchases made on credit?

The brainstorms should be the opportunity to explore issues in broad terms not to focus at great length on an individual's experiences or personal problems. However such personal issues and needs may require to be managed and treated sensitively and appropriate referrals made.

Explain that the session is to help people to think more carefully about credit arrangements and to give them some help to understand calculations.

Revision of key points (30 min)

1. Revise percentages with the group.

   10% of 100 is ...

   3% of £2,000 is ...

   The car costs £6,000. The credit arrangement means paying the total price at 10% for 3 years. How much is paid back?

2. Try the following exercise with the whole group, explaining clearly how each part of the decision is reached.

   Jim wants to buy a £12,000 car, should he go to garage A or B? How do you reach your decision?

   Garage A offers: Trade in of £1,250
                        Interest free credit over 3 years

   Garage B offers: Trade in of £2,000
                        Credit at 10% over 3 years

   Check that the learners understand and then approach the two problems which Brian faces about purchases on credit.

Brian's purchases (40 min)

Read though sheet MM13 with the learners and check they understand what they have to do. They should work in pairs. Ask the group what answers they have arrived at and why. Check everyone understands the principles. The next activity **MM14** again concerns Brain's purchases. Read through the sheet to ensure the learners understand what is required. Again check on the answers the pairs reach and their reasons for them.

Group rules (10 min)

Conclude the session by asking the group to come up with some key points for themselves and other learners. If you are thinking of buying on credit, what should you do?

Session Seven: Savings

 Trainer's notes

The same need for clear thinking about credit arrangement applies to working out how best to save money. Again there will be a need to explain the financial language which is used to describe savings arrangements.

Definitions (10 min)

Show the learners some adverts about savings opportunities. Ask them to identify any terms with which they are not familiar or any language which is unusual.

Explain the difference between **net** and **gross**, i.e. after and before tax and the ways in which one rate can look more attractive than another because one may be expressed in gross terms.

Gross, net and penalties (40 min)

Use the following exercise in the group to find the best savings option and to explore some of the restrictions about the various savings schemes. The group needs to understand the penalties which are sometimes involved in withdrawal of savings.

Write the following on the flipchart so everyone can see. Explain and discuss each savings account so everyone is clear about the issues.

Savings account A:
> Interest on amounts over £10,000 is 5% gross.
> Easy Access. No penalties.

Savings account B:
> Interest on amounts over £10,000 is 5.5% gross. 6 withdrawals a year.

Savings account C:
> Interest on amounts over £10,000 is 4.5% net. You cannot make a withdrawal for 8 months.

Ask the group to work in pairs and set the following problem:
You have £10,000 to save, you are not sure what your financial needs are over the coming years but know that you will need to use some of this money. You want to get the best deal you can to make your money work for you.
What should you do?

Ask the pairs to feedback to the group their choice of A, B or C and to give reasons. Link this information about savings back to work on budgeting and the importance of having some money saved. Go through the various options for saving and places for depositing savings. Have some leaflets available for the learners to read through.

Session Eight: Drawng the threads together

As a group summarise the key points about:
- budgeting
- debt
- avoiding debt
- using credit
- having savings

Check if there are any who are not clear about any of these areas. Find out what information the learners still need to know. Make sure that there are no outstanding issues which had been identified in the first session or which have emerged through the module. Clear up any areas of confusion.

Find out how many do not have a post office, bank or building society account and have information available for these people. Ensure that any learners who need copies of handouts can have them. There should be copies of:
- monthly/weekly budget form
- yearly calendar of expenses
- how to tackle debt
- any resource leaflets which you have collected
- phone numbers of local Citizens Advice Bureau and Money Advice Centres.

Emphasise that being financially secure is not necessarily about being rich but is about being *moneywise*. It is about planning, savings and living according to income.

MM1: Managing my money

Read the statements below and tick the column which applies to you

	I never do/ I don't	I often do/ I can
I work out a budget for each week		
I plan my budget and stick to it		
I have good intentions about being careful with my money but these do not last		
I do get into debt quite often		
I run out of money and have to go without things		
I know how to use the bank/building society/post office		
I understand my payslip/benefits		
I know how to borrow money cheaply		
I know how much I spend on things like the phone, electricity, TV		
I have lent money and don't get it back		
I buy things without thinking and regret it		
I know I waste money		
I use credit cards frequently		
I borrow money despite its cost		
I never go without things even if I have to borrow		
I will borrow from friends		
Sometimes I don't repay people		
I know roughly what I will need to spend in a year		

MM2: My approach to money

Pick out the cards which apply to you and put them to one side

I don't know what's in my bank or building society account today	I don't know my weekly or monthly expenses	I couldn't tell you what I spent yesterday
I don't know what a budget is	Money goes through my fingers like water	I keep a note of what I spend each day
I have borrowed money and have had trouble paying it back	I couldn't tell you the five things I spend most of my money on	I always run out of money partway through each week
I shop using a calculator	I check my bank statements	I don't think money is interesting
I have a savings account but don't use it	I have a savings account and try to put something by regularly	I don't mind buying on credit
I enjoy looking after my money	I'm the sort of person who always has money left at the end of a holiday	I consider I am careful with my money
I have got a lot of credit and store cards	I prefer to wait until I can afford something	I know what I need for food, heating and rent/ mortgage each week
I have a budget for day-to-day expenses	Easy come – easy go. That's my view on money	I can't see why people fuss about money
I spend more than I get each week	I can cope with an emergency because I have some savings	I don't plan for things like Christmas, birthdays or holidays
People think I am tight. I think I am sensible	I get laughed at for planning my money	My friends think I am a soft touch

Photocopy onto thin card and cut out each of the cards

MM4: My monthly spending

The things I buy most regularly each month are:	Each month this costs	As a % of my income each month this is
1.		
2.		
3.		
4.		
5.		
6.		
7.		
8.		
9.		
10.		

The things I should spend my monthly income on are:

Now ✓ the items that you should spend your money on and which you actually do spend your money on

Which items do you spend money on but should not spend money on or should spend less on?

MM3: Summing up your approach to money

✓ which applies to you

	Yes	No
I am confident that I can:		
Control my own spending		
Control household spending		
Get the best/cheapest credit		
Repay any loans		
Save from any current income		
Avoid debt		
Claim all the benefits I am entitled to		
Talk sensibly about my finances to a bank manager or finance adviser		
Plan how I should spend my money for the next year		

Overall I think that I manage my money (✓ which applies to you)

- ☐ very well
- ☐ quite well
- ☐ not very well
- ☐ badly

I think this is because:

It would help me if I knew more about:

1.

2.

3.

MM6: Weekly/monthly budget

INCOME

Date	Type of Income	Amount

Total

OUTGOINGS

Date	Type of Expenditure	Amount

Total

Total Income

Total Expenditure

Money in debt/credit

Other expenses to be taken into account:

MM5: John Williams' income and expenditure

As a group, decide on the following figures:

John's weekly

income   £

rent/mortgage   £

food bill   £

transport   £

money towards bills, like electricity   £

Any other money will be used for savings or other expenses.

1. What money does John have for savings or other expenses?
   What short of things might he use this money for?

Item	Amount

2. Should he be saving any money?
   Why?

3. John has had an increase in his weekly income of £10.00 but the cost of bus fares has also increased by £2.00 per week. Calculate how much money is left over for spending.

4. John's weekly income has increased by £20.00. He wishes to take out a loan to purchase a stereo system and will have to pay £5.00 per week.
   Using the original figures calculate:
   a. How much money is left after all other expenses have been paid?
   b. How much money is left after allowing for the loan repayment?

MM8: Money management summary sheet

Three things I have found out about myself and money management are:

1.

2.

3.

Three things I have found most useful are:

1.

2.

3.

Three things I would like to be able to do or to know more about are:

1.

2.

3.

MM7: Yearly calendar of income/expenses

January	£

February	£

March	£

April	£

May	£

June	£

July	£

August	£

September	£

October	£

November	£

December	£

MM10: Tackling debt

Debt can be caused by:

- changes in your circumstances
- not having some savings for an emergency
- wanting more than you can afford
- having too many things on loans and credit
- trying to get rid of one loan with another loan
- not seeking advice of trained debt counsellors
- not looking realistically at your finances
- not budgeting
- not taking responsibility for your money

Take steps to deal with debt:

- make a list of essential expenses, decide what you can do without
- do not take on more loans or credit
- seek proper help from e.g. the Citizens Advice Bureau, some have Money Advice Centres or contact National Debt Helpline 0121 359 8501
- don't get involved in short-term quick ways to make money – it could make your situation much worse
- don't just try to sell off possessions, pawn possessions as a way to get money fast. Get advice first
- find out if you can re-plan repayments to spread your commitments

If you don't deal with debt it:

- will get worse
- may lead to legal action
- may lead to repossession of goods or home
- may mean loss of services like heating, electricity, telephone
- could push you into doing illegal, dangerous or silly things which will in the longer-term cause harm
- could mean you get caught up with people who want to exploit your situation

MM9: Joe Brown in debt

Joe Brown lost his job. He had some savings, about £150, but he spent this quickly without thinking how long it might be before he got another job. He still has two outstanding loans, one for a motorbike and the other for a TV/video. He is single but has a steady girlfriend.

Someone in each group needs to be Joe Brown.

- How is he going to try to deal with his problems?
- Who is he going to ask for help?
- How might he avoid getting into worse debt?
- What should he do right away?
- What should he plan to do longer-term?
- Who might offer to help him?

MM11: Managing difficult situations

Summarise the situation:

List as many options as you can:

What action would you recommend and why?

Action steps to better managing the financial situation

Describe each action step – list sources of available help	Start date

---

MM12: Cases

1. Harry is 27. He has been living in the same rented flat for two years. The rent has gone up at the same time that his company is stopping overtime. He has a HP arrangement on a drum kit. He is now struggling to cope.

   What should he do?

2. Jenny is a single parent. Jon is three years old. Jenny's rent is paid by housing benefit. She has very little income and has a regular HP commitment for a washing machine. She is having problems coping.

   What should she do?

3. David and Annie have been living together for three years. Annie is now pregnant and will be stopping work in five months. Dave's job as caretaker in a community centre has been cut to part-time. They have various financial commitments to HP companies and a £500 credit card debt for a recent holiday. They have been spending heavily on things for the new baby. They have no savings.

   What should they do?

4. A family of four, Jerry 8 and Lisa 3 with both parents out of work are finding it increasingly hard to cope. Sandra and Jim are fighting about money most of the time. Jerry is getting more demanding about things he wants. They live in rented accommodation and get various benefits.

   What should they do?

MM13: Brian's stereo

A Brian has £150 a week to live on and has the following essential expenses:

Rent	£50
Food	£30
Transport	£30
Bills	£12

Work out how much money he has left over.

B Brian has decided to try to save £5 a week and use the remainder of the money for himself. How much does he have?

C Brian still wants to save £5 a week but wants to buy a stereo system. He has seen an offer for the system he wants

(a) interest free credit for 12 months or

(b) 17.6 % interest over 24 months

State whether he can afford (a) or (b) or neither.

Brian still wants to save £5 a week until he has saved enough money. He will have to wait a long time until he has saved enough money, costing £200 paying back:

MM14: Five years later

After living in a furnished flat for a considerable time Brian has managed to save approximately £500 and has purchased a number of small electrical items. He now wants to move to another area. The flat he wants is the same rent, but only partly furnished and he therefore needs to purchase a suite of furniture. There are a number of furniture stores in the area with various offers of credit or he could buy from a second hand shop, which will only accept cash. Which of those listed should Brian choose, giving reason(s) for your answer. Remember, Brian still wants to carry on saving £5 per week and his day-to-day extra money is only £15 a week. The suite is exactly the same in all stores.

A. Furniture Land — Cost of suite £500

Interest free credit over 4 years

Paying back on a monthly basis.

B. Suite Place — Cost of suite £400

Interest free credit over 3 years

No repayments for 12 months after date of purchase

C. Bargain Suites — Cost of suite £350

No deposit but H. P. at 15%

Start repayments 3m months after date of purchase

D. Cosy Seats — Cost of suite £350

Deposit of £50 required but interest free credit over 3 years

A similar style suite in a used but good condition is in a secondhand shop in the High Street priced at £100 cash.

Identifying personal and transferable skills

The module is divided into four sessions:
1. What are personal and transferable skills and why are they important? (1 hour)
2. What are my personal skills and strengths? (2 hours 55 min)
3. What are my transferable skills? (1 hour 35 min)
4. Developing your skills (1 hour 20 min)

The module makes use of the following training and learning activities:
- self-assessment activities
- action planning
- discussion and brainstorming
- pair work
- role-play

Trainer's notes

This module aims to encourage the learners to:
- identify and appreciate the full range, value and potential of their personal skills and qualities
- identify and consider skills and qualities which they have, and would like to develop through, for example, paid or voluntary work, further training or within their personal lives
- identify any aspects of themselves or their lifestyles which are blocking what they would like to develop
- consider qualities and skills in relation to their life goals
- take themselves seriously and appreciate the value of lifelong learning and taking control of their personal development
- draw up clear personal profiles and statements and a development plan

Why consider personal and transferable skills and qualities?

People are forced to develop new skills and to adapt old ones to manage new situations, without so doing they would not cope. Much development and adaptation is not done consciously so people fail to appreciate what they have achieved and fail to recognise what is involved in the process of applying what has been learned in one situation to another situation. As people change in response to or to manage different situations, it is important to encourage them to periodically take stock of their developing skills and qualities, to note those which have fallen into disuse and those which are changing or those which are new.

People must be able to talk about and evidence their skills and qualities; for example when they are in an interview situation. It is important that people understand the ways in which skills may be developed and used in other situations. This encourages a sense of competence, self-confidence and an awareness of potential future directions.

This module encourages the learners to undertake work which will enable them to be more clear about what they can do and why they can feel confident to manage new situations in their employment, training or personal lives.

Definitions

Personal qualities are features of an individual such as being empathetic to others, being loyal, being trustworthy and having a willingness to try out new activities. These qualities are strengths which have value in their own right and which may be transferred into the workplace or into other situations.

Transferable skills are learned responses and ways of managing which can be applied in a number of situations. For example, an individual may have been employed in a shop and therefore have a number of people management skills. For example, the person may be able to listen carefully to what is wanted and respond appropriately, be polite and assertive while dealing with an angry or difficult customer. Such skills could be identified and transferred into a job such as a receptionist, which demanded similar skills while the particular job-related skills of receptionist would have to be learned.

Session One: What are personal and transferable skills and why are they important?

Introductory brainstorms: defining terms (30 min)

Ask the group what they understand by:

> ## Personal skills and qualities

The group should consider the difference between *skills* and *qualities*. Skills are learned or developed and qualities are attributes or characteristics. They are somewhat different and the learners should be able to distinguish between them.

The brainstormed list should cover a huge range of skills which people are able to offer and personal attributes which they have. Examples might be:
- being self-confident
- being organised
- making others feel at ease
- being able to lead and influence others
- being persuasive in an argument

The group can be asked why skills and qualities are important. They may suggest:
- the more personal skills and qualities a person has the more able they will be to cope with a range of situations
- the more skills, the more likely the one to feel confident in facing difficulties
- the more skills and qualities a person has the more likely they are to have an interesting life and be interesting to others

Brainstorm what is meant by the phrase:

> ## Transferable skills

The group should reach the conclusion that the phrase means quite simply a skill developed in one area which can be applied to another. Ask for examples of transferable skills. The group may suggest skills such as:
- being able to maintain cars for self and friends
- managing the household budget
- being involved in the local theatre group
- having the skills to do small repairs and decorating at home
- arranging and managing the local football group
- being numerate
- organising a family and going to work or a training course

- being a good communicator
- being good with animals
- being a good cook

Find out if the group thinks that transferable skills are important. It should be suggested to the group that transferable skills are important:

- For an individual because they will enable him or her to apply skills to different situations at home and work.
- In a work situation because they make employees more flexible and able to do different things.
- They show a potential employer that experience and aptitude has been gained in one area and that these can be applied to another. This makes employing an individual a safer option for the employer.
- They make an individual confident about being able to cope with a number of situations.

Anecdotes (20 min)

Ask the group if they can offer examples from their own lives when they were able to apply skills learnt in one situation to another. Note on the flipchart these examples of transferable skills.

Prompt with examples from your own life if the group gets bogged down in the activity.

Introduction to the module (10 min)

Explain that the module will be asking the learners to think about their own personal skills and qualities and the extent to which these may be transferable. The module encourages learners to take a positive view of themselves, to describe and evidence their skills and qualities. The outcomes of the module will be:

- having a clear profile of personal strengths and qualities which can be evidenced to others
- developing a personal profile which can be used with employers and others
- having a clear understanding of personal skills and the connections between them which the learner can make use in his or her own life
- thinking about the skills which can be developed and having a strategy for doing this

Ensure that the learners are comfortable with the concepts and reasons for the module, that they understand why knowing about their own personal and transferable skills will be of value to them.

Session Two: What are my personal skills and strengths?

This session relies on the learners being self-honest and making the most of the opportunities to undertake some self-assessment activities. There are several self-assessment checklists and exercises which should be undertaken by the learners working alone.

The first activity asks the learners to consider some of the high points in their lives so far and to make a list of things which they have achieved. This can be done by drawing a lifeline similar to one which may have been done during work on Time management. Ask the learners to draw a lifeline marking the highs and lows of their lives so far. The highs being those occasions when they felt that they achieved something important to them.

The exercise may require some brainstorming before they begin. It is likely that the learners may not recognise their achievements as such.

Brainstorm (10 min):

Achievements in life

Record the responses on the flipchart as a reminder for the lifeline activity. Suggestions could cover:

- learning to drive
- passing an exam
- making a success of the allotment
- rebuilding a motorbike
- winning the photography competition
- getting a poem printed in the paper
- learning how to decorate the living room
- managing to live to a budget and save enough money for a holiday
- learning to cook
- getting on the football team
- bringing up a child well
- dealing with an illness or disability
- caring for a mother when she was ill
- getting married
- getting a better job
- setting up and running a business

The achievements are high points on personal calendars and part of everyday life. It is important to encourage the flow of suggestions so the learners can find a number of things of which they are proud.

Lifelines and listing (20 min)
After the brainstorm ask the learners to work on their own to complete their lifelines and describe their achievements. They may want to work on A1 sheets of paper.

Pair work (15 min)
As the learners finish they may want to talk in pairs to describe their lifelines. The partner may have ideas about other things which could be added ase achievements on the lifeline.

Achievements into skills
1. Group activity (15 min)
Ask the learners to look at those things listed as achievements and ask volunteers to suggest a couple of examples. Write these on the flipchart and ask the learners to work out the range of skills or personal qualities which they think are involved with that achievement. An example is worked through below:

e.g. Achievement: Captain of a games team
The skills and qualities involved would include:

- organising events – arranging times of matches, liaising with other teams, booking accommodation
- dealing with money – collecting subscriptions from players, arranging and paying for practice sessions, for other necessary facilities, buying any necessary equipment, looking for the best price and keeping accounts

- arranging fixtures
- using communication skills to: explain, give clear instructions, listen well
- being assertive
- using written communication skills: writing letters, doing posters, memos
- using IT skills to produce posters or the team newsletter
- contacting and persuading people to play and act as reserves
- publicising the team
- delegating and asking others for help
- coaching and encouraging others, helping with technique, supporting players when morale is low, praising when things are going well
- persevering – dealing with difficulties in the team or with matches, encouraging others through difficult times when the team may not be succeeding
- managing time, own time and others' time
- being interested in others and the good of the whole team
- being personable and not bossy
- good communication skills, listening, persuading, being clear with others
- loyalty

2. Working alone (25 min)

Each learner should consider a few of their achievements and record the various skills and qualities which went into their realisation. They can work on their lifeline sheet or on **PT1**. It is important that the learners work through a couple of their achievements in great detail so they understand the various skills which they have shown and can describe them.

3. Checking in pairs (20 min)

Ask the learners to return to their pairs and to work through the selected achievements each checking through the lists of skills and qualities. The partners should be able to help each other in not overlooking skills and qualities. For example perseverance in order to learn the skill in the first place; careful planning and budgeting which preceded being able to have the allotment; being able to organise time and personal resources sufficiently well to manage a small child and take the part-time course which meant that the exam was passed.

Skills and qualities developed through work (paid or unpaid), training, home and in leisure activities (40 min)

Ask the learners to work on another copy of **PT1** and to think about the activities rather than achievements in their lives. They need to consider their experiences at home, work or training if appropriate, during periods of unemployment and leisure activities. These experiences may not have been highspots but they represent the day-to-day acquisition and practice of skills and demonstration of qualities. The learners should work through a few different activities and experiences to tease out the skills and qualities which they demonstrate.

Again the learners may need to begin with a brainstorm or working through an example as a whole group. If the learners get stuck they can work in pairs.

Part 3: Personal portraits
Working alone (20 min)

Having collected together these various ideas of personal skills and qualities and spent time in finding the evidence to support them it is essential that the learners summarise the information they have found out about themselves. Use **PT2** for this. The learners need to retain this.

Closing round (10 min)

Close this session of the module with a round of:

> *Something I found out about myself today was ...*

Ask the learners to offer an item of evidence to support the statement they make about themselves. The statements should be positive ones.

Session Three: What are my transferable skills?

 Trainer's notes

So far the learners have been thinking carefully about their achievements and experiences and the ways in which these can be described as demonstrable and learned skills. This session asks the learners to focus on skills they have and to appreciate them as transferable ones. Remind the learners again what transferable skills means and work through an example of such a skill.

Self-assessment: working alone (35 min)

Give each learner a set of choice cards (**PT3**). Ask the learners to read through these cards and to create two piles. One of skills in which they consider that they have competence and another of skills in which they have less competence but feel would be useful to develop.

During this period the trainer should be providing assistance with any difficulties in reading or understanding the cards. The trainer should ask for examples of evidence to back claims of competence or limited competence.

Part way through the sorting session the learners could be asked as a whole group to offer examples of the types of evidence for certain of the transferable skills or for definitions of certain of the skills. This will help all the learners by discussing areas of competence and encourage them not to miss any in their own lives.

Summary (10 min)

The learners need to summarise their findings. An analysis sheet is provided for this activity.

Small groups on transferable skills (30 min)

Working in threes the learners should brainstorm the types of work activities which the individual learners might do with the transferable skills they have identified. The time should be shared equally so each learner has a chance to describe their transferable skills and receive the consideration of the group.

Each learner should record the group's occupational ideas for themselves.

 Trainer's notes

Some small groups will need help in identifying appropriate occupational outlets for the transferable skills they have identified. A selection of simple outline careers leaflets or materials clustering a range of types of occupations should be available. Check with the local careers company or learning partnerships for such resources.

This session aims to raise awareness and interest. It is not intended to find specific occupational solutions for individual learners.

Group feedback (10 min)

Ask for each group to offer an example of a skill and its applications. Others in the whole group may have some additional ideas.

Summary activity (10 min)

Individual learners should keep a record of their skills which have been explored and the range of activities into which they can be transferred on sheet PT5.

 ## Trainer's notes

Find out from the group how many would be interested in receiving information on occupational training. Consider inviting in representatives from local employers, Employment Services, education and training providers, APEX Trust, NACRO, local careers companies and services and learning partnerships.

Session Four: Developing your skills

The learners need to use summary sheets PT2 and PT4 for this session. They will have identified personal and transferable skills and will have identified some skills which they wish to develop. This session is devoted to exploring those areas which they would like to develop.

Working alone and then in pairs (20 min)

The learners should review the skill lists created so far and generate a list of the skills which they would, given no constraints such as time or money, like to develop. In creating their list of skill development, they should try to think of some way in which such skills could be developed. The learners should prioritise their top five development areas.

In pairs the learners should review the lists, each helping the other with additional suggestions for ways to develop the skill areas. Learners should use PT6. These sheets will be used again in the final session.

As a group (30 min)

The learners should each offer an example from their top five skill development areas. These should be recorded on the flipchart. The group session should then be devoted to a collective review of the most important development areas for that group and to a problem-solving session about they ways in which individual learners may be able to develop certain skills. It may be the case that a significant number have identified areas such as not being assertive enough; wanting to work on developing communication skills; learning about better money management or finding out about computing. Such areas may be ones for which programmes can be run. This group session should enable the trainer to identify these types of learning needs.

Other areas may be particular to individual learners. For example one may want to develop skills in book-keeping or to take a skill learnt and practised for a club activity to a level which would be thought of as sufficient by an employer. Another may want a qualification in basic cookery or food preparation in order to extend a personal interest in catering for family and friends, into a commercial activity.

In order to help learners explore more individual developmental needs, the group, with your support, will need to think in broad terms how these may be met.

Brainstorming may come up with possible solutions for a number of individual learner needs. Brainstorming solutions for individual learners may generate such suggestions as:

- evening classes
- day release activities
- getting a formal qualification
- undertaking voluntary work
- contacting the WEA
- contacting a trade union or other specialist group
- making use of the reference section in the library
- using the Yellow Pages
- sending speculative letters to possible employers
- building up a portfolio of evidence; for example, photographing work or asking people to write statements about completed work
- advertising skills etc. in the local paper
- advertising in the local shop for people with similar interests and so on.

🍎 Trainer's notes

The opportunity should be taken during the session to explore with the learners how they would find out information about:

- occupational areas
- acquiring job search skills
- joining job clubs
- further education or training
- courses run by voluntary bodies

The trainer should produce a key contacts list for vocational training, employment search and educational organisations in the area.

Final review and one-to-one (30 min)

The learners should further review skills they would like to develop and consider further, how in light of the discussions, they would do this.

There should be reference materials to hand whenever possible about courses which are available to the learners, open learning materials which can be accessed, information about libraries, Citizens Advice Bureaux, agencies looking for volunteers, careers guidance facilities and job clubs.

One-to-one reviews of sheets **PT6** need to be undertaken so the trainer has a clear sense of the learner's continuing needs and the appropriate referrals to make.

PT2: Personal profile: summary of personal skills

Personal skill	Evidence of use of skill		
	In home life	In work/training voluntary activities	In leisure activities

PT1: Recording types of skills

Describe the achievement or expertise	Description of skills involved and how they are used
1.	
2.	
3.	

Cooking for large numbers	Can make people feel special	Self-reliant
A good eye for colour	Leading people	Have an eye for detail
Able to work at heights	Good with electrical things	Quick thinking
Reading and finding out information	Working in a team	Working well with routines
Making opportunities for other people	Teaching people things	Like repairing things
Like to know how things work	Well co-ordinated	Good at estimation
Will apply all the rules and not cut corners	Calm in a crisis or under pressure	Can sell anything
Making things	Good at estimation	Listening carefully to people
Finding things out	Influencing people	Like communicating with others
Driving all kinds of vehicles	Supervising others	Supporting and helping others
Able to do several different things in a job	Use resources economically	
Creative thinking	Working with people	Learning languages
Taking responsibility	Making decisions	Working with ideas

Photocopy onto thin card and cut out each of the cards

Activity sheet PT3: My skills

Stack the skills with which you rate yourself as being most competent in one pile

Stack the skills with which you rate yourself as less competent but interested to develop in another pile

There are a few blank cards for you to write in any skills which you have but which are missing from these cards

Good with figures		Able to follow instructions
Working to deadlines	Organising people to do things	Managing money
Willing to have a go at new things	Looking after people	
Can make people laugh		Managing budgets
Good with animals	Physically fit	Working alone
Can imagine what things will look like when they are done	Can use power tools	Consider others
Can draw patterns	Writing things	Solving problems
Can use hand tools	Computer skills	Well co-ordinated

Photocopy onto thin card and cut out each of the cards

PT5: My transferable skills

Skill	Ways in which skills can be used in whole or part or as a basis for development in an occupational area

PT4: Summary of transferable skills

Competent at:	This skill is useful because ...	I show this by ...	Less competent at:	This skill is useful because ...	I show this by ...

PT6: Key development areas

Areas to develop	Reason for importance/ value of this skill area
1.	
2.	
3.	
4.	
5.	

Strategies for development of key areas	Start date/ source of help
1.	
2.	
3.	
4.	
5.	

Review date:

Identifying and developing personal support networks

 The module is divided into five sessions. These are:

1. What are personal support networks? (1 hour)
2. Identification of personal support networks (1 hour)
3. Developing and strengthening support networks (1 hour 5 min)
4. What I can offer others (1 hour 45 min)
5. Action plan and close (1 hour)

It links with the work on understanding and developing relationships covered in the manual *Developing Social Skills*. In this manual the module links with Developing Positive Attitudes and work on improving personal chances in the final module.

 The module makes use of the training and learning activities of:

- self-assessment activities such as completing checklists
- large group discussion and brainstorming
- working in pairs and small groups
- information giving including use of OHTs SN5–7 and handouts
- action planning

Trainer's notes

This module aims to help learners to:

- identify the various important people and agencies in their lives
- understand the importance of building up, maintaining and developing networks of individuals and agencies which can offer to support them
- understand a range of ways through which they can find people and agencies to support them
- think about the ways in which their relationships with others can be improved
- think about the ways in which they can become supportive to others
- think about the importance of developing their own skills and qualities which they can offer to others
- think about the importance of personal networks in developing self-esteem, self-confidence and a sense of personal direction

Note:

The trainer will need a comprehensive list of local and other agencies to draw upon during the action planning session to assist those learners who have identified particular areas of need in developing their personal support networks. The trainer will need up to date information about the availability of such resources and ways to access them in order not to raise false expectations.

The module will help the learner to think about the nature and quality of their relationships with others. The module encourages the learner to take some responsibility for making themselves an adequate and satisfying social and support network. Without such networks the individual learner may be at risk of not sustaining the changes to behaviour or lifestyle which they have identified as wanting to make. Without networks learners may become isolated and therefore vulnerable.

Session One: What are personal support networks?

Opening brainstorm: Who's important? (15 min)

It is often said that 'no man is an island', that everyone has links with someone else. Ask the group to brainstorm a list of people and agencies with whom they have links and connections.

The group will come up with list of family, friends, workmates, cell mates, co-residents, probation officers, employers, team mates, social workers, landlords, people at NA, education and training staff. They should think about the widest possible range of people who may have significance in their lives. Ask for any examples of the ways in which the people listed are of importance to them. Record their ideas on a flipchart.

Why have networks of people? (15 min)

Ask the group to think of all the situations in which it is essential to have people around them and to consider the types of help and support which others can offer.

The list should include events such as: dealing with times of change or stress; dealing with bereavement; helping to make personal changes, e.g. better money management, dealing with drink problems; learning new skills; undertaking practical tasks, e.g. decorating or repairing a car; and helping to solve problems, e.g. working out personal finances.

Explanations (30 min)

Introduce the module outlining why it is important to think about personal support networks and why they could think about developing their own networks.

Work through the material on OHTs SN5–7 and have copies of this information to offer as handouts for the group.

OHT SN5 is an illustration of the way in which Maslow, an American psychologist, thought that human beings' needs could be classified. He suggested that we need to look after basic needs for food, shelter and safety before we move to address other levels of needs. Many of these other levels of need are to do with building good relationships with other people – emotional safety, love, affection and a sense of belonging within a community.

According to Maslow's hierarchy of needs we all need to think most carefully about how we build up, develop and maintain our personal support networks with other people. Ask the group what it thinks about Maslow's categorisation of human needs. Can needs be put into different levels? Are the levels in the right order? Would they have included anything else?

Some of the work you will have done with the group will have been about taking support and help from others. The work which the group will do later in the module will be about the qualities and skills which they have to offer others. The reciprocity in relationships and the development of opportunities to give to others is a significant part of developing self-esteem.

Giving to others and playing a part within a community of friends and others is important for the ways in which people think about themselves and their self-esteem.

OHT SN6 looks at good self-esteem and the ways in which involvement with others encourages this. OHT SN7 looks at poor self-esteem and will help the learners to see that part of developing a poor sense of self-worth depends on the ways in which they get on with and interact with other people. Work through the two cycles of developing and diminishing self-esteem.

Check if the group can find those accounts make sense to them and if they have examples of things that you have said which they would like to share with others in the group. Check if there are any questions or any points which are not clear to them.

Session Two: Identification of personal support networks

Self-assessment activity (40 min)
Give out handout **PSN01** and ask the learners to read it through with you. Check that they understand what is wanted of them. The learners will need to undertake a several pieces of work with the chart they draw for this activity. They should be provided with A1 paper and coloured pens and told to use the whole sheet of paper for their diagram.

Ask the learners to work alone for 20 minutes producing a diagram of their own personal support networks. They can make use of symbols and words which have meaning to them. They need to be honest.

As the learners finish ask them to add to their diagrams by considering their personal support networks of 5–7 years ago. They may find that some people are still in their lives and that others have gone. They might like to add these past relationships in by using a different colour.

They have a further 20 minutes for this activity and should answer the three questions on **SN1**. They will need to compare their two networks and to consider why there have been changes.

There may have been reasons for changes; for example, moving city, spending time in a residential setting, taking up a new lifestyle, getting divorced or separated, getting married or moving in with someone. Not all the changes in their networks will be good and not all bad. They might like to consider what they think has happened for the best and what for the worst. They might consider how far they were involved in or responsible for the changes in their relationships.

Working in pairs (20 min)
Ask the learners to move into pairs to consider their two diagrams. They should work through their answers to the questions, the changes in their relationships and explore the types of lines on their diagrams. The pairs will need to work co-operatively and sympathetically. If there are some group members who seem not to have any or many support networks they could work together.

If this part of the exercise is likely to be destructive then it would be wise to ignore it.

Session Three: Developing and strengthening support networks

The learners will need to continue to work with their diagram. As they are adding information about their future networks they might like to do so in another colour.

Looking forward (30 min)
Having considered their current and past situations the learners should work on their own for a while to think about the ways in which they would like to develop their networks in the future. You can suggest:
- there may be aspects of themselves which they would like to change and they may need help to do this. For example they might like to get involved with NA or AA, they might like to get training in a vocational area or develop their literacy or numeracy.

- they might like to become part of a work group either on a paid or unpaid basis.
- they might like to develop a broader range of friends or to join some activity group.
- they might like to develop certain of their relationships or get to know current friends or family better. They should indicate that these relationships need strengthening on their charts.

Having completed this they need to take ten minutes to work on SN2. Here they need to list all the new relationships or links with others on one side of the handout and to note the ways in which they could achieve this on the other. They need to complete a similar listing exercise for those relationships which they would like to strengthen.

Working in pairs (20 min)

Assuming that the previous pairs worked well the learners should return to those pairs and then take turns to discuss their future personal support networks. They will each have their diagrams and their action lists. Their partner can help to make suggestions about the ways in which they can develop and strengthen their relationships. They may have other ideas about the sorts of relationships and links with others which they would like to add to their networks or to strengthen in their existing networks. This piece of joint working requires tact and sympathy. The results can be most impressive where the two partners act as effective referral agents for each other.

Group feedback (15 min)

Ask the group to work together to record the types of relationships and links with others which they would find it beneficial to develop. Ask for any examples of such links and any information they would need to build up such networks. There may be information needs about how to get a particular type of help in order to make them more able to improve a personal relationship or they may want to develop a link with an organisation as part of strengthening a change they would like to make in their own lives.

Trainer's notes

During the group feedback session you will need to make a note of any agencies which have been identified as likely to be supportive. You will need to make use of a break between sessions to check out details, phone numbers, addresses and how to access such agencies. This data will be needed during the final planning session.

Session Four: What I can offer others

The success of this session will depend on the extent of the learners' self-honesty and their willingness to acknowledge that they have a range of good qualities to offer others and strengths to develop.

Acknowledging my qualities and skills: a card sorting exercise(15 min)

Give each learner a set of cards SN3 and ask them to think about particular qualities or skills they have or would like to have. They should sort the cards into qualities and skills they have and those they would like to develop.

There are several blank cards for them to add any of their own skills or qualities which have not been included. At the close of this exercise they should review the skills and qualities which they have and then pretending they are someone else write a few lines which could be used as a sales pitch about themselves.

In pairs (20 min)

In pairs each learner should offer the other the couple of lines about marketing themselves. The pairs should then review the cards which each has selected and discuss what was chosen or discarded and how realistic the choices seem to be. Each should then again review the other's sales pitch and decide whether more should be added.

Group feedback 30 min)

1. Ask for some learners to volunteer their statements to the group. Thank them and accept them. They do not need to be commented upon.

2. Ask the learners what it was like to think about their skills and qualities. Then ask them what happened and how they found it when they were working on their selections and statements in pairs. For example, is it hard to be positive about oneself? Does it feel uncomfortable?

3. Ask the group members to volunteer some of the various skills and qualities they have. After you have a couple of dozen examples, ask the group to select things which they particularly value in friends and others they know and qualities which they would like to see as part of their own personal support networks.

At this point introduce the idea of the importance of giving back to others as a means of developing support networks. Remind the learners of Maslow's hierarchy and the levels which related to self-esteem and to belonging to others.

Giving back may be in terms of personal qualities to offer friends, by developing skills to offer others and developing support networks with others who may not be friends but who are people with whom skills and qualities can be traded. For example, one may offer help and support to deal with a drink problem in exchange for gaining help to decorate a flat. There could be a trade of small plumbing repairs for window cleaning and so on.

Strengthening my links with others (20 min)

Ask the learners to return to their diagrams of their networks and to consider how they need to add to their networks the qualities which they have to offer others. They need to think carefully about what they have to offer others in terms of:

- their personal qualities as family members or friends
- their skills which they could exchange with others
- the skills or qualities which they would like to develop to be able to offer others as part of a relationship or as part of a skills exchange network

Many learners may find this hard and so will need support from the trainer. They may want to work in pairs on this exercise to help them be positive and creative in their thinking.

Working in small groups (20 min)

In small groups of four ask the learners to discuss what they have added to their diagrams and consider if there are any other qualities or skills which they have to offer but which they have left off their charts.

The learners may want a few final minutes to complete their diagrams.

Session Five: Action plan and close

The learners need to make use of the planning sheet which is included as **SN4**. Check that everyone understands how to use the planning sheet and that they understand the principles behind it. These are, in summary:

- That the goals should be limited to one or two.
- The goals should be very clearly defined and should be **SMART**: Small, Measurable, Achievable by that individual, Realistic and within the current means of that individual not as they would like to be. The goals need to be Timebound. The individual needs to be able to know when they start working on the goal and when the time is up for its completion. No-one wants to see a goal way ahead in the distance.
- Each goal should be broken down into SMART action steps.
- Sources of help should be identified. This is not to take the work or the responsibility away from the individual but it will help them to know that they are not isolated in pursuing their goals.
- A review date should be included so they can formally appraise themselves and others of their progress. Ideally the review should be part of their on-going development work with their trainer. Informal and brief reviews should form part of the on-going contacts with the learners.

The learners should work alone for 20 to 30 minutes on their plans. They may need the support of the trainer while they are trying to gather information for their plans. The trainer should certainly check on the progress of each plan as it is being written. The trainer should sit alongside the learner and ask helpful questions, point out where there are inconsistencies or too great a set of assumptions, or where the goals are too large.

Where possible information leaflets about local agencies should be available for the learners to read.

The learners might also benefit from spending 10 minutes talking through their plans with a partner to collect additional ideas. You can suggest that the pairs might act as support for each other to progress their plans.

Closure

Complete the session with a round of:

One thing I have learnt about myself today is ...

Ask the group members to be honest and positive about themselves as they offer up their one observation.

Thank them all for their contribution and attending.

SN2: Developing my personal network

New relationships to develop	How I should do this?

Current relationships to strengthen	How I should do this?

SN1: My networks

On the sheet of A1 draw out a diagram like the one below in which you show all of those people, groups or agencies which are there to support you and are part of your life.

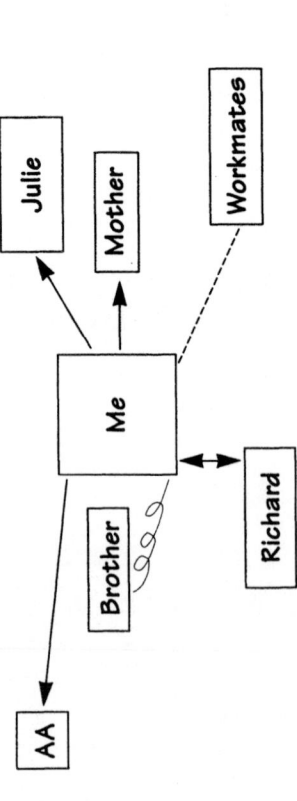

You should add some words or a key to show the type of relationship which you have with each and the strength of the relationship.

For example if the relationship is one way – someone supporting or giving to you then have a line with an arrow going towards you; if it is you doing all the giving then have the arrow pointing towards them

If the relationship is not as strong as it could be or you would like it to be have a dotted line

- - - - - - - - - - -

If the relationship is difficult then have a wavy or twisted line.

Add more symbols to suit your own networks with others.

When you have completed your diagram of current and past networks please answer the following questions:

1. Looking at your support networks now and in the past list out what have been the main changes.

2. Why have there been these changes?

3. How much do you think that these changes are because of you and why?

Being hospitable		Not just assuming that other people will do what you want
Knowing when people have reached their limit and not pushing them	Sharing workload and difficulties	Being concerned for the world
Taking others seriously	Being physically fit	Taking yourself seriously
Taking care to develop your skills	Coping with pressure	Seeing the funny side of things
Being able to budget	Being willing to do things for others	Helping others to deal with stress
Having conversational skills	Having a good imagination	
Making an effort to look your best	Managing time well	Being organised
Not getting crushed when things go wrong	Having a sense of perspective	Having goals and working towards them
Not always asking for support from people		Being sensitive to others' mood and feelings
Being able to be interested in new things	Being patient	Not mocking others' beliefs

Photocopy onto thin card and cut out each of the cards

SN3: Skills and qualities

Select the skills and qualities which you have to offer others – stack them in one pile

Select the skills and qualities which you would like to offer others – stack these in another pile

There are some blank cards for you to add any skills or qualities which you think are important but which are missing

Practical skills eg. gardening, decorating, baby sitting, repairs	Artistic skills: graphic, drawing, decorating furniture	Making things from wood
Plumbing	Building skills	Hairdressing
Catering	Reliable	Punctual
Honest	Loyal	Humorous
Knowing your own feelings	Being truthful	Computing skills
Considering others	Being able to cope with changes in plans	Being a good listener
Taking an interest in other people	Being musical	Being outgoing and interested
Taking care of people when they are ill or low	Being appreciative of things people do for you	

Photocopy onto thin card and cut out each of the cards

SN4: Action plan

My key areas for improvement are:

1.

2.

The plan to tackle these areas

List detailed SMART action steps	Start dates

Who can help you and with what?

I will know I have made progress when:

I will review my progress on: _____

SN3: Skills and qualities – continued

Making time for others	Helping others to complete forms and letters	Respecting the environment
Sticking with things to see them through	Gentle	Being able to make decisions
Content with your lot	Respecting others' wants and needs	Sharing your things with others
Kind	Good at house cleaning	Being brave
Good at telling people how to do things	Being thoughtful	Good at car repairs
Plastering	Bricklaying	Being able to repair and reuse household items
Tiling	Being quick witted	Being good in an emergency
	Electrical skills	Knitting
Carpet laying	Good with young children	Driving
Printing and making leaflets	Removals	Making and selling things

Photocopy onto thin card and cut out each of the cards

Good self-esteem:
A positive self-image. A sense of strengths and weaknesses. A sense of self-value. Able to cope with negative experiences and learn.

External self-confidence. Clear about needs, wants and opinions. Projecting a clear sense of self-worth. Not being put down/shut up.

Internal self-confidence. Feel secure, valued and wanted. Able to offer more to others, take an interest and be generous.

Better self-esteem. Treated with respect, care and interest so see self as of worth and value. Take self seriously. Have more to offer others.

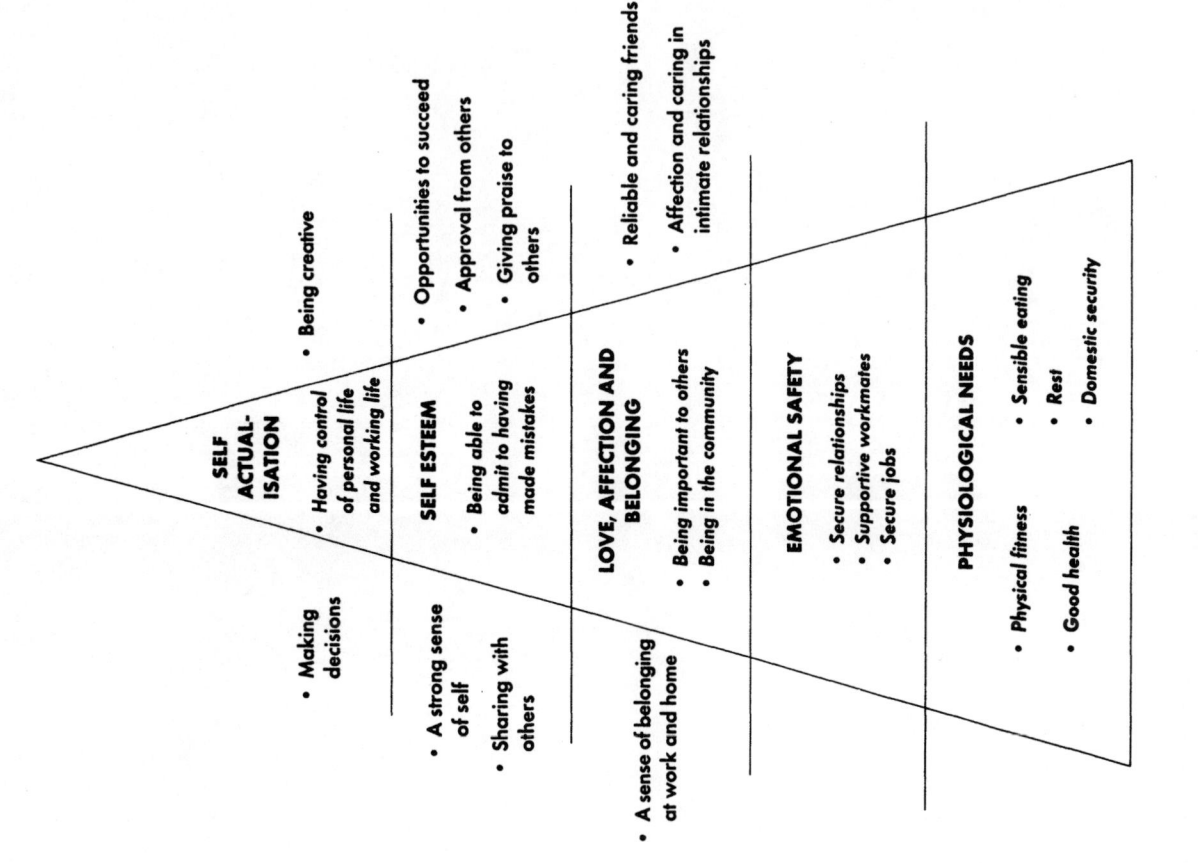

SELF ACTUAL- ISATION
- Having control of personal life and working life
- Being creative
- Making decisions
- A strong sense of self
- Sharing with others

SELF ESTEEM
- Being able to admit to having made mistakes
- Opportunities to succeed
- Approval from others
- Giving praise to others

LOVE, AFFECTION AND BELONGING
- Being important to others
- Being in the community
- A sense of belonging at work and home
- Reliable and caring friends
- Affection and caring in intimate relationships

EMOTIONAL SAFETY
- Secure relationships
- Supportive workmates
- Secure jobs

PHYSIOLOGICAL NEEDS
- Physical fitness
- Good health
- Sensible eating
- Rest
- Domestic security

SN7: Poor self-esteem and low self-confidence

Poor self-esteem:
Poor self-image, limited awareness of own value and that of others. Easily disappointed and failing to learn from experience.

Outer self-confidence.
Not clear about own worth, ideas or wants. Confused messages to others. Not presenting well or attractively to others.

Low self-esteem.
People are not interested in you. You are not involved with others. Increasingly fearful and anxious and anticipating rejection and disappointment.

Internal self-confidence.
Feeling of little value with little to offer. Poor relationship skills and relationships worsen. Feel uninvolved with others.

Developing and maintaining positive attitudes

The module is divided into six sessions. These are:

1. Introduction to positive and negative thinking (3 hours 45 min)

2. The power of negative thought (1 hour)

3. Self-esteem, positive and negative attitudes (3 hours)

4. Positive projections into the future (2 hours 25 min)

5. Supporting the development of positive attitudes (1 hour 20 min)

6. Drawing together learning points and planning positive actions (50 min)

The following training and learning activities are used:

- self-assessment activities

- role-play

- small and whole group discussion

- brainstorming

- action planning

Trainer's notes

This module aims to raise the learners' awareness of the importance of developing and maintaining positive attitudes about themselves, their lives and towards others around them. It encourages learners to think about the ways in which they may get others to respond to them by conveying positive or negative messages about themselves. It encourages learners to realise the importance of the ways in which they respond to events within their lives and to other people as a result of their own self-created messages. The module also helps learners to consider the ways in which they can undermine their self-view and can come to view the world around them bleakly. It explores the links between a positive attitude and creating high self-esteem. Learners are asked to think critically about their situation, themselves and the ways in which they respond to events and to think of ways in which they can more actively take control over events and over their responses to them.

The module seeks to:

- raise learners' awareness of the importance of creating and maintaining positive attitudes

- encourage awareness about self-esteem and how to attain high self-esteem

- enable learners to apply understanding about self-esteem to themselves

- help learners to think about the ways in which they can enhance their positive attitudes

- encourage awareness of the ways in which learners can undermine their own positive attitudes or allow themselves to be undermined

Session One: Introduction to positive and negative thinking

Opening activities: two brainstorms (35 min)
Brainstorm One
Ask the group to consider **what might be meant by positive thinking or having positive attitudes**. Record the group's thoughts on the flipchart.

The learners may make suggestions such as:
- thinking well of others
- looking for the good in a situation
- being optimistic
- not always anticipating the worst
- living life as it comes
- when things go wrong finding out why and doing it differently next time
- expecting that things will turn out for the best
- taking it easy and not always worrying about things before they happen
- expecting to be successful and not expecting failure or rejection
- assuming that difficulties can be sorted
- taking on a problem as if it is a puzzle – looking for solutions

Brainstorm Two

Ask the learners to brainstorm **the ways in which people with a positive attitude or who are positive thinkers may behave or may appear to others**. Again, record their thoughts on the flip chart. Their responses may include such as:
- having a sense of humour
- being ready to have a go at the same thing again to get it right
- not giving up
- being ready to see the funny side in a situation and sharing it with others
- having ideas about what else could be tried
- learning from a situation
- being open and relaxed
- not taking things or comments to heart or taking them personally
- having a number of things going on in their lives
- not dwelling on difficulties or upsets
- having things to look forward to
- being ready to talk to others

Having completed the two brainstorms ask the group to consider **what common ground there is between the two lists and what overall comments the group make about those people who think positively.**

Note these on a flipchart sheet. Tape the completed brainstorms to the wall. The learners will need to refer to these lists in the role-play activity at the close of this session.

The power of negative thinking

Reflection alone (30 min)

Ask the learners to think on their own for a few minutes about several occasions when they have been able to undermine themselves, 'talked themselves down' either before or after an event, allowed others to undermine them or have been pessimistic about something they were about to do.

Ask for some volunteers in the group to offer a couple of examples of events or situations when they undermined themselves or allowed others to undermine them. Ask them what happened next and what it felt like. Did they feel a sense of relief or a sense of the inevitable having happened? Find out if once one thing went wrong or was thought to have gone wrong, the learners then found other things did not go well or that they expected things to go badly.

Ask the learners to complete **PA01** which asks them to think about three negative triggers and the effects of these triggers. Explain what is required by the Activity – see below, *Trainer's notes*. These sheets need to be kept for later activities. The trainer should check on the learners' progress as they complete the activity.

 Trainer's notes

The trainer will need to work through one or two examples on the flip chart/whiteboard so that the learners understand how a trigger event may stimulate feelings of being negative, and how past experiences or buried feelings have an impact on current behaviour, thinking and feeling and thus the way in which events are then shaped. It is important that the learners understand clearly what is wanted. This exercise can seem complicated and difficult for some people.

An example is worked below:

Trigger: Event/feeling	Once you start	Feeling negative:	What happens?
	What do you do?	What do you say to yourself?	
Loss of job	Blame myself Smoke and drink more Hide away Think about the other times I've lost jobs Begin to behave in the ways I have done before when I have been redundant	It always happens to me I can never keep a job I've let the family down again All they want is money	Get bad tempered Get more depressed Stay away from people I know no-one else will have me Don't bother looking Money gets tighter It gets more tense at home There are more arguments and outbursts and blaming just like last time Want to leave the wife and kids

Group feedback (30 min)

Explain that the purpose of the session is to consider what has been learnt from the previous session. There is no need for learners to disclose anything they do not want to, as some of the material they have covered may be too personal. The feedback session needs to be managed so that individuals do not feel compromised and so that no single group member is able to dominate the group, seeing it as a session to look at their problems rather than a consideration of general principles.

The feedback session needs to cover the learning points:

- that negativity can feed negativity
- from the response to a single incident, attitudes and the things that people say to themselves and the ways in which they behave can make the rest of their lives seem hopeless
- a current set back can remind people about past set backs and awaken old feelings of negativity, despair, inevitable defeat or uselessness

- past ways of dealing with situations (which may not have been the most effective at that time) can be used again – just because they are familiar
- once a person is thinking negatively it is easy for future actions to be stalled or to be sabotaged by thinking negatively. For example, I won't get that job – who'd want me? I'll never go out with anyone else again – who'd want me?

The group should be able to reach the point of acknowledging that negative thinking is powerful. They may be able to reach the point of deciding that for some people negative thinking is easier than positive thinking.

Pair work (10 min)
Write the following questions on the board:

How do people who have negative attitudes appear or behave:

- to themselves?
- to others around them?

Ask the group to work in pairs to generate five statements for each of the questions. The pairs should be prepared to offer these statements back to the group during a feedback session.

Group feedback (10 min)
Ask for volunteers to offer their thoughts. Try to ensure that everyone in the group participates.

The power of negative thinking and the importance of positive thinking
Group summing up (10 min)
Ask the group to sum up the learning points so far.

The group has had an opportunity to reflect on negative and positive thought. Discuss with them how easy it is to think of the ways in which people can be negative about themselves and others around them, and how it is often more difficult to think of ways in which people think positively and project a positive attitude. Ask why they think that this may be the case?

Consider with the group why being negative is such a powerful and destructive state of mind.

Ask the group what would happen if instead of being negative people were positive about themselves and others. What would the effect of this be? Brainstorm the group's ideas.

Role-play activity (1 hour 10 min – depending on the numbers in the group)
Use the ideas and the lists of positive and negative thinking and behaviours as material to stimulate and prepare the learners for the role-play activity.

Divide the group into pairs, give the learners one of the situations on **PA2** or **PA3**. The four situations are the same on each card but the learners are asked to enact the scene they are given from the point of view of having a highly positive outlook or an intensely negative outlook.

In each role-play the characters with these opposing views of life meet, consider the situation in which one or both find themselves and discuss what might be done.

Allow five minutes for each learner to work alone to think about the situation and the ways in which the character would interpret it. The learners need to use the ideas generated through the earlier group brainstorms to get in the right frame of mind. Each will need to maintain their view against the opposite view which will be offered by their partner.

A further five minutes should be allowed for the pairs to think how they will play the scene together. Then ask each pair to present their scene. After each scene ask the players **in role** to consider:

- How realistic they thought their interpretation as a positive or a negative character to have been?
- Did they have any sympathy with the point of view of the character they were playing and why?
- How did they find playing against the highly positive/highly negative character?
- Were they beginning to become infected by the other's view of the world?
- What solutions to the issues were suggested – were the ones most likely to be adopted those which were positive or negative and why?

Check these responses with the audience.

At the close of all the role-plays ask the group which interpretation positive or negative they found more powerful. What might this tell them about themselves?

Summing up and finding starting points for the module (20 min)
Take a few minutes to quickly outline the work covered so far. Then ask the learners why they think that a module on developing positive attitudes will be of use to them. Record these ideas on the flip chart.

Ask the learners what they would like to achieve by the close of the module. Again record these thoughts and come back to them in the last session, Session Six.

Session Two: The power of negative thought

The learners should now be aware of the differences in outlook between positive and negative thinkers and the power each type of thought exerts. This session asks the learners to consider more deeply the ways in which they may have disabled themselves in various situations by their own negative thinking. It asks the learners to consider some of the ways in which they may speak to themselves and others or describe events and incidents to themselves and colour them with negativity.

Working alone: selecting statements (20 min)
Ask the learners to work with the pre-printed statements on cards PA4. Ask them to sort through the sorts of statements which they may make about themselves and others. From the statements which they have selected ask if the learners can find any patterns in the ways in which they think about themselves and others? Ask them to record this on sheet PA4.

Working alone: completing statements (15 min)
Ask the learners to complete the statements about the ways in which they may respond to situations on PA6. Again they should record their findings on sheet PA5. Ask the learners to complete the box at the foot of PA5 about the types of negative things which they would like to change about themselves.

Working in pairs: comparing attitudes (15 min)
Ask the learners to work in pairs to compare the ways in which they think they view the world, themselves and situations around them. They should base their discussions on activities PA4–6. The learners should feel completely in control of sharing what they want to share and not feel that they have to disclose too much.

Depending on how well the pairs know each other they may be able to comment on how true they find their partner's views. Have some learners been overly hard on themselves? What does this tell the learners?

Group feedback (10 min)

Explore the following questions with the group. Ask for volunteers to share their experiences of the activities they have just completed.

- How useful did the learners find the activity?
- What sorts of things did they find about themselves?
- Are there particular things about which, or ways in which, the learners had negative attitudes?
- Were these reasonable?
- What solutions might the group suggest to turn the negative into positive?

Session Three: Self-esteem, positive and negative attitudes

Trainer's notes

This session explores the links between developing and maintaining a sense of good or high self-esteem and the power of positive thinking. It encourages the learners to see that there are links between maintaining a positive attitude and feeling good about oneself and others. It encourages the learners to think about what constitutes self-esteem for themselves as individuals and how they may best maintain it.

Learners may want to discuss what self-esteem is and why it is important. It is worthwhile having some thoughts prepared to be able to enter into discussion to demonstrate that considering self-esteem is important. Some notes on self-esteem follow below.

Definitions and self-esteem

Self-esteem is the feeling that a person has about themselves. It is a sense of overall self-worth. While self-esteem may fluctuate it is desirable to maintain a sense of high self-esteem and a sense of feeling good about oneself. This comes from feeling loveable, likeable, worthy of such feelings and able to accept them from oneself and others. It also comes from a sense of feeling capable and able to undertake tasks and from being acknowledged as capable.

Low or poor self-esteem is the opposite of this. A person feels neither loveable nor likeable by others or by themselves. The person does not feel capable or competent and therefore feels that no-one values them.

A quotation about self-esteem defined by D. Corkille Briggs runs as follows:

> "A person's judgement of self, influences the kinds of friends he chooses, how he gets along with others, the kind of person he marries, and how productive he will be. It affects his creativity, integrity, stability, and even whether he will be a leader or a follower. His feelings of self-worth form the core of his personality and determine the use he makes of his aptitudes and abilities. His attitude toward himself has a direct bearing on how he lives all parts of his life. In fact, self-esteem is the mainspring that slates each of us for success or failure."

A sense of good self-esteem is about making choices in life, having control over aspects of life, feeling that life is being lived properly and to the full. High self-esteem means that the person feels that they have opportunities and are making the most of them. High self-esteem means feeling worthwhile, and so not being afraid or guilty about taking opportunities and good things in life.

Brainstorm: Feelings (10 min)

Ask the group to suggest how it feels when they have a positive attitude and when they have a negative attitude. Divide a flipchart sheet in half longitudinally and record the group's thoughts. At the close of the brainstorm compare the two lists and see how many of the suggestions on each of the lists are the opposite of each other.

The brainstorm may run as follows:

Feeling positive	Feeling negative
Energetic	No energy for me, anything or anyone
Able to get more done	Don't really want to be with anyone
More able to give to others	Depressed
Happy with what's going on	Bored
Interested in others and the world	Life doesn't seem to go well
Feel better about myself	What's the point – it'll probably go wrong
Ready to have a go at new things	Don't want to try anything new
Ready to make the changes I've been meaning to make for a while	Little enjoyment of life
Able to make new friends and tackle new things	Can't make changes to habits or lifestyle
Feel a more interesting person	Defeated and down

Ask the group which set of feelings they would rather have and why.

Brainstorm: Self-esteem (15 min)

Ask the group what they understand by the term 'self-esteem'. Record the answers on the flip chart. Compare this brainstorm with that on feeling positive and feeling negative. Ask the group if there are any similarities between the lists and where there are similarities.

Explanations (10 min)

Explore with the learners the links between having high self-esteem and having positive attitudes about oneself, others and aspects of one's life. Remind the learners of activity **PA01**, when they considered the ways in which an event, memory or thought which triggered a negative response could lead into a number of other negative things, into thinking negatively, doing negative things towards others and being negative about the future. Those feelings and negative attitudes could be viewed as part of developing low self-esteem.

Individual work on negative self-esteem (25 min)

Explain to the learners that they are going to look at the spiral of negative self-esteem and how one act or idea may feed another until someone feels really bad about themselves, about their life and its opportunities and about their ability to control their own life and have a positive influence on the future.

Ask the learners to look at activity **PA7**. Work through the downward spiral looking at the questions and considering how the spiral works. It may be useful to then work through an example on the flip chart having drawn out the spiral on the chart. A trigger event from the lists produced for activity **PA1** could be used for this example and when they are thinking about what might spark off an episode of low self-esteem. Ask the learners if they understand how to complete the spiral of negative self-esteem and allow 20 minutes for them to complete the spiral. Move from learner to learner checking on understanding and progress and asking for points to be explained.

Pair work (20 min)

Ask the learners to share what they choose to share with a partner. Ask them to consider:

- how does the spiral of negative self-esteem work for them?
- what starts the spiral off – is it often or always the same thing?
- what can happen, or can be done, to stop the downward spiral?

Group feedback (10 min)

Ask for the group to feedback what they have learnt from completing and discussing their spirals. Take overall learning points and brainstorm:

> **Are there any solutions or suggestions of things which may be done to interrupt a downward spiral?**

Write up the suggestions and keep these.

Positive self-esteem – working alone and then in pairs (40 min)

Explain that the learners are to repeat the process but this time completing a spiral of positive self-esteem. They should take 40 minutes in total to work alone and then in pairs. Once in pairs they should consider:

- how does the spiral of positive self-esteem work?
- what starts the spiral off – is it often or always the same thing?
- what can happen, or can be done, to stop the upward spiral?
- how can things which would stop the spiral be prevented?

Group feedback (20 min)

Ask for the group to feedback what they have learnt from completing and discussing their spirals. Take overall learning points and brainstorm:

> **What things may happen to stop an upward spiral once it has begun?**
>
> **What can be done to stop the spiral being interrupted?**

Write up the suggestions and keep these. Compare these with the suggestions from the work on negative self-esteem and explore any similarities between the lists of suggestions. Find out if the learners think that intervention is harder to prevent positive esteem slipping or to turn negative self-esteem into positive self-esteem. Find out why they think one may be harder. Ask for examples of the interventions which the learners make or have made in the past.

Goal setting (15 min)

Ask the learners now to consider the types of things which they have written down about low self-esteem. They will have had the opportunity to consider what they might do to stall or turn round negative self-esteem with a partner and as part of the whole group discussion. Ask them to complete **PA9**, a goal setting exercise to work on discouraging low self-esteem.

The learners may want to work in pairs to gather extra ideas after working alone for some minutes.

Whole group feedback (15 min)

Ask for some examples of the goals which the learners have set themselves and some of the things which they will do to achieve these goals. Find out what suggestions others in the group may have to help the individual learners in their goal setting. Allow some time at the close of this feedback session for the learners to add to their goal setting charts.

Session Four: Positive projections into the future

 ## *Trainer's notes*

This session requires that you work with the learners to think about the tactics they could develop to help them to manage how they think about themselves, others and situations in a more positive way. There are a number of ways in which people can think more positively about themselves and their futures. This session relies on the trainer explaining each strategy and helping the learners to practice it.

There are some notes about these techniques on handout **PA10**. This can be copied and given the learners.

Ideally the learners should consider these changes to their thinking within the learning session and should then set themselves goals to practice in their daily lives before the next learning session. The learners should be encouraged to set goals, to record and review their progress. They should have the opportunity to discuss what happened with each other and with the trainer. Such practice and discussion will help new ways of thinking to become established. Needless to state it takes more than a week to change a way of thinking, but the more conscious the learner can be made about they ways they view their situation, finding some ways to consider how they may look at it differently and having the opportunity to discuss what they have been consciously practising helps them to integrate these new ways of thinking into their lives.

If follow-up sessions are not possible then the learners should nevertheless be asked to work with **PA12** an exercise to trial new thinking.

Explain there are a number of ways in which people can influence events by thinking positively about the ways in which they wish things to happen. In thinking about the ways in which they wish events to turn out they can encourage them to do so. For example, in deciding that a particular job has their name on it, thinking about being successful at a job interview, anticipating the questions that may be asked, thinking about how it would feel to get the job and what could be done in the job will all help the person to go into the situation feeling more confident and more assured of success. This confidence helps the person project themselves better, discuss the sorts of things they would do in the job and encourage the interviewers to view them in this way.

Telling anecdotes (25 min)

Ask the group to think about times when they have wanted something to turn out in a particular way and it has. Ask them to work in threes to swap stories.

Then ask for a couple of volunteers to share their stories with the whole group.

When the events turned out as they hoped they would, how did it make them feel?

Record these feelings which may be ones such as: good, powerful, more confident, sense of accomplishment, "I could do anything". Briefly, link these back to the work on the cycle of positive self-esteem.

Explanations (40 min)

Refer back to the notes at the opening of the session. Explain that the anecdotes have shown the power of positive thinking (the power of negative thinking and the ways in which the learners have illustrated how they have encouraged things to go wrong for themselves by having negative attitudes will have been amply demonstrated). The power of positive thinking is a way for the learners to make use of their own energies to encourage good things for themselves. The positive feelings about something good happening and the ways in which this gathers momentum for the individual was considered when looking at the positive spiral of self-esteem.

Thinking positively about the future and about how events should best turn out may be approached by:

- scripting
- visualisation
- affirmations
- setting appropriate goals and being aware of positive qualities and strengths

Spend time outlining with the group the meanings of the above. The following notes may help in these explanations. During each explanation:

- check that the learners understand
- find out if any have tried the techniques and with what results. An advocate in the group will be the best advert to encourage other learners to experiment
- ask how learners may try out the technique and offer some of your own examples. The more concrete the explanation and the examples the more clearly they will be understood and the more likely to be adopted
- pause to allow the learners time to take in the information and to check that they understand the handout or if they want to add anything to the handout

1. *Scripting* – imagining what will happen in an encounter and work out what you will say, what might be said by others and how you will deal with things which are said and still manage to work the situation to achieve what you would like.

   The learner will have rehearsed what may happen and how this will be dealt with. The learner will therefore feel more confident in knowing what they are is aiming for and what the result would look like. He or she will feel encouraged that they have some power and control over the future and able to manage an encounter.

2. *Visualisation* – this involves imagining what an individual would like to see happening in their future or as an outcome to a particular issue. The learner needs to concentrate and work hard on focusing on the desired outcome. The learner should be encouraged to think about a number of details to support the visualisation. The frequent repetition of the visualisation will encourage the learner to move in that direction and to make changes. The changes become more possible because they have already been mentally rehearsed. The barriers to making changes will have been crossed and the ground on the other side explored, at least mentally, thereby reducing fear of change. The learner will have a clear sense of direction, set of reasons for doing something and a sense of what the outcome looks like.

3. *Affirmations* – find a statement which sums up what is wanted. The statement needs to be easy to remember and to repeat. The learner should be able to support the statement with images of success and realisation of their goal. The learner should find opportunities to repeat the affirmation regularly. This should re-channel thinking in the direction of the affirmation and away from alternative or negative statements. An easy way to illustrate an affirmation is to ask the group to consider some negative affirmations which they often repeat. They will already have considered some of these as part of negative thinking. They will know the power of repeating negative statements – I won't get that job; no-one likes me; I just mess new things up; and so should be convinced by the power of repeating positive statements. Positive statements work in a similar way.

Positive self-reminders to the individual that they have skills, qualities and a vision will encourage positive thinking and a sense of personal power.

Considering personal futures through any of these techniques requires the learner to focus on what they are doing rather than have a mind cluttered with other things. The learners should be introduced to the idea of relaxation and some basic relaxation techniques before they work on any of these activities. Relaxation is a useful way to unclutter the mind and calm the individual. Relaxation is considered in the module on Exercise and well-being.

For visualisation and for supporting the affirmations with images the learner should take a step further and learn how to meditate. Some learners may resist this and block the possibility of visualising anything. Some may not be able to conjure a clear mental image, others may have a clear picture, some may hear or sense something which seems right for them. Others may not be able to actively see, hear or sense anything and may just receive impressions or a sense. There is no one right way to visualise.

The learners should not force themselves to work at these techniques for a long time. Short practice periods and frequent repetition will be of longer term benefit.

4. *Setting appropriate goals and being aware of positive qualities and strengths.* The learner needs to undertake a stock-take of their personal qualities, skills and achievements and from this sound foundation of knowledge they can plan what could be undertaken next. The stock-take informs further learning and developmental needs, and it helps to define what are realistic goals. The goals are then subdivided into small and specific action steps. The goal setting can be part of the visualisation and the affirmation which the learner can use along with an action plan to successfully project themselvesf into the future.

Pair working (25 min)
Ask the learners to look at the situations printed on PA11 and to decide which of the strategies they would like to try to use in that situation. Work through one as an example with the group before they begin to work in pairs.

Group feedback (15 min)
Ask for some examples of the ways in which the learners approached particular situations and see which of the approaches were most frequently suggested. Check that any reasons for the learners not using an approach was not one based on a lack of understanding.

Personal futures (30 min)
Take the learners as a group through a simple relaxation routine (see module on Exercise and well-being). Ask the learners to then focus on their own futures, an aspect of it or an issue which they would like to resolve. They should consider what outcome they would like and then think through what they have undertaken in the session and how they are going to make use of one or more of the tools they have been offered.

Once they have thought through in some detail what they are going to do, ask them to write this down (PA12). This can be added to and should be reviewed in the subsequent week to see how progress may be being made. Ideally the learners should be able to discuss this with the trainer and with others in the group to resolve any difficulties they are having and to share successes.

Feedback (10 min)

A brief feedback session to check that the learners have understood what they are doing, share and summarise the ideas discussed to date.

Session Five: Supporting the development of positive attitudes

 Trainer's notes

Explain that there are several ways in which people can help themselves to develop positive attitudes. These include some of the areas looked at so far and a number of other practical things which people can do for themselves.

Brainstorm (10 min)

Ask the group to suggest a number of the ways in which people can feel better about themselves and the ways in which they view others and their lives. Put at the centre of the brainstorm:

> **Ways to make myself feel better**

The list should include some of the issues which have been covered so far and others. Tell the learners they will all have ways to make themselves feel better/stronger. Gather as many ideas as possible:

- thinking positively about the future – having a focus and goals
- knowing what makes me feel bad and avoiding it or tackling it
- knowing what makes me feel good and not messing this up
- good relationships with others
- looking after myself
- taking exercise

The list may include a number of negative or potentially negative tactics:

- self-medication – drink/drugs
- running away
- denial of a situation
- blocking
- repression

There may be a need to explore and to challenge some of the long-term and actual effects of some of their suggestions. The brainstorm should introduce some of the items which are the subject of the penultimate session.

Summarising and checking (15 min)

Revise with the group the three following mainstays for developing positive attitudes:

1. Identifying what encourages a sense of self-esteem and doing these things.
2. Identifying positive things about oneself, saying positive things to oneself and to others about oneself.
3. Avoiding those things and people who undermine self-esteem.

Check that the learners can identify what makes them feel a sense of high self-esteem and that they have positive things to say to themselves and sayings which they may like to use as affirmations.

Allow the learners ten minutes to complete PA13.

Effective relationships (15 min)

Explain that many of the things which the learners will have identified as of importance to helping them feel good about themselves will have centred on relationships, but only on relationships which go well. Working relationships will create feelings of acceptance, warmth, giving to others, trust, belonging, a sense of well-being and protection.

Many of the things which learners will have identified as leading to poor self-esteem will centre on relationships going badly, being in a poor or dysfunctional relationship and encountering friction or conflict in various relationships from those with partners or friends or problems with those in authority.

Ask the learners to complete PA14. This is a communications skills and relationships checklist. The assessment should help both trainer and learner to identify any areas which could benefit from further work. Record any findings from this activity for better planning individual and group programmes.

Note:
The importance of helping the learners to become more aware of the range of relationships and the ways in which they can better manage them is at the heart of the manual *Developing Social Skills*. The module in this manual, Developing communication skills, touches on a number of the key issues in the better management of communications with others. This session with the learners should be to encourage them to highlight the importance of relationships to their sense of positive or negative well-being.

Another area which the initial brainstorm may have covered and the final area for this session are those aspects of looking after oneself which learners may often neglect.

Brainstorm (10 min)

Ask the learners should identify areas in looking after themselves which they think are important. It may be necessary for the trainer to add others. The learners should be thinking about what encourages a positive outlook on life, a sense of good self-esteem and what contributes to low self-esteem and a negative outlook on life. The brainstorm should be wide ranging covering such issues as:
- healthy eating
- exercise
- getting proper sleep and rest
- maintaining a good appearance
- dealing with money and avoiding debt
- getting and keeping a job
- having a good time
- not being bored
- feeling useful and not useless
- not feeling left out or isolated
- having a sense of purpose
- maintaining a comfortable and attractive home environment
- working on use of time, having and realising goals and developing leisure interests
- recognising and valuing personal skills and qualities
- knowing how to manage stress
- not being anxious about money

- not feeling out of control
- feeling good about the way the children are growing up
- having a goal

Identification of skills and needs (10 min)

Ask the learners to construct three lists (see PA15). The first list should show aspects of looking after themselves which they would say they were good at. The second list, the things they feel they should develop and would like help in so doing, and the third list the things they were less good at but did not care too much about improving upon.

Group feedback (10 min)

The lists can be used to determine if there are common learning needs within the group and to help learners with certain needs to pair up with another learner. Some areas can be met from other modules in this manual. The self-help pairings would need overseeing but may be useful as starting points for skill acquisition.

Individual needs analysis sessions (10 min per learner)

The lists are a useful tool. The areas which the learners do not want to work on are as important as those which they have self-identified as needing work. The list will need reviewing with individual learners and the reasons for wanting to improve or not to improve would need to be discussed as well as asking for evidence for competence in certain areas.

Session Six: Drawing together the learning points and planning for positive actions

 Trainer's notes

The learners have made a number of lists and undertaken several goal setting activities in the course of this module. The final session should be to review these lists and plans, and to prioritise this will be the area for action as a final goal setting exercise.

Review and planning (20 min)

The learners should review all their lists and plans and create a final action plan for working on their own development of positive attitudes. A planning form is PA16. The learners should be reminded about the importance of only setting achievable goals, for determining their own success criteria, and the importance of deciding when an action will be started and when it will be reviewed.

Summing up the module (20 min)

Remind the learners of the two lists they created at the close of Session One.
1. Why they thought a module on developing positive attitudes would be of use to them.
2. What they would like to have achieved by the close of the module.

Discuss with the learners what else they would now add to the first list and whether they feel that the module was useful to them in achieving the goals they set at the outset. Check that what has been covered is understood and that there are no problems in implementing it.

Closing round (10 min)

Go round the group and ask each learner to volunteer one positive thing they have learned about themselves from working on the module.

If it is appropriate then the group could be asked to offer one positive thing they have learned about another person, or a positive thing they have appreciated about another person. It is important to manage this so that everyone is mentioned, so once one person has been commented on, that person cannot be mentioned again.

PA2: Situations for positive thinkers to role play

1. You are someone who always tries to see the good in others and likes to find a way to make the best of a situation.

You have been involved in a painful but not too serious sports accident. The others on your team are ready to turn on the opposition. They think that it was a case of foul play.

What are you going to do about it? What is going through your mind? How do you deal with the friend and team player who you talk to about this situation later that afternoon?

2. You always look for what can be made from a bad situation or to find what you can learn from it.

You have just finished three months in a new job but the manager has told you today that you and the other new person will have to be laid off. There haven't been the orders coming in. The manager is very sympathetic to your disappointment. She promises that if the work picks up, she will contact you.

What are you going to say or do? What do you say to the other new person who has been laid off but who has a completely different view of the situation to you?

3. You are the type of person who has a good opinion of yourself and you like to think that the best will happen to you.

You have been for an interview for a job which interests you and which has good prospects. You and the other candidate are sitting in the waiting room waiting for the decision. The interviewers have so far taken an hour deciding what to do.

What is going through your mind? How are you going to keep yourself going until they tell you the decision? What decision do you expect to be made? What if it is negative what will you think or do?

Imagine the conversation you have with the candidate who is with you in the waiting room. What sorts of things will you find out about each other?

4. You have tried to take life as it comes, to roll with the bad times and make them as good as possible. You enjoy the good times and tend to have more good than bad in your life.

You have just been told by your partner that they are sorry but they have decided to take a job in another town, 70 miles away, and do not want to be persuaded out of the decision. The job means a promotion and more money. Taking the job may not mean the end of the relationship.

How do you react? What is going through your mind? What do you think will happen? How will you deal with the situation? You meet with a friend in the pub and talk about the situation. Your friend has a negative outlook on life and tries to influence you. How are you going to respond?

PA1: The effects of thinking negatively

Think of three occasions when you become negative and complete the boxes below.

What triggers you to become negative? What is said or done? What do you think about or remember?	Once you start feeling negative:		What happens?
	What do you do?	What do you say to yourself?	

Activity sheet PA4: How do I tend to think about myself?

What statements reflect the sorts of thoughts you have or the ways in which you think? Select these cards and stack them in one pile

What statements reflect the ways in which you think or talk about other people? Select these cards and stack them in another pile

There are a few blank cards for you to use if your favourite or most common sayings about yourself or others are not written down

I often go over things which have gone wrong	I like to try new things	I tend to put myself down to myself and to others
I tend not to value what I do very much	I don't take compliments well	I don't often feel in control of what I do
I like to do things even if they are not always 100% successful	I think I am going to fail even before I have done anything	I just don't let anyone walk over me
I think people laugh at me	I often think that life will throw bad things at me	I find it hard to forgive others
Other people are interesting and often have good ideas	I don't mind telling people what I am good at	Others have just had more advantages and chances than me
I often think I'm no good	People just let you down – so why bother?	I am good at considering others' feelings
I like to take an interest in other people	I know people like being with me	I am not very good at ...(finish the sentence with anything you like)
Other people always seem better or more in control	I am not very good at making friends	I try not to draw attention to myself

Photocopy onto thin card and cut out each of the cards

PA3: Situations for negative thinkers to role play

1. ***You are someone who can't always see the good in others. You often suspect that someone is out to get you. You don't react well to difficult situations.***

Your friend and fellow team player has been involved in a painful but not too serious sports accident. The others on your team are ready to turn on the opposition. They think that it was a case of foul play. You often see the bad in people and tend to agree with the other team players. Your friend is the opposite and has a quite different view of what is going on and what should be done. It is irritating to you. You talk about the situation that afternoon.

What are you going to do? What is going through your mind? How do you want to inflect your friend and fellow team player?

2. ***You often experience bad situations. There is rarely anything which can be made from such situations and you can never really find anything to learn from then. Bad things just seem to happen.***

You have just finished three months in a new job but the manager has told you today that you and the other new person will have to be laid off. There haven't been the orders coming in. The manager is very sympathetic to your disappointment. She promises that if the work picks up, she will contact you.

What are you going to say or do? What do you say to the other new person who has been laid off but who has a completely different view of the situation to you ?

3. ***You are the type of person who does not have too high an opinion of yourself and you tend to think that if something bad is going to happen then it will happen to you. You've given up hoping for good things.***

You have been for an interview for a job which interests you and which has good prospects. You and the other candidate are sitting in the waiting room waiting for the decision. The interviewers have so far taken an hour deciding what to do.

What is going through your mind? How are you going to keep yourself going until they tell you the decision? What decision do you expect to be made? What will you think or do then? What happens if it is positive?

Imagine the conversation you have with the candidate who is with you in the waiting room. What sorts of things will you find out about each other?

4. ***You don't really take life as it comes, you worry a lot about the future, often expecting the worst. You just know that bad things happen and that they often outweigh the good things.***

Your friend whom you meet in the pub this evening tells you that they have just been told by his/her partner that they are sorry but they have decided to take a job in another town, 70 miles away, and do not want to be persuaded out of the decision. The job means a promotion and more money. Taking the job may not mean the end of the relationship.

How do you react to what you are told? What things do you remember from your past or that of friends? What is going through your mind? What do you think will happen? How will you tell your friend to deal with the situation?

I expect people to value me and what I do	No-one does anything for nothing	I just feel down and I don't know why
Most things are rigged against you	I find it hard to say no if someone wants me to do something	People just don't explain what they want from me very clearly
Hard work, honesty and so on aren't recognised so why bother with them?	There's no point in worrying – things will work out	It's usually someone else's fault and I get blamed for it
People think I'm stupid	Other people have more things and better money – it's not fair	People don't give me a chance to show how well I can do
People are prejudiced against me	School let me down	There's no point in trusting anyone
	I just don't get on with other people	I don't get the right sort of help that I need
I always attract the wrong sort of people	I can't deal with my drugs/drink problem	
I tried once but it didn't work so I didn't try again	I always know that something will work out for the best	If I wasn't so unhappy then I expect I could do something about…eg. my weight/smoking
People are just out for themselves	People don't listen to me	My family has always been behind me
Most people want to do a fair day's work for a fair day's wage	Most people are kind	Most people are honest
	Most people will cheat if they can get away with it	If I ask for help, people will usually help me

Photocopy onto thin card and cut out each of the cards

I like being with other people.	I find it hard to give compliments to people	Often I think people don't think I can do anything very well
There's no point in me learning new skills I just won't cope		Some people just have all the luck – I'm not one of them
I often find I am saying sorry for things – even if they are nothing to do with me	I find it hard to forgive myself	I think that I should be able to enjoy things
I just let things get on top of me	I try not to blame myself	There's not a lot fair in this life
I don't get the chances others have	I don't have a sense of proportion – little things just seem big to me	
I try not to blame others	I think that I am better than other people	I don't always assume that it's been my fault
I just can't keep a relationship going	With beginnings like mine it's hardly surprising that I've not got anywhere	I think that I respect other people
I like to have goals and work towards them	It's not my fault	I don't get crushed when things go wrong
I don't mind a challenge		If it goes wrong I try again
If others did more I wouldn't have to do everything	Other people can hold down jobs I can't	I think that a lot of it is my parents' fault
I spend more time thinking about what I cannot do than what I can	I let others blame me for things	I made a mistake once and it's never gone right since

Photocopy onto thin card and cut out each of the cards

PA6: Look at the situations and think how would you respond to them

1. Faced with the loss of my job I would...

2. If I have to try something new then I feel...

3. If I have to look for work then I feel...

4. When someone does something which I do not like then I...

5. If I had to move to a new town then I would feel...

6. If I was to have an accident tomorrow then I think I would react by...

7. If someone I really liked grassed on me/rejected me then I would...

8. If I meet someone I think will be a friend then I...

9. If I had to look after someone who was ill then I would...

10. If I have to deal with a problems about council tax/benefits/the electricity bill then I know that...

11. If someone is nice to me then I...

12. The hardest thing I could do is....................I think that I would be okay/fail/not do it very well/could manage/would do it well (fill in the blank and cross out the words which do not apply to you)

13. If I overheard someone criticising my appearance, I would...

PA5: The ways I think about myself and others

Consider any patterns which you may have discovered about the ways you think about yourself and others during the learning activities.

The four main things I think about myself are:

1.

2.

3.

4.

The four main things I think about other people are:

1.

2.

3.

4.

Looking at the ways I think about situations then I think that I am:
more positive then negative or more negative than positive? (cross out one which does not apply)
Give some examples to support your statement.

Thinking about the ways in which I am negative, I would like to improve on...

PA8: Creating the upward spiral of positive self-esteem

So now you're really on top of things
Describe the situation you are in.
What does it feel like to have reached this point?
How do you feel about yourself?
How do you feel about others?
What do you think others feel about you?
What was it that was worth feeling that bad about?
What can you do about it now you are here?

So what could you do now to muck things up for yourself?
Why won't you do this?

So you are really going up
How do you feel about yourself?
How do you feel about others?
What are you doing now to keep on making things better for yourself or to encourage you to see things as really good?

So what could you do now to muck things up for yourself?
Why won't you do this?

So you are on your way up
How do you feel about yourself?
How do you feel about others?
Identify what are you doing to make things good for yourself or to see things as good?
How do others around you feel?

Your triggers
Describe the thoughts, feelings, memories incidents or events that start you feeling good about yourself and the world around you.

PA7: Creating the downward spiral of negative self-esteem

Your triggers
Describe the thoughts, feelings, memories incidents or events that start you feeling bad about yourself and the world around you.

So what could you do now to make things better for yourself?

How you are on your way down
How do you feel about yourself?
How do you feel about others?
Now be honest:
What are you doing to make things worse for yourself or to see them as worse?
What do you think others feel about you?

So what could you do now to make things better for yourself?

So you are really going down
How do you feel about yourself?
How do you feel about others?
Now be honest:
What are you doing now to make things yet worse?
How do others around you feel?

So now you're down
Describe the situation you are in.
What does it feel like to have reached this point?
How do you feel about yourself?
How do you feel about others?
What do you think others feel about you?
What was it that was worth feeling this bad about?
What can you do about it now you are here?
Think of a six point plan to get yourself out of this situation.

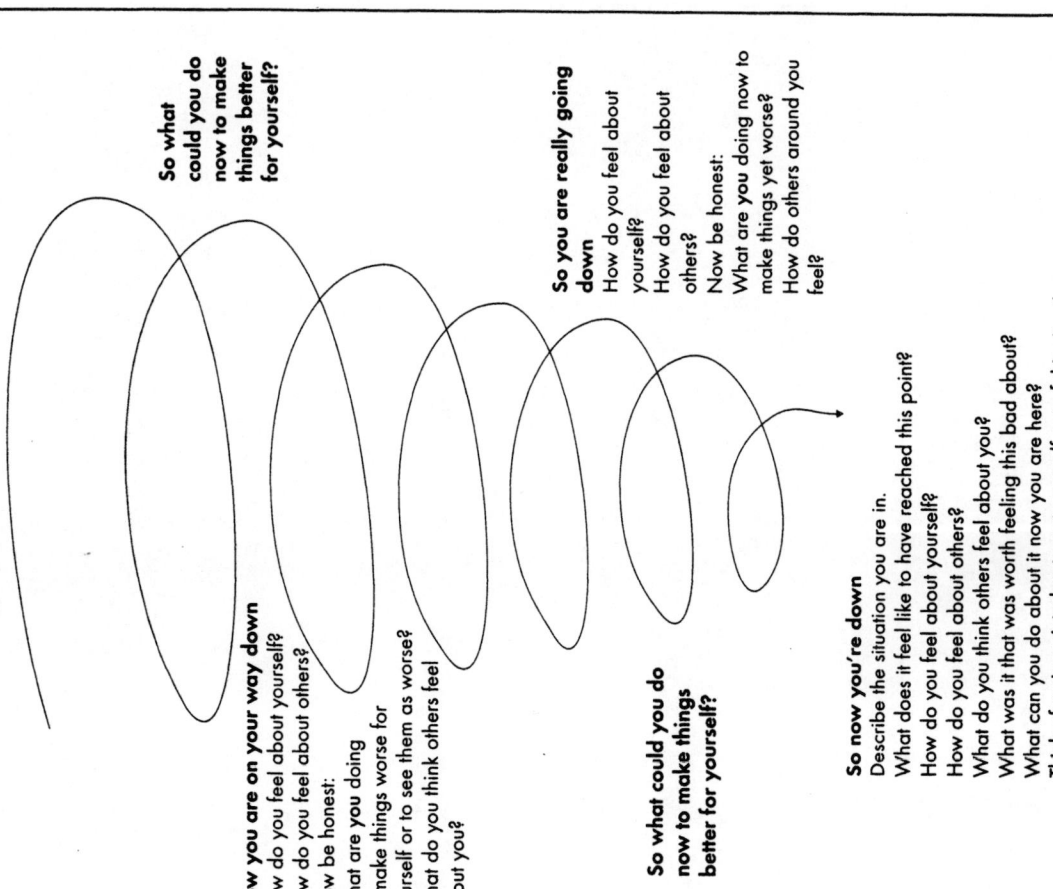

Handout PA10: Strategies for working with your future

There are four ways offered to help you think more clearly about what you would like in your future or how you might like an issue to be resolved.

These ways will help you to be clear about what you want to happen and how you want it to happen. This is a long way to getting what you want and where you want to be.

- scripting
- visualisation
- affirmations
- setting appropriate goals and being aware of positive qualities and strengths

1. Scripting – imagine what will happen in a situation. Think about what you would like to achieve. Consider what others may say and how you will reply. Write the script of the ideal outcome from your point of view and then use that script.

2. Visualisation – imagine what you would like in the future, how you would like something to be. Put in as many details as you can to make it feel as real as possible to you. Thinking in this way will help you to work out what changes you need to make and why you are making them. You have a clear picture of what you want to achieve.

3. Affirmations – find a statement which sums up what you want. Make it easy to remember and to repeat. Think about supporting the statement with images of what you want. Repeat your affirmation to yourself many times a day to remind yourself of what you want to do and what you can do.

4. Know your own strengths, what you need to do and what you can do. Decide on your goals and action steps and how you will get there. Work to your plan and check on your progress.

PA9: Goal setting

What triggers a spiral of low self-esteem?

What could you do to make the trigger less strong?

Who could help you?

List the things which you could do to avoid making the spiral worse

How will you do these things?

PA12: Your future

Describe in detail what you would like to achieve or to change

Which method will you use? How will you use it?

After a week
Describe your progress. What have you done? How did the method help you? What did you find difficult/hard?

What will you try next?

PA11: How might these situations be managed?

1. You have been going to a class to learn about creative writing. It is something you enjoy doing. Your work is praised by the tutor. You think it is something you can do in the future.

2. You are bored in your current job but you like working for a big company. Your boss has noticed you are interested in computers.

3. Your partner has recently left you. You are still feeling shocked and depressed. You have begun to give up going out and seeing friends.

4. An injury has made it impossible for you to carry on playing golf as well as you would like. This is getting you down. You miss the exercise, fresh air and the skill of the game.

5. You have seen an advert in the local paper for a new Sainsbury's superstore. You know you should apply but your confidence is low at the moment.

6. You and your partner have not been getting on very well. The relationship looks shaky, you are arguing a lot and your partner is very tense. It is making you stressed and bad tempered.

PA14: Relationships and communications

This checklist will help you to consider how good you are at getting on with different types of people and using your communication skills
✓ *which applies to you*

I get into a mess at work by not listening			
I don't listen to other's points of view very often			
I fly off the handle quickly			
I never really have a serious conversation with my partner			
I tell my kids what to do – I don't often listen to them			
I often interpret what people say as criticism			
I find it hard to talk to people I don't know			
I tend to want my own way and ride over other people			
I don't talk about my feelings			
I can hold my own in most situations			
I can't stand up for myself			
I have few real friends			
I often feel put down by people in authority			
I enjoy talking with my mates			
Situations often turn into conflict or hostility			
I don't manage myself very well with other people			
I am a good listener			
I am not phased by someone in authority			

PA13: Reminding myself

Key things to remember to do to help my self-esteem are:

Key things to avoid which damage my self-esteem are:

Four positive things about myself are:

Something positive I would say about myself is:

PA16: Planning ahead

_____

Assessment of strengths and areas to develop:

Main goals for action and reasons for action:

Action steps: what you would like to do

Start dates

Review date: _____ _____   Name: _____

PA15: Looking after myself

_____

I am good at looking after myself in these ways:

I would like to get better at looking after myself in these areas:

I am not so good at looking after myself in these ways – but I do not mind about this:

Food and nutrition

 The module is divided into eight sessions. These are:

1. The importance of food and the range of food types (2 hours 25 min)
2. Introducing nutrition (40 min)
3. Reasons for making changes in eating habits (45 min)
4. Food hygiene lecture (1 hour)
5. Food hygiene quiz (40 min)
6. Consolidation and making changes (1 hour)
7. Safe ways of working in the kitchen (20 min)
8. Practical cookery sessions (suggestions for five 1 hour sessions)

 The trainer could link work in this module to that on Exercise and well-being and to DIY: improving your appearance.

 The module makes use of the training and learning activities of:

- brainstorming
- working in pairs
- information giving, including use of handouts
- discussion
- planning changes
- an end of session quiz
- practical cookery activities

Trainer's notes

This module aims to help learners to be more:

- aware of the importance of food and good nutrition
- aware of food hygiene
- able to understand why they should want to makes changes to their diet and handling of food and how to do so
- able to cook simple and nutritious food and to do so safely

A potential difficulty for trainers working in residential settings may be that learners have little control over what they can eat and they may become highly critical of the quality and quantity of the food they are given. The trainer must be aware of these dangers, deflect criticisms and consider practical ways in which improvements may be made in the learners' current situations. The trainer should spend time stressing the importance of the work for more independent living in the future and the value of taking control over those aspects of diet which can be influenced now, for example the types of snacks which are eaten, the value of not overeating and taking sufficient water each day. If a criticism is that food handlers engage in unhygienic practices, then the trainer may suggest to the appropriate authority that a food handling course is offered to those people handling food.

The practical work

The module offers information and the chances for the learners to consider the type of foods they eat and how they may improve their diet, it also offers of opportunities to consider the safe handling of food. These learning opportunities are valuable in themselves. These sessions conclude with consolidation and planning changes exercises. The remainder of the module offers some suggestions for practical cookery activities. This will be enjoyable and is a chance to bring a number of the lessons about food values, the importance of a balance of foodstuffs and hygienic handling of food to life. The practical working with food will give the chance to immediately implement the session based learning. It will give opportunities for the learners to consider food purchase and the use and saving of foodstuffs as part of practical budgeting.

But please check that:
- you have the authority to undertake such work
- you have been cleared by your line manager to do the work
- you are trained to manage the health and safety issues and
- you are trained to train the learners how to use equipment

As a trainer you will need to be confident in the cookery room. Ensure that you know the rules governing the safe keeping of tools. If a learner has to leave the group for another activity ensure that all tools are present. Keep potentially dangerous tools locked away when they are not needed. As a trainer you will need to be able to practice all that which you will have taught the learners about the safe keeping of food and managing foodstuffs and preparation areas in a hygienic way.

You will need to consider beforehand how to manage the practical cooking sessions, to be clear about the training which the learners may need in using the equipment and what if any training records they will need to sign. You will need to be clear about the budget you are working within and to have ready assembled the foodstuffs needed for the session. You will need to be clear about the types of rules which are important for the kitchen and to be able to work towards an agreement about these with the learners before they begin any practical work. Finally, you will need to be clear that you can manage the group in this learning setting, that your instruction giving skills are high, that you are able to stop the group if you need to and are able to change activities if that is necessary.

There are five practical sessions. Each one lasts about an hour. This includes:
- preparation time
- costing the food stuffs
- explanations about the techniques used
- explanations about how left-over food may be stored and re-used
- proper clearing away
- cooking and eating the dish

Where the practical session cannot be completed, the recipes can be discussed and some of the learning points drawn from the activity.

Session One: The importance of food and the range of food types

Brainstorm (15 min)

This brainstorm is designed to highlight for learners the importance of food in our lives. Ask the learners to suggest:

> **What are the main things which we need to live?**

You may be surprised at the types of suggestions which the learners offer – money, alcohol, drugs etc. They may take some time to come round to ideas of food, air, water. You can ask the group to prioritise the five most important things. It may be that they take food and other essential items for granted. If this is the case ask the learners to consider what all types of life, i.e. human and animal, needs to sustain itself.

The five items which the learners should eventually have are:
- food
- air
- water
- shelter
- appropriate temperature

Once such a list has been generated on the flipchart discuss how quickly the learners considered food. Move to the next brainstorm:

Brainstorm (15 min)
Ask the learners:

> **Is knowing about food and nutrition important? If so, why?**

Check that the learners understand the meaning of nutrition. Again, encourage as many ideas as possible, record on the flipchart and leave these visible during the course of the module. You will want to refer back to this list in Session Five.

Learners may mention health, growth of babies and children, enjoyment of food, appearance (certain vitamins are connected with the maintenance of healthy skin), controlling weight, having energy and feeling good about oneself. Some learners may know that aspects of certain lifestyles have an impact on the body's ability to benefit from nutrition. For example, heavy drinking interferes with the absorption of calcium.

Good nutrition can make us feel better, increase our lifespan, and help to avoid certain illnesses and diseases. Everyone will know that vitamin C helps to fight off colds, and some may mention that a good intake of fibre will help to prevent cancer of the bowel. Explain that some of these issues will be considered later in the module.

Considering food

1. Pair work: favourite foods (15 min)
Ask the learners to work in pairs to make two lists, one of their favourite meals (e.g. fish and chips) and the other of their favourite foodstuffs (e.g. chocolate). They should each make five suggestions for each list. If they have time they should write down the reasons for the meal or the type of foodstuff being a favourite one for them.

Once this has been done, ask each person to highlight their most favourite meal and their very favourite food.

Group feedback (10 min)
Quickly go round the room asking for examples of the most favourite meals and foods. Record these on the flipchart. Ensure that the lists generated by learners are kept safely as these will be needed in a subsequent activity.

The range of foods (15 min)
Ask the learners to look at the lists on the flipchart and to think about the range of different types or categories of foodstuffs. Ask the learners if they can name any. Stress that at this stage you are interested in types of foods not in the things which can be derived from food like protein and carbohydrates. Some learners, especially those keen on exercise may know a lot about the components of foodstuffs and their uses. Encourage these learners to let others have the opportunity to raise their awareness of food and not dominate the session.

Reach the point where a list of six types of foodstuffs have been created. This list should cover:

1. fruits
2. meat, nuts, eggs, poultry, fish, dry beans
3. vegetables
4. bread, pasta, rice, cereal
5. milk, cheese, yoghurt, cream, butter
6. fats, oils, sugars

Analysing learners' favourite foods
Ask the learners to work alone using the lists of their favourite meals (30 min)
1. Ask each learner to consider two meals which they would like to have in any one day.
2. Ask them to list out the types of food groups into which their two favoured meals fall.
3. Ask them to consider how much of each type of food group is represented by the two meals.

They should then fill in **FN1** for their two favourite meals. They should use space 6 for the most often eaten foodstuff in any one day and working up to space 1 for the least eaten foodstuff which is in their two favourite meals. The learners may have some of the numbered spaces as blanks.

Group then pair work (30 min)
Handout **FN2** which is a completed food pyramid showing the amounts of each type of food which are needed daily. Go through the food pyramid with the learners. Ask them if they are surprised about any of the amounts of the different types of food. Then ask them to work in pairs to decide:

1. What they should add to their diet to balance it and to suggest how they will do this.
2. What they should remove from their diet to balance it.

Feedback (15 min)
Work round the pairs asking the learners to list those things they need to add and those they need to take out from their diets. Record these on the flipchart. Ask the learners what they have learned from the activity and what, if anything, has surprised them.

Session Two: Introducing nutrition

 Trainer's note

Different types of food meet our different nutritional needs. For example, some give us protein which helps us with growth when we are children and repair of body tissue throughout life. Other types of food are rich in minerals which can be used for such things as bone and haemoglobin formation. These activities below will help to alert the learner to the reasons why they need to have a properly balanced diet and to consider meeting the demands of the food pyramid when planning meals.

Brainstorm (20 min)
Another way to look at foods is to think about them in terms of the type of nutrition which they are able to offer us. Ask if learners can suggest what these might be. Write these on flipchart paper, using one sheet for each heading. Ask for examples and write lists under the headings (e.g. Carbohydrates). The lists you write need not use the same wording as suggested below, and need not have so many examples.

1. Carbohydrates   bread, cereal, rice and pasta
2. Proteins   meat, fish, eggs, cheese, milk, yoghurt and nuts, dry beans, Quorn
3. Vitamins   present in many foods including fruit, yeast and wholemeal bread

4. Minerals   present in protein foods and others

5. Fats   present in oils and fats (e.g. butter) as well as in meat, cheese etc.

6. Water   present in all liquids and in most foods

Information giving (10 min)
Give out handout FN3 and work through this with learners to ensure understanding.

Pair work (10 min)
Ask learners in pairs to look back at the food pyramid (FN2) and work out which types of nutrition everybody should have and in which proportions each day.

 Trainer's notes

A balanced diet must contain roughly 20% protein, 20% fat and 60% carbohydrate and an adequate amount of water. Some of the learners may be confused about the need for 20% fat when the food pyramid says that fats and oils should be used sparingly. This is because so many foodstuffs are high in fat; e.g. cheese and some meats.

Session Three: Reasons for making changes in eating habits

Pair work (10 min)
Ask the group to work in pairs to consider the changes they might make to their diets as a result of their work so far. Ask the pairs to record the changes they would make on a piece of flipchart paper. Once they have had 10–15 minutes, ask one from each pair to present their conclusions to the group and pin up their piece of flipchart paper.

If the group becomes stuck or the learners are not sure, then try to tease out some of the learning points to date.

Information giving and discussion (35 min)
Ensure that the following have been covered. This can be done as a question and answer session. For example, the trainer may have to supply the main heading (e.g. less fat) and can then ask the group how changes could be made.

Eating less fat, especially saturated fat
Half-fat cheese can be bought; cottage cheese or Edam can be eaten instead of the higher fat cheeses such as Cheddar and Stilton; semi-skimmed or skimmed milk can be used instead of full-fat milk. Use polyunsaturate margarine instead of butter. Visible fat can be cut off meat before cooking. The skin should be removed from poultry, as most of the fat will come away with it. Avoid higher fat meats such as hamburgers and pork pies. Buy less, and leaner meat, for meat dishes and add pulses and other vegetables. Have fewer chips. Eat low fat yoghurt instead of cream.

Eating more fibre
Wholemeal bread, fruit, pulses, vegetables and cereals. Substitute half wholemeal flour for ordinary flour when baking. Choose wholegrain cereals. Try eating cereal without sugar and use a banana or dried fruit to sweeten it. Make use of peas, beans and other pulses (including baked beans). These are cheap, high in fibre. Eating jacket potatoes, unsalted nuts, dried fruits and wholemeal bread will increase fibre intake.

Eating less salt
Too much salt has been linked to heart disease so use less salt when cooking and to flavour food use lemon juice, herbs, spices or mustard instead of salt. Cut down on salty snacks, such as

crisps and nuts. Look at the labels on canned and packet foods and do not buy those that have a lot of salt.

Eating less sugar

Cut down, or stop taking sugar in tea and coffee. Use unsweetened fruit drinks, and low calorie soft drinks. Choose fresh fruit rather than fruit canned in syrup. Cut down on sweets, biscuits, cakes and chocolate. Use less sugar in cooking, this may not work in all recipes, eg. jams and meringues. Read the labels on tins and jars and don't buy those foods which are high in sugar.

Eating sensibly

Eat breakfast. Eat healthy snacks, e.g. not crisps or peanuts. Don't eat your last meal of the day after 7pm.

The learners can be given FN4 as a handout to remind them about some of the changes they might like to make to their diet.

Session Four: Food hygiene

 Trainer's note

The information on the next few pages can be supplemented with other materials which you have. However, these notes should be sufficient to enable you to deliver a useful and factual talk to ensure safe food handling by preventing the spread of bacteria. Depending on the group, you could ask them to take free notes during your talk or to fill in spaces in pre-prepared notes which you have made for them. There is a quiz which you can use after you have given the talk and revised its key points to ensure that the learners have understood and absorbed what you have said.

Keeping yourself healthy, keeping food safe – managing bacteria in the kitchen

Before starting, ask the group if they know what bacteria are.

Bacteria are microscopic organisms. Some are harmful and some are not. Some are essential for our health. They live everywhere – in the air, on and in people and animals, on food and in soil as well as in water. When thinking about food hygiene, we are thinking about the bacteria that spoil food and cause illnesses. For example, diarrhoea and vomiting and in severe cases death by food poisoning.

Ask the group if any of them have had food poisoning, and if so to describe what it was like.

We can take several simple measures to avoid becoming ill.

Ask if anyone in the group knows what these measures might be.

Measures to manage bacteria

1. *Store food correctly.* That is in fridges or freezers set at the correct temperatures, i.e. fridges under 5°c and freezers between –18°c and –25°c.

    Also ensure that all food is covered. Do not store food in tins in the fridge. Ensure that raw meat cannot drip onto food stored below it (this won't happen if all food is covered or kept in plastic containers). Bacteria is not killed by low temperatures, but merely remains dormant. Some bacteria is killed by very high temperatures above 63°c but some bacteria are able to produce spores which can survive high temperatures.

2. **Bacteria need** four things to survive. *Ask the group if they know what these four things might be.* These are:
   - warmth
   - food
   - moisture/water
   - time

These also help them to multiply.

Our systems can usually cope with small numbers of potentially harmful bacteria, but the danger increases as the number of bacteria increase. A single bacteria can multiply by dividing itself into two. It can do this every ten minutes. You can work out the sum on calculators, but roughly a million bacteria can be produced from a single bacteria in about three and a half hours.

Bacteria love high protein foods such as meat and cooked rice, but they can live on damp teatowels and in water.

The best temperature for bacteria is 37°c, but they can still live and grow between 10°c and 60°c.

Ask learners why 37°c is familiar – it is the temperature of the human body.

3. **The main sources of bacteria are ...**

   Ask the learners if they know any sources of bacteria.

   The main sources of bacteria are: humans, raw food, animals, insects and the environment. These are discussed below.

   a. Humans by touching ears, nose, skin, hair, mouth, coughing, sneezing, rubbish, animals, etc. or using the toilet and then handling food without washing hands.

   It is no use thinking that washing your hands does not matter for you and your family as you share germs. The bacteria you spread from touching your hair and so on, will not be harming you where it is, but will harm you once it is allowed to grow in food. The bacteria are not yours, they merely live on you. Once they are allowed to grow in food they can cause serious illness and even death.

   Do not lick your fingers while cooking, or breathe on glasses to make them shine, or smoke over food while cooking it. If you have cuts, spots or pimples, these must be covered. A sneeze can propel droplets 20 feet.

   b. Raw food must be stored correctly, and be kept separate from cooked food.

   c. Animals must not be allowed access to food that is intended for people, or to food preparation surfaces or equipment.

   d. Insects must be kept away from food, as must rats, mice, birds etc. Again proper storage is needed.

   e. The environment must be kept clean. Bacteria are found in soil so vegetables etc. must be thoroughly washed; as bacteria also live in the air, food must be covered.

   Bacteria cannot move by themselves they need help from humans, animals, the environment or insects. The trainer should stress this.

4. *Washing your hands* is most important. Hands should be washed in hot water, using a nail brush and ensuring that they are clean between the fingers and on their backs, before and after touching any food. They should also be washed after touching rubbish, using the toilet, combing or touching your hair, touching animals, before you start to cook, no matter what you have been doing and so on. Keep nails short and towels clean and dry (bacteria live on damp towels). Using paper towels is ideal as these are thrown away.

5. *As bacteria can also live in the environment* keep cloths, surfaces, equipment etc. clean. After cleaning use a sanitiser, especially if there are small children or elderly people in the house. Keep rubbish covered. Clear up any spillages immediately. Use a dishwasher if possible as these wash at higher temperatures than hand washing up. If washing up by hand, use water as hot as possible, rinse and air dry the dishes.

   Do not store food on the ground. Keep food in sealed containers. Watch for mice, signs of which may be gnawed food, spillages or droppings.

6. *Keep food at the correct temperatures* and observe the rule of food rotation – in fridges first in, first out. Ensure that fridges and freezers are defrosted and cleaned, not forgetting door seals. Do not overstock fridges or freezers as this will prevent the movement of cold air and the temperature will increase. Do not put hot food in fridges as this raises the temperature of the fridge and thus damage food.

7. *Defrost all food thoroughly before using.* When cooking, e.g. poultry use a thermometer to ensure that joints of meat are cooking at a high enough temperature in the middle.

   Revise with the learners the four things bacteria need for growth and how to stop each of them.

Session Five: Food hygiene quiz

 Trainer's note

When you are confident that your learners have had the best possible opportunity to absorb and understand the information you have offered, then work through with them the quiz which appears as FN5. You should take 20 minutes to administer the quiz and to allow them time to write the answers on their FN5. The answers are printed below. Spend a further 20 minutes going through the answers with the group relating them back to the talk you have given.

1. *What are bacteria?*
    Bacteria are organisms so small that you need a microscope to see them.

2. *Where do bacteria live?*
    Everywhere – in the air, on and in people and animals, on food, in water and in soil.

3. *Are bacteria harmful?*
    Some are and some are not.

4. *Can you name a use that humans have for bacteria?*
    Making cheese, beer, bread, yoghurt etc.

5. *What harm can bacteria do?*
    Spoil food and cause illness

6. *How can we kill bacteria?*
    Cleaning and sanitising and very high temperatures.

7. *At what temperature should fridges be set and why*
Below 5°C as at this temperature bacteria are dormant (asleep), but this does not kill them. They 'wake up' once the food is at room temperature again.

8. *What are the main sources of harmful bacteria? (Name three)*
The main sources are humans, animals, insects, raw food, and the environment.

9. *Name three things that should not be done when handling food.*
There are many. For example, sneezing, touching hair, leaving food uncovered and out of the fridge, storing raw and cooked foods together, not washing hands after using the toilet and so on.

10. *What groups of people are especially susceptible to food poisoning?*
Babies, the very old and anyone who is unwell.

Session Six: Consolidation and making changes

Pulling the threads together (20 min)
Working as a group, ask the learners to review what they have learned about:
- types of foodstuffs
- the nutritional value of different foods and combinations they should eat
- ways to better look after themselves
- ways to avoid food poisoning.

Ask the group to suggest five things under each heading in order to create a group summary of the learning so far. Compare the summary sheet with the second group brainstorm exercise. Is knowing about food and nutrition important? If so why? Stress how much learning has taken place.

Planning personal changes (15 min)
Ask the learners to work on their own with worksheet FN6. Check that each person understands what is required of them before they start working and check on individual progress during the 15 minutes.

Group feedback (25 min)
1. Ask for some volunteers to suggest the changes they will make, why they will make them and how. Record these on the flipchart.

2. Check to see if the group can think of any other ways in which changes can be made and maintained.

3. Find out if anyone in the group had problems in thinking about how to make the changes they wanted to make. Record these on the flipchart. Ask the group to offer suggestions to overcome these problems.

4. Finally, check that the group knows what pitfalls or problems they make face in making dietary and food handling changes. Ask the group to work with you on a brainstorming exercise. Draw up a list on the flipchart paper, as below. Ensure that for every problem discussed, that the group can come up with some solutions and can suggest reasons for not going back to past practices. The flipchart list might look thus:

Problems	Reasons to make changes/ solutions to problems
Easier to get take-aways	Wasteful of money; high fat content... Learn how to make a few good, simple meals
Like fish and chips	High fat; expensive. Balance a meal of fish and chips every now and again with healthy, home-made and cheaper food
Can't cook where I live	Think about making meals which do not involve cooking, e.g. salads, nutritious sandwiches
Cleaning materials are expensive	Not to buy cleaning materials is to put your health at risk
Buy supermarket brands and when on special offer
Buy just washing-up liquid and bleach

Session Seven: Safe ways of working in the kitchen

 Trainer's notes

Before cooking with your group, work with them to devise a set of sensible rules for the kitchen. If you are not confident that they understand the rules and will abide by them, *do not* risk allowing them to work in the kitchen.

Pair work (10 min)

Ask learners to work in pairs to devise 'Ten commandments' for working in the cookery area or kitchen.

These may include:
- not running
- clearing up as you go along
- leaving the room clean and tidy
- taking turns to use the equipment, not pushing and shoving
- listening to instructions on the safe use of equipment, and signing to say that they have understood
- using all equipment for the purpose for which it is intended. For example, using oven gloves to remove articles from the oven, rather than using a teatowel
- washing hands before cooking
- keeping raw and cooked food separate. Washing knives, boards, surfaces, etc. immediately after using on raw food
- correct use of all tools. Carrying knives point downwards, ensuring saucepan handles are placed safely, etc.

As a group, discuss and agree the ten rules (10 min)

Manage the feedback in order to arrive at the ten rules you want, including rules that are specific to your place of work. Once these rules have been agreed, they should be displayed in a prominent place. If it seems appropriate, ask each learner to sign a copy of the rules.

Session Eight: Practical cookery sessions

 Trainer's notes

The following sessions cover:

- meals with little cooking
- a soup
- two main meals
- two puddings

You should emphasise the appropriate storage of leftover foods, or the importance of throwing certain things away. You should ensure that the learners work out the approximate cost of the meal which they have prepared. Where possible, contrast the cost of home-made food with a ready-made or take-away meal. Again, where possible, consider with the learners the reasons for the higher nutritional value of home prepared food.

Meals with little cooking

Russian salad:	using leftover vegetables 2 cupfuls cold, cooked mixed vegetables, e.g. peas, beans, carrots, potatoes, turnips

First: Chop the onion. Chop cold vegetables
Second: Mix onion, mayonnaise and cold mixed vegetables
Third: Sprinkle with parsley and serve

Coleslaw:	1 small white cabbage	1 small onion
	1 medium carrot	$^1/_2$ cup mayonnaise
	sea salt and freshly ground black pepper	

First: Grate the cabbage and carrot and finely slice and chop the onion with a sharp knife
Second: Season with sea salt and black pepper and mix in the mayonnaise

This is a much cheaper option than buying pre-made coleslaw. It is fresh and of greater nutritional value.

Grated carrot salad:	2 large carrots	1 orange
	sea salt and freshly ground black pepper	
	$^1/_2$ tablespoon olive oil	

First: Grate the carrots finely and season with salt and freshly ground pepper
Second: Cut one half of the orange into slices and extract the juice from the other
Third: Dress the carrots with a few drops of olive oil and the freshly squeezed orange juice
Fourth: Mix to spread the dressing through the carrots

These salads can be served with:

- cheese
- cold meats
- cold eggs
- cold pies (beware fat content)

The following Greek salad has cheese already incorporated.

Greek salad:
1 large green pepper	2 oz (55g) olives
2 large firm tomatoes	soft white or Feta cheese
1 large onion	oil and vinegar dressing

First: In a salad bowl make layers of sliced green pepper, tomatoes and onion
Second: Add a few olives and top with some soft white cheese (cottage or curd cheese, or Feta cheese)
Third: Dress with olive oil and a little vinegar or lemon juice

The following are quick economical foods and may be used with the salads.

Stuffed eggs:
4 eggs	2 oz (55g) black olives
1 oz (30g) butter	1 tablespoon parsley, chopped
$\frac{1}{2}$ teaspoon cayenne pepper	1 tablespoon pimentos
Juice of $\frac{1}{2}$ lemon	4 slices wholemeal bread
1 tablespoon grated cheese	

First: Hard boil the eggs and when quite cool slice in half lengthways
Second: Remove the yolk and pound with butter, salt, cayenne pepper, lemon juice, grated cheese, and the stoned and finely chopped olives
Third: Pile back into the whites and decorate with a little chopped parsley and pimentos
Fourth: Serve on a croûton of toast spread with the leftover filling

Herb potato cakes:
The herbs can be selected to taste. Use for example parsley, chives, tarragon, chervil and thyme.

1lb (455g) potatoes	wholemeal flour
butter	1 egg, beaten with 2 tablespoons milk
sea salt and freshly ground pepper	wholemeal breadcrumbs
3 tablespoons fresh herbs	

First: Boil the potatoes or use leftover potatoes. Mix with butter. Season with salt, pepper and finely chopped herbs
Second: Form the mashed potato into flat cakes
Third: When reasonably firm dust with flour, dip in the beaten egg and milk mixture and cover with breadcrumbs. Fry in a little vegetable oil until golden and serve immediately

A soup

Lentil and carrot soup:
25g butter	salt and pepper to taste
1 medium onion	2 teaspoons lemon juice
1 clove garlic	about 150ml milk
2 carrots (100g)	parsley (optional)
2 sticks celery	150g red lentils
1 litre vegetable stock	

First: Peel and chop onion and carrots
Second: Heat butter in pan and gently fry onion and garlic for about 5 minutes with the lid on
Third: Add carrots and lentils and stir for a few minutes. Add stock. Cover pan and cook gently for about 40 minutes

Fourth:	Liquidise. Pour back into a saucepan
Fifth:	Add lemon juice and thin with milk. Season with salt and freshly ground black pepper
Sixth:	Add a little chopped parsley, if liked

Learning points:
1. What value as a food stuff do lentils have?
2. What could be used instead of a liquidiser?

Main meals

Chicken curry:

1 onion	1 clove garlic
1 tablespoon vegetable oil	2 chicken breasts
1 eating apple	2 teaspoons ground ginger
2 tablespoons curry powder	1 pint stock
1 pint apple juice	1 tablespoon sultanas
1 pinch salt	freshly ground black pepper
1 tablespoon desiccated coconut (optional)	

First:	Chop the onion and fry in oil with garlic – cook gently
Second:	Skin the chicken and slice in thin (5cm) strips. Peel apple and quarter, removing the core and then cut into 5mm cubes. Add the curry powder and ginger to the pan of onions and garlic and stir well. Add chicken, apple and apple juice, stock, sultanas and coconut if using. Stir well
Third:	Turn up the heat until mixture bubbles, cover with lid and simmer for 20 minutes, stirring occasionally. Remove lid and simmer for 5 more minutes, stirring occasionally. Add salt and pepper to taste
Fourth:	Prepare rice. Bring water to boiling point and add rice. A mug of rice will give two generous portions. Brown rice has more vitamins and fibre but takes longer to cook, about 30 minutes, easycook white rice takes about 10 minutes

Variations:
Vegetarians can use Quorn or potatoes and a mugful of lentils instead of chicken; other meats can be used.

Learning points:
1. Check with the learners how they would store any leftover curry – when would they refrigerate it? What would they do with the rice?
2. Ask the learners to cost this meal and compare it with a take-away curry or prepared and frozen curry and rice from a supermarket.
3. Why would the chicken skin be removed?

Tuna Pasta:
(serves two)

100g (4oz) pasta	1 medium onion, chopped
200g (8oz) tin tuna in brine	1 clove garlic, chopped
oil for frying	75g (3oz) mushrooms, chopped
1 glass white wine and water mixed	2 sticks celery, chopped
$^1/_2$ teaspoon dried mixed herbs	1 small tin tomatoes
pepper and salt to taste	

First:	Boil water and then cook pasta as directed on the packet. Once cooked take from heat.
Second:	Chop onions and garlic and fry in oil until soft.
Third:	Cook chopped celery and mushrooms with small tin tomatoes, wine, water and herbs. Simmer gently do not boil juice away.

Fourth:	Once celery is soft add tuna, salt and pepper to taste. heat for five minutes.
Fifth:	Mix with pre-cooked pasta. Heat both pasta and tuna together until hot.
Sixth:	Serve with salad

Variations:
Chopped ham rather than tuna can be used.

Learning points:
1. Cost this dish with one similar purchased from a supermarket. Consider benefits other than cost to home-made dish.
2. What happens if six people are to be served? Compare cost of home-made and pre-bought dishes.
3. What food value is there in this meal?

Puddings

Apple crumble:	675g or 5 dessert apples	1 teacup flour
	2–3 tablespoons sugar	1 teacup rolled oats
	1 handful raisins or sultanas (optional)	
	$\frac{1}{2}$ teaspoon ground cinnamon(optional)	
	2 heaped tablespoons soft vegetable margarine	

First:	Preheat the oven to 190°c/375°F/Gas 5. Boil a mugful of water in a pan. Peel, remove core and chop apple. Add to the pan and boil, then cover and simmer for four minutes.
Second:	Place flour and margarine in a bowl and rub in the margarine. Add the oats and one tablespoon of the sugar.
Third:	Remove the apples from the heat and stir in one tablespoon of the sugar. Taste and add more sugar, if needed. Stir in raisins or sultanas.
Fourth:	Place apple mixture in a pie dish and sprinkle over the flour mixture. Bake for 15–20 minutes until brown.

Serve with custard, using custard powder and low fat milk, or with yoghurt, not cream.

Spiced bananas:	2 bananas	brown sugar
	lemon juice	cinnamon powder

First:	Cut each banana lengthways and lay on a piece of foil which has been lightly rubbed with low fat margarine to prevent sticking
Second:	Squeeze some lemon juice and sprinkle some brown sugar and cinnamon over each banana. Fold foil over the bananas
Third:	Bake the parcels in a preheated oven, Gas Mark 4 (180°C/350°F) for 25 minutes
Fourth:	Serve in the foil

FN2: The food guide pyramid

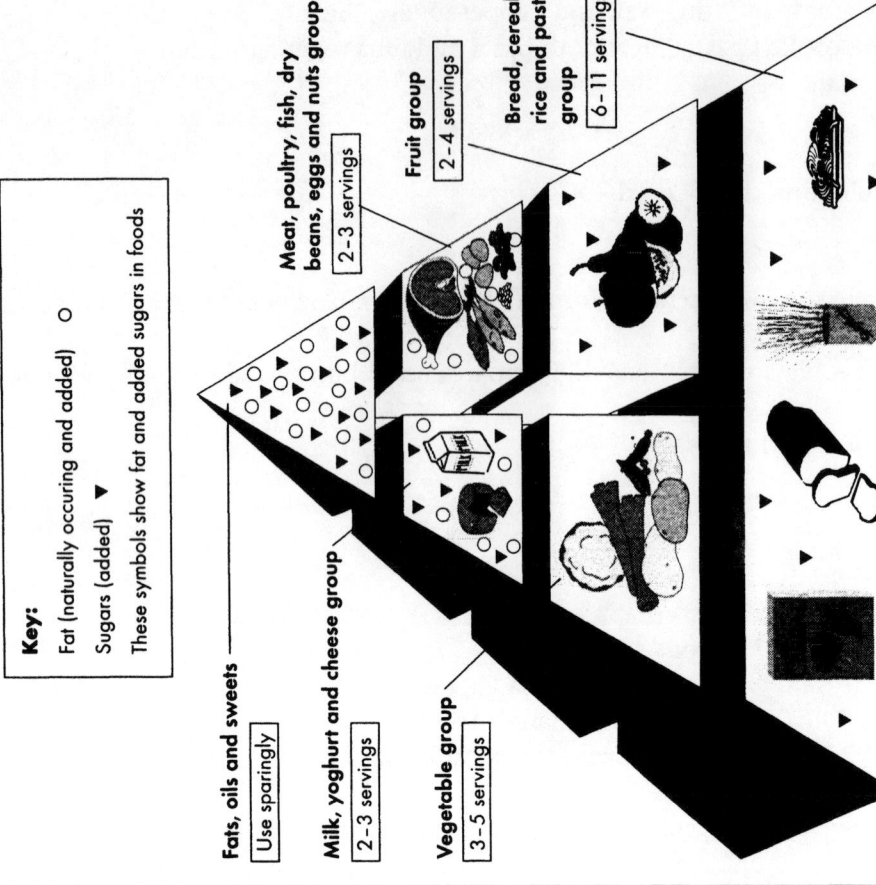

Key:

Fat (naturally occuring and added) ○

Sugars (added) ▼

These symbols show fat and added sugars in foods

Fats, oils and sweets
Use sparingly

Milk, yoghurt and cheese group
2–3 servings

Meat, poultry, fish, dry beans, eggs and nuts group
2–3 servings

Fruit group
2–4 servings

Vegetable group
3–5 servings

Bread, cereal, rice and pasta group
6–11 servings

Daily serving sizes:

Dairy group: 2 oz processed cheese, 1 cup (8 oz) milk, 1 cup yoghurt, 1.5 oz natural cheese, 2 oz cottage cheese (low fat)

Vegetable group: 1 cup raw leafy veg, 1/2 cup other veg, 3/4 cup veg juice

Protein group: 1 egg, 2-3 oz lean fish, meat or poultry, 1/2 cup cooked dried beans

Fruit group: 1 med apple, pear, orange or peach, 1/2 cup tinned or cooked fruit

Grains group: 1 slice bread, 1 oz ready to eat cereals, 1/2 cup cooked cereal, pasta rice

---

FN1: Types of foods eaten in two meals

1.

2.

3.

4.

5.

6.

Fill in the pyramid by putting the food type you would eat most of in a day in space 6 and the food type you eat least in space 1

FN3: Nutritional groups

1. **Carbohydrates** – bread, cereal, rice and pasta

2. **Proteins** – meat, fish, eggs, cheese, milk, yoghurt and nuts, dry beans, quorn

3. **Vitamins**

Vitamin	Deficiency effects	Source
A (fat soluble)	Poor skin, night blindness	Green vegetables, milk, butter, fish liver oils
B (thiamin)	Disorders of the nervous system, muscular atrophy	Yeast, wholemeal bread, peas and beans
B2 (riboflavin)	Disorders of the skin and digestive system	Yeast, meat, milk, liver, eggs
B12 (cobalamin)	Pernicious anaemia	Liver, fish, eggs
C (ascorbic acid)	Scurvy – internal bleeding, swelling of gums	Citrus fruits and vegetables
D	Rickets – bones soften and become pliable	Fish liver oils, eggs, butter. Formed by the action of sunlight on skin
E	Embryo fails to develop	Wheatgerm oil, eggs, liver, green vegetables
K	Failure of blood to clot	Dark green vegetables

4. **Minerals** (there are more than the examples on the list below)

Mineral	Use	Source
Calcium	Bone formation	Cheese, milk, bread
Magnesium	Formation of bones and teeth	Most foods
Zinc	Formation of insulin	A trace element in plants
Iron	Formation of haemoglobin	Liver, kidney and eggs
Flourine	Formation of tooth enamel	A trace element in water

5. **Fats** – Provide energy and insulation for organs. Fat can be stored under the skin. Fat is found in butter, lard, cheese, suet, fish oil.

6. **Water** – Dissolves foods, and is needed for chemical reactions in the body. Water is found in all liquids and most foods.

FN4: Nutrition notes for learners

1. Eat foods in the proportions recommended by the Food Pyramid.

2. Many favourite foods, for example spaghetti bolognese, are low in fat and healthy. Eating higher-fat foods such as fish and chips, bacon and eggs is all right in moderation.

3. If possible, always eat breakfast to fuel your body for the day. Try to eat regular meals as this will make unhealthy snacking less likely. (Unhealthy snacks are likely to be high in fats and sugar, eg crisps and sweets. Some snacks are healthy, eg dried and fresh fruit.)

4. If possible, sit and eat at a table to aid digestion and to help your body to absorb the full nutritional value of your food. Try to avoid eating as you move about.

5. Ensure that you eat enough fibre. This is essential as it is used in the bowel to absorb water and to aid in expelling waste products from the body. To avoid constipation and to keep fit and healthy it is recommended that we eat plenty of fibre. Keeping your bowels working well, will help to avoid cancer of the large bowel. Fibre is found in wholemeal bread, brown rice, peas and beans (particularly the skins) potatoes and root vegetables and green vegetables and fruit.

6. Eat more bread and potatoes. They are high in fibre, relatively low in fat and cost little. Eat fruit and/or vegetables daily.

7. Eat wholefoods wherever possible. For example, eat wholemeal bread rather than white bread. Wholefoods are higher in fibre and have better nutritional value than processed foods.

8. Drink as much water as you want. Try to drink between six and eight glasses every day.

9. Learn to stop eating when you have had enough. Don't just keep eating to clear your plate, or to please someone else.

FN6: Taking control over my diet and well being

The positives and negatives about what I eat and how I make food:

The changes I want to make:	Why I want to make those changes:

The main change goals

Goal 1

Goal 2

Action steps	Date for starting

Success in Goal 1 means:

Success in Goal 2 means:

FN5: Food hygiene quiz

1. What are bacteria?

2. Where do bacteria live?

3. Are bacteria harmful?

4. Can you name a use that humans have for bacteria?

5. What harm can bacteria do?

6. How can we kill bacteria?

7. At what temperature should fridges be set and why?

8. What are the main sources of harmful bacteria? (name three)

9. Name three things that should not be done when handling food.

10. What groups of people are especially susceptible to food poisoning?

Exercise and well-being

The module is divided as follows:

Exercise

1. Introduction (1 hour 40 min)
2. The importance of exercise (2 hours 20 min)
3. Exercising (2 hours 10 min)

Well-being

4. Raising awareness and improving personal well-being (1 hour 15 min)
5. Sleep (1 hour 15 min)
6. Relaxation (1 hour)
7. Well-being in the round (1 hour 40 min)
8. Closing session (50 min)

 This module links with those on stress, positive attitudes and food and nutrition.

 ## Trainer's notes

This module aims to help learners to understand the importance of exercise and well-being. Exercise will help the learner to:

- gain or maintain good self-esteem
- feel good about themselves
- have more energy
- feel in more control of themselves
- look good
- prepare for employment
- make a good impression on others
- manage stress more effectively
- improve their body functioning, e.g. heart, lungs and metabolism
- lose weight

The well-being part of the module will help the learner to consider their lifestyle and perhaps make changes to increase their level of well-being.

Groundrules

The trainer and group participants need to be sensitive to people's feelings when discussing body size, shape and fitness. Allow those who wish to volunteer opinions and experiences to do so, but do not push others too hard. It is important to work with the group before commencing the first exercise in order to agree group groundrules. For example, not making personal comments to, or about, other group members and respecting confidentiality.

Resources

For collage work, magazines, newspaper supplements, basic art materials such as felt pens, crayons, scissors, paste, A1 and A3 paper, need to be available.

A word of caution

This module should only be used if you feel confident with the material.

Be sure to stress that if anyone has a medical condition (diabetes, a heart condition, a bad back and so on) they *must consult their doctor* before taking exercise. Also be sure to stress that learners must stop an exercise if they are in pain. The expression 'no pain – no gain' is worse than nonsense, it is damaging.

If learners intend to walk/jog/run outside ensure that they are familiar with the necessity of wearing supporting running shoes and suitable clothing both for their comfort (that is natural fibres such as cotton) and to ensure that they are visible to motorists. Running with a personal stereo can be dangerous as traffic will not be heard.

The work on devising exercise programmes should only be undertaken if the trainer understands what is involved or can arrange for a fitness expert to be in attendance.

Session One: Introduction

Introduction and groundrules (30 min)

Once groundrules have been established, explain the contents of the module to the learners and encourage some observations from the learners on why a module on exercise and well-being would be of value to them.

Discuss with the group which groundrules would be important. As a group decide upon the groundrules and if appropriate display these on a flipchart.

Explain that you are giving them handout **WB1** ahead of time, as you want them to fill this in for each day between now and the time you begin the well-being sessions. Go through the chart with the learners so they understand how it should be completed and why. The chart allows the learners to record at hourly intervals mood, levels of energy and how these are related to various activities. These may include exercise, an afternoon nap, eating a heavy meal, the day after a heavy night's drinking, during a stressful day, e.g. job interview, preparation for a court appearance and so on.

The learners should then be able to detect over the period of a week a pattern or relationship between mood, energy, sense of well-being, activities undertaken, food eaten and so on. Various factors such as their sense of self-esteem, positive or negative attitudes, use of time and nutrition taken will link together. The exercise will be demanding for the learners but will provide valuable material for them to consider how to improve their well-being.

Defining terms (20 min)

Ask the group to define:

- fitness
- exercise

Record the responses on the flipchart. These may be worthwhile revisiting during the module to see how the learners' ideas develop or change.

Thinking about fitness (40 min)

Ask the group to work in pairs to produce a drawing or collage representing fitness or its opposite. If one member of the pair wishes to draw and the other to find images from magazines, the two can be combined. Once the work has been completed each pair should say why they have chosen, or created, particular images and what these mean to them. The resulting drawings or collages should be displayed throughout the session. Allow the learners time to look at these.

Drawing the threads together (10 min)

Explain that fitness levels change for all of us over the course of our lives, depending on how physically active we are. Being fit enables us to lead our lives with less strain and to increase our chances of living longer, healthier lives by strengthening our hearts, lungs, muscles, circulatory system and metabolism. Good levels of fitness improve both the quality and the quantity of a person's life.

Emphasise that any individual's starting point is irrelevant. Each of us can improve our fitness without it costing very much, other than time. There are many excellent and inexpensive gyms run by the local council where individuals can be given professional advice and where they can benefit from a range of equipment. Most of these gyms charge per session and are used by a cross-section of the community including Down's Syndrome teenagers, older people where doctors have recommended exercise, as well as the young and the physically fit and beautiful. There is absolutely no need to buy expensive specialist fitness wear (other than a sensible pair of shoes). Track suit bottoms, leggings, shorts and T-shirts are ideal. The address of such gyms can be found in the local phone book, by ringing the council or library, or by phoning the local information number. Have some information about local leisure services available.

Session Two: The importance of exercise

 ### Trainer's notes

This session links exercise to physical health. It looks at weight and heart disease. The session closes with an informative quiz.

Brainstorm (15 min)

Ask the group to brainstorm

> **Is exercise important? If so why is it?**

Record the suggestions, or ask a learner to do so.

Reasons for exercise being important might include:

- makes you feel good
- makes you look good
- helps to keep stress levels down
- helps you to sleep
- it's enjoyable
- keeps you fit
- self-esteem
- taking control
- helps with weight control
- passes the time
- it's about valuing yourself
- helps prevent aches and pains
- helps prevent illness e.g. heart disease

The next activity considers one of these reasons. The management of weight and development of a healthy body.

Exercise and weight: are you overweight? (30 min)

Give out **WB2** and go through how the table works. Ask the learners to assess for themselves whether they are overweight. Stress that the more overweight a person is, the more health problems they are likely to have. These might include: high blood pressure; diabetes; less resistance to infections and illnesses; unnecessary stress on the heart; less effective metabolism and overall greater stress on the whole system of respiration, muscles. Check that these reasons make sense to the learners and ask what other ideas they have.

Working in pairs (10 min)

Ask learners to consider if they are happy with their body weight and its shape. What changes might they like to make? How might they make them?

Discussion on exercise (20 min)

As a group

Ask the learners if anyone has had experience of a regular exercise programme. If there is a volunteer(s) ask them to say:

- why they exercised regularly
- what they felt they achieved through it
- are they still exercising? Why? Why not?
- what do they think are the benefits of exercise?
- what do they miss by not exercising?
- what stopped them exercising?

For those with little or no experience of exercise activities ask:

- why exercise does not appeal?
- what they feel they might gain?
- what they would have to give up to do exercise?
- what they would need in terms of help, support, advice, confidence to start exercising?

Have available information about exercise facilities, and be prepared to help the learners to take the first steps towards beginning an exercise programme.

Diet (20 min)

Brainstorm with the learners:

> ## Why do people diet?

Discuss with them their experiences of diets, whether diets work and why they do or do not.

Explain that diets have little effect on their own because when you are on a diet, you will lose only a little fat before the body's natural self-defence mechanism kicks in. The body needs a fat store to guard against hard times, and it needs fat to cushion the internal organs. If the supply of fat is suddenly cut, the body will break down protein (muscle) and lose water weight. So if you give your body too few calories, it will prevent loss of fat and will burn muscle. Once you lose muscle, your metabolism will slow down, making it almost impossible to maintain the weight loss. It is muscle that burns fat. Diets do not work in the long run unless they are accompanied by exercise.

Weight loss and a healthy body can only be gained by combining diet and exercise. OHT **WB1** may help explain the value of exercise.

Exercising to raise the metabolic rate means burning up calories to fuel the body. Raising the metabolic rate and eating earlier in the day will mean the fuel is burnt up during the day and not stored during periods of rest or sleep at night. If possible, do not eat after 7pm.

A sensible guide to eating can be found in the Food guide pyramid in *Food and nutrition*.

Protecting your heart

 ### Trainer's notes

Diet and exercise are also important for maintaining a good inner, as well as outer self. Diet and exercise play a crucial part in the battle against heart disease.

Heart disease is the biggest single killer disease in this country today. This section encourages learners to become aware of what coronary heart disease is and to think how they can better manage themselves and their lives to prevent it.

Note: Care should be taken not to upset any learners who may have lost relatives/friends in this way.

Opening brainstorm (10 min)

Ask the learners what the heart is and what its function is within the body. Their answers should include the facts that the heart is a muscle which acts as a pump to move blood around our bodies. As a muscle the heart can be strengthened and exercised. Many learners are interested in knowing about their bodies and are often quite uncertain about how their bodies work or where one organ is in relation to another. There are many educational posters, three-dimensional charts and structures which you can buy.

Brainstorm: Coronary heart disease (15 min)

Ask the learners to pool their ideas about heart disease.

There are four types:
1. **Angina** occurs when the heart has a reduced supply of oxygen as the blood flow is reduced due to a narrowing of the arteries.
2. **Thrombosis** is a blood clot in a blood vessel.
3. **Arteriosclerosis** is a disease where there is hardening and thickening of the artery walls.
4. **Acute heart attack** (myocardial infarction) is when sticky blood forms a clot in a narrowed artery and prevents blood getting to the heart. The heart may stop, causing death.

Brainstorm (15 min)

Can the learners list out the factors which contribute to heart disease?

These should include:
1. Ageing
2. Hereditary factors
3. Gender
4. High blood pressure
5. Physical inactivity
6. Diabetes
7. Obesity
8. High serum cholesterol
9. Stress
10. Smoking

Risk factors, group discussion and information-giving (20 min)

Ask each learner to star the risk factors that they feel they have control over. These should be 4, 5, 7, 8, 9 and 10 from the list above.

We cannot change our age, our genetic inheritance or our sex but all the other factors are amenable to being determined, to some extent, by our behaviour.

Look at each in turn, asking learners what they think can be done.

4. High blood pressure

Would someone know if they had high blood pressure? The answer is no, there are no obvious symptoms. However, it is not difficult to get blood pressure checked.

What can be done to prevent high blood pressure? *Answer:* regular aerobic exercise has been shown to lower blood pressure.

5. Physical inactivity

Ask the learners how many of them take regular exercise. By this is meant at least 20 minutes in the moderate zone, three times per week. Nationally seven out of ten men and eight out of ten women take significantly less physical activity than they should in order to protect their hearts.

6. Diabetes

Diabetes can be inherited or being overweight may cause it. The link between heart disease and diabetes is unclear but adults with diabetes are over three times more likely to get CHD than others.

7. Obesity

Obesity is being seriously overweight and over a third of British women are obese. Obesity is a major risk factor leading to CHD. It is linked with diabetes, high blood pressure, higher cholesterol levels and so on. Cutting down on fatty foods and exercising will reduce obesity.

8. High serum cholesterol

A sensible diet and exercise will reduce cholesterol levels.

9. Stress

Exercise will reduce stress.

10. Smoking

Stopping smoking, or not smoking at all, will reduce your risk of CHD. Discuss issues learners raise, such as not being able to stop smoking at the moment because of being in a high-stress situation, or being surrounded by other smokers. Perhaps ask whether it would be possible to cut down, or to plan to give up at a later date.

There are many free leaflets from Health Education Councils, supermarkets, chemists etc., on heart disease, exercise, smoking and sensible eating. A ready supply of these should be available to the learners. Posters on the effects of smoking and alcohol may be useful learning aids.

Fitness quiz: Trainer's copy with answers

Work through the following questions. The learners' copy is **WB3**. The learners can work alone or in pairs for 15 minutes. Then take 10 minutes discussing the answers.

1. *Children are less fit today than they were 40 years ago. True or False?*
   True

2. *Men and women are very different and should have very different fitness programmes. True or False?*
   False. However, generally men will be able to lift heavier weights.

3. *Taking exercise is good for you. True or False?*
   True. You will look and feel better if you exercise.

4. *Taking exercise will enhance your self-esteem. True or False?*
   True. Taking control of your life and your physical appearance, and spending time on yourself, will make you feel better about yourself.

5. *Exercise is for the young. True or False?*
   False. Anyone who is reasonably healthy can exercise, even if they take most of their exercise indoors, perhaps sitting down if they are elderly.

6. *Keeping an exercise diary is a good idea. True or False?*
    Many people find it most helpful and encouraging to keep an exercise diary in order to see the improvement in themselves.

7. *Should you train if you feel unwell?*
    No. You are more likely to have an accident or do yourself an injury. Your energy is needed for repair and for dealing with infections etc. and should not be used on exercise routines.

8. *Is it better to run on grass or on the pavement?*
    Grass as it is a soft surface and puts less strain on joints. Appropriate shoes are needed whichever type of running surface is used.

9. *Give the pulse level used by athletes. That is, what is the maximum pulse? How can this be broken down?*
    220 minus your age to find your maximum pulse. Take a percentage of this figure to find your appropriate level: Easy = 60–70% of the maximum pulse; Moderate = 70–80%, Hard = 80+%.

10. *Should beginners walk a minute, jog a minute? Why?*
    Yes, if they find that a sustainable pace, or they may jog a minute and walk for two minutes. The combination of brisk walking and jogging will be different for each person. The important thing is to exercise by raising the pulse rate for a short, sustained period.

11. *Should you stop if something hurts?*
    Yes. Always.

12. *If you stop exercising, muscle turns to fat very quickly. True or False?*
    False. Muscle cannot turn to fat; it can only shrink.

Session Three: Exercising

Gains from taking exercise (30 min)

As a group brainstorm the various ways exercise can be taken. For example:

cycling	walking	jogging
running	gym-steppers	weight lifting
rowing	swimming	aerobics
cross-country skiing	stationary cycling	cricket
yoga	basketball	football
badminton	table-tennis	

Ask the group to decide what is gained from each type of exercise – which ones are weight-bearing? Which ones are aerobic? Which ones increase suppleness? Which ones increase stamina? Which increase strength?

Then discuss what each of these terms mean and why they are of importance.

Strength – being strong enough to lift heavy weights which might include having a well muscled, good looking body. The strength of muscles can be increased by weight lifting.

Suppleness encourages flexibility or stretchability. A supple person looks young for longer and is less likely to suffer from aches and pains. These exercises are especially good for weight lifters as lifting weights shortens the muscles and stretching lengthens them. Stretching prolongs ease of movement and helps a person look graceful and poised.

Stamina and improved cardiovascular performance are linked. The benefits include being able to keep going for longer without tiring. The heart muscle will be stronger and pump blood more efficiently around the body. This will benefit all the organs, including the brain, as freshly oxygenated blood is supplied to the brain tissues as well as the rest of the body.

Devising an exercise plan

Trainer input (20 min)

Using **WB4** and any other materials you have go through with the learners the constituent parts of an exercise plan. These are: warm up, cool down, aerobic exercise to raise pulse to appropriate level, gradually increasing what is done, improving on suppleness, and weight-lifting. Emphasise the importance of a steady build up of pace, time and difficulty; if learners try to do too much too soon they may damage themselves or may put themselves off taking further exercise.

Stress the importance of only trying suppleness exercises once warmed up.

Point out the importance of seeking professional advice if the learners have physical problems or are unsure of what to do.

If learners have limited space or no access to facilities running on the spot is excellent exercise, as is skipping. If running on the spot, once a degree of fitness is achieved, the runner counts and jumps each time the right foot hits the ground on 20. The jumps can start at two and work up to ten. Keeping this up for 20 minutes will provide the necessary aerobic exercise.

Pair work/small group work (30 min)

Ask the learners to work in pairs or small groups to devise an exercise plan to suit their situation and needs. Stress that it should include warm ups and cool-downs and should be working towards strength, stamina and increasing suppleness. Most importantly it should be a realistic plan, which they would enjoy following, which will challenge them but not damage them. They need to take into account their starting level of fitness.

Give the learners **WB4** with guidance and examples of different types of exercises. This handout should be retained by the learners for reference. But it is to be stressed that they should take advice on how to do the exercises.

Feedback and discussion (40 min)

Ask one person from each pair or small group to report back to the whole group, and record ideas on a flipchart/whiteboard. Discuss, as a group, the merits of each plan.

Give out handout **WB5**.

Discuss the advice given. For example, why is it necessary to drink so much water? The answer is that a person will sweat more when taking exercise. The fact is, the fitter you are, the more you sweat and the sooner you will sweat in your workout.

Why is it important to take professional advice? The answer is to get a fitness programme tailor-made to the individual and their lifestyle and that takes account of any medical problems. If learners are not in a position to get professional advice, they can buy a book or borrow one from a library to supplement the information in this module.

Drawing the threads together (10 min)

Summarise the learning about gain from exercise. These are:

- improved stamina
- improved strength
- improved suppleness (in most cases)
- improved self-esteem and appearance
- increased alertness/less fatigue
- improved sense of well-being
- improved functioning of internal organs
- enhanced health

Session Four: Raising awareness and improving personal well-being

Trainer's notes

The work here is applicable to most people. However your group may have special needs which will have to be addressed. If it does, you would be wise to address these needs. For example, you may have a group of middle-aged women who are concerned about the menopause; or a group of young men who are concerned about relating successfully to young women; or a group of teenage mothers, and so on. Whatever the composition of your group, it is likely that your local Health Education Council will have some suitable material for you to use in conjunction with this module.

Opening brainstorm (10 min)

Brainstorm with the learners

> ### What is well-being?

This may include:

- feeling energetic
- no aches or pains
- feeling good about self
- high energy levels

- feeling in control of self and life
- feeling rested
- able to sleep
- feeling able to cope with pressures

Reviewing personal well-being logs

Working alone (20 min)

Look through the seven logs (WB1) and decide what patterns or relationships the learners can find between well-being and for example:

- eating
- sleeping
- nights out drinking
- purposeful and enjoyable activity
- stressful and unenjoyable activities

Working in pairs (20 min)

Ask the learners to compare what they have found. Each pair should decide how they can improve on a sense of well-being by increasing certain activities, doing other things with their time or reducing those things which make them feel less well.

The pairs should be ready to feed this information back to the group.

Group feedback (15 min)
On the flipchart record, for example

Detracts from well-being	Contributes to well-being
• not eating regularly • eating junk food • drinking too much • not enough sleep	• seeing friends and relatives • caring for someone else • being organised • eating well

Working in pairs (10 min)
Ask the learners to look through their logs and decide if the time of feeling low in energy or depressed can be related to particular times of day or to particular activities. This work may link well with work on better management of time, living in harmony with values and goals and should be remembered for a final planning activity.

Session Five: Sleep

 ### Trainer's note

One factor which will contribute to a sense of well-being is having adequate rest and sleep.

Opening discussion (20 min)
Introduce the idea of the importance of sleep. Draw out a grid as below on the flipchart and go round the room with each learner saying where they fit in.

Name	Trouble getting to sleep	Disturbed sleep	Early waking	Sleep well

Tell learners that the average person needs 7–8 hours' sleep a night; some people can manage on 5–6 hours' sleep, and much more rarely there are people who report being able to manage on less than five hours' sleep. At certain times in our lives, for example, when we are babies, children, pregnant, old, ill or very stressed, we will need more rest and sleep than at others.

Ask learners why they think we have to sleep. They may suggest that it is to rest the body, when the body can repair itself, or to dream. All are correct as far as they go, but nobody really knows exactly why we have to sleep. However, we all know from our own experience that we cannot function without sleep.

Stress that everyone has trouble sleeping at some time in their lives, and that this should not cause undue concern.

More effective sleep

Brainstorm (10 min)

Ask the learners to brainstorm any ideas which they have to improve the quality or quantity of sleep.

Information-giving and discussion (45 min)

Give the learners **WB6** and work through each of the suggestions. Some of the learners may have tried some of the methods. Ask for their experiences. Check for understanding and ask how these suggestions could be incorporated into their daily lives.

Session Six: Relaxation

 Trainer's notes and explanatory material (20 min)

Relaxation is important for people because it contributes to a sense of emotional and mental well-being. Relaxation is recommended as a route to achieving some of the techniques for developing positive attitudes such as visualisation.

Relaxation has an impact on body and brain helping relieve stress and increasing a sense of balance and well-being in life by creating some times for personal restoration.

There are a number of ways in which people may choose to relax. Two examples are offered below. The first is a visualisation exercise, the second concentrates on muscle stretches and relaxation.

Make sure that you are warm and comfortable and unlikely to be disturbed. This may be in a bath, or a room alone. Close your eyes and consider how lucky you are to be warm and safe. Think of a time that has happy associations, or just drift, perhaps visualising yourself on a beach or in a favourite place. Nothing structured has to happen. Time can pass without your being aware of where your mind has been.

Head rolls:

- drop your chin onto your chest as you breathe out
- now rotate you head slowly clockwise as you inhale
- when you head is back in an upright position exhale and continue to exhale as you rotate your head until your chin is again on your chest
- do this three times and then repeat three times in the opposite direction
- do all actions slowly

Head and neck stretches:

- slowly move your head from side to side while keeping it level
- gently move your head forward and back as far as is comfortably possible
- move it to the left and the right. Feel the stretch on the muscles

Shoulders stretch:

- place your right hand on your right shoulder and your left hand on your left shoulder
- bring your elbows together in front of your chest and make slow large circles first in one direction and then in the opposite direction, drawing a large circle in the air with your elbows

Take the learners through a few techniques. Explore how relaxation could be integrated into their daily lives.

If practical a demonstration session could be tried. An example follows below:

Relaxation exercise (40 min)

Be sure that everyone has a comfortable spot to lie down in, away from draughts and the possibility of disturbance.

Ask the group to close their eyes. Say the following in a slow calm voice, allowing a pause between instructions. Incense can be burned.

Relax into the floor, trusting it to support you.

Tense your left foot, screwing up the toes as tightly as you can. Hold this … (repeat) hold this tension … and now relax the foot.

(Repeat this for both sides and all of the body including the calf muscle, upper thigh and buttock, shoulders, head, arms, neck, face – screwing up eyes, cheeks, tensing mouth).

Once the physical relaxation exercise is finished say to the learners:

Allow your body to relax further and further into the floor, to prepare for an inner journey.

Allow your mind to consider one or two things that are troubling you in your life at the moment.

Now you have identified these things, mentally put them in a box. There is no need to think of them further.

Now imagine yourself undertaking a journey. You are at the edge of a wood and your task is to find the wise man who lives in the wood and who is able to help you.

Imagine the walk. The weather is good and the wood is calm.

As you walk, you see small flowers, magnificent trees, rabbits playing.

In the distance you can hear a small waterfall.

There is someone ahead, dressed in white. You approach and ask the way to the wise man's hut.

You follow the route, and come to a clearing as the person in white said you would.

It is very calm. Bees are buzzing, birds singing.

In the centre of the clearing is a small, clean, clear pool.

You approach the pool, and bend down to look into it.

The face of the wise man looks back up at you.

Relax now, keeping your eyes closed.

(Here, you can play some quiet 'spiritual' music for 3-4 minutes)

Keeping your eyes shut, wriggle your left foot … move your left leg.

Now wriggle your right foot ... move your right leg.

We are nearly finished now. Keeping your eyes shut, rub your hands together.

Once your hands are warm, cover your eyes. Open your eyes into the darkness of your hands.

In your own time, roll over and sit up slowly.

Session Seven: Well-being in the round

 ### Trainer's notes

So far discussion of well-being has considered:
- the ways in which people can enhance or depress their own sense of well-being by an analysis of the personal logs
- sleep
- relaxation

Exercise was considered as part of helping improve physical well-being and sense of self-esteem. This session asks learners to put all of these things together and also to consider values and use of life or time.

Explanations (10 min)

The World Heath Organisation's definition of health is *Health is a state of complete physical, mental and social well-being and not merely the absence of disease or infirmity.* Write this on the whiteboard/flipchart for all to see. Ask all learners what they think. There is nothing about spiritual well-being in the above definition – should there be?

Working alone: values (20 min)

Ask the learners to work on WB7. Ensure they understand what is wanted.

Feedback (10 min)

Ask for some examples of what is important and why and for definitions of what each state of well-being means.

Brainstorm: Improving well-being (20 min)

Using definitions from the previous activity decide on ways in which each area of well-being could be enhanced. List these on the flipchart.

Reviewing well-being: explanation, working alone and planning (40 min)

Remind learners that ideally there should still be one third of our lives after work and sleep. Introduce the group to the idea that we each have a pie of time and energy each morning and we use it up as we go through the day. If there are eight hours of time and energy that are our own to use as we wish, what do we do with them?

Ask the learners to look again at their well-being logs and lists of what encourages or depresses well-being. Ask the learners to consider how their use of time currently helps them to improve their physical, mental and social well-being? Ask them to work on Action plan WB8 to think what they may do to improve each area of life. An example is worked below. Check on each learner's progress, helping as required.

Action Plan

1. Main goal   *to lose weight*
Steps:
1. *Find a sensible diet. I will start next Monday.*
2. *Take exercise – join gym or ask Jim to help me. I will do this Wednesday 20th.*

2. Main goal   *enjoy myself more*
Steps:
1. *Consider what I enjoy – music, seeing friends, eating.*
2. *Make time to listen to music – join library and borrow some for free – maybe learn to play piano. Invite friends for meals. From today I will make time for at least one of the things I most enjoy.*

3. Main goal   *get a better job*
Steps:
1. *What job would I really like? Realistically ...*
2. *What do I need to do to stand a chance of getting that job?*
3. *Breakdown of (2) above. Enrol in evening class, or distance learning. Ask boss if work will pay for this, or pay half with me. I will have started this by Wednesday 27th.*

Session Eight: Closing session

Round the module off with a final health quiz and summary exercise.

Health quiz (30 min)

The learners should work in pairs in small groups to answer the quiz. Once they have had enough time, ask them to report back to the whole group.

Allow discussion around each point before stepping in with the facts.

Answers to true/false questionnaire (WB9)

1. *This is difficult.* Who determines how fit anyone should be? Most people would probably claim to be 'fit for life' (i.e. able to work and enjoy life). However our death rate from heart disease and cancer of the large bowel is worrying and much higher than in third world countries.

2. *False.* Being unemployed affects men's and women's health differently. Men are more likely to suffer from heart disease but women suffer from anxiety and depression.

3. *True.* The NHS needs sufficient resources to function as well as possible. However, who decides how the money is spent? Heart surgery is very expensive; would it be better to spend the money educating people about how they can prevent themselves getting heart disease?

4. *True.* Smoking is also linked with cancer and heart disease. One person smokes and needs an operation for a condition directly linked with their smoking, another person does not smoke and needs an operation as a result of a car accident. If there is only sufficient money for one operation, which person should receive treatment?

5. *False.* Health is more than this. The World Health Organisation defines health as *Health is a state of complete physical, mental and social well-being and not merely the absence of disease or infirmity.* Ask the group to consider the role of exercise in achieving the WHO's definition.

6. *True.* But is it the employment in itself, or the lowered standard of living? Or a combination.

7. *True.* Especially so in a recession as unskilled manual workers are those most likely to have to face the problems of unemployment.

8. *True.* Unemployment affects us mentally as well as physically.

9. *True.*

10. *True.*

Summary exercise (20 min)

Finally ask the learners to complete the summary sheet **WB 10**. Ask each learner to contribute something they have learned and why it is of value. Ask each learner to say one change they wish to make and why they would like to do this.

Thank the learners for their hard work.

WB2: Height/weight chart

Height without shoes ft in	Small frame st lb	Medium frame st lb	Large frame st lb
WOMEN			
4 10	7 2	7 12	8 7
4 11	7 4	8 0	8 10
5 0	7 7	8 2	8 13
5 1	7 10	8 5	9 2
5 2	7 13	8 7	9 5
5 3	8 2	8 10	9 8
5 4	8 6	9 0	9 12
5 5	8 10	9 5	10 2
5 6	9 0	9 10	10 6
5 7	9 4	10 0	10 10
5 8	9 8	10 5	11 0
5 9	9 12	10 10	11 5
5 10	10 3	11 2	11 10
MEN			
5 3	8 10	9 4	10 0
5 4	8 13	9 7	10 3
5 5	9 2	9 10	10 6
5 6	9 6	10 0	10 10
5 7	9 10	10 4	11 1
5 8	10 0	10 8	11 5
5 9	10 4	10 12	11 9
5 10	10 8	11 2	11 13
5 11	10 12	11 6	12 4
6 0	11 2	11 10	12 8
6 1	11 6	12 0	12 13
6 2	11 10	12 5	13 4
6 3	12 0	12 10	13 9

WB1: Monitoring your well-being

Please complete this before attending the first session on well-being

Date: _____

Day number: _____

Time	Activity e.g. sleep, exercising, eating, spending time in way you like or not	Energy level 1–5 (5 = high 1 = low)	Mood you are in e.g. calm, tired, stressed, good, great, unhappy, depressed
0100			
0200			
0300			
0400			
0500			
0600			
0700			
0800			
0900			
1000			
1100			
1200			
1300			
1400			
1500			
1600			
1700			
1800			
1900			
2000			
2100			
2200			
2300			
2400 (Midnight)			

WB4: Elements for an exercise plan

Warm-ups

In order not to damage muscles, warming up is always necessary before taking aerobic exercise or stretching. Start running on the spot quite gently for a few minutes, or alternatively skip fairly slowly until you feel warm.

If you are intending to do aerobic walking, jogging, running or stepping as your main exercise then use the same type of exercise but at a lower intensity as the warm-up.

The main exercise

Once warmed up, exercise at the appropriate level.

To work out what is an appropriate level, use the following.

Pulse

220 minus your age to find your maximum pulse. Take a percentage of this figure to find your appropriate level: Easy = 60-70% of the maximum pulse; Moderate = 70-80% of the maximum pulse; Hard = 80+% of the maximum pulse. Stopping for one minute to take your pulse is necessary. Once you have done this for a few times, you will be able to predict fairly accurately what level you are working at without taking your pulse.

If you are unused to exercise, exercise at the easy level for five minutes and then a moderate level for ten minutes. Gradually work until you can work for twenty minutes at a moderate level. Then build on this until you are working twenty minutes at the hard level. Each step should be incremental and gradual. For example, once you are able to work-out for twenty minutes at a moderate level, try ten minutes at a moderate level, five minutes at the hard level, and then a final five minutes at a moderate or easy level. Gradually increase the number of minutes worked at the hard level.

The exercise you choose is not so important, other than ensuring that a good proportion of it is weight-bearing. (Swimming is a good exercise, but not weight-bearing.)

If space is limited, you can skip, run on the spot or step up and down on the bottom step of stairs.

Aerobic exercise increases the amount of oxygen you use, the calories you burn up. It makes fuller use of your lungs, exercising the heart as well as the other muscles.

Cooling down

As with the warm-ups you can continue with the chosen exercise, but gently until your breathing returns to normal.

Part of the daily programme may include stretching. After using muscles for aerobic activity, stretches mean using the muscles differently so giving them a chance to do other work.

Always ensure you warm up before stretching.
Some examples of stretches are given overleaf.

WB3: Fitness quiz

*Consider the twelve questions and decide upon your answer **and the reasons** for your answer.*

1. Children are less fit today than they were forty years ago. True or False?

2. Men and women are very different and should have very different fitness programmes. True or False?

3. Taking exercise is good for you. True or False?

4. Taking exercise will enhance your self-esteem. True or False?

5. Exercise is for the young. True or False?

6. Keeping an exercise diary is a good idea. True or False?

7. Should you train if you feel unwell?

8. Is it better to run on grass or on the pavement?

9. Give the pulse level used by athletes. That is, what is the maximum pulse? How can this be broken down?

10. Should beginners walk a minute, jog a minute? Why?

11. Should you stop if something hurts?

12. If you stop exercising, muscle turns to fat very quickly. True or false?

Weight lifting

Always warm up before lifting weights.

Dumbbells can be bought quite reasonably from department stores. If you wish to build muscle, use heavier weights; if you wish to tone, use lighter weights and do more repetitions.

Two exercises are given below. If you buy a set of dumbbells, an exercise chart will be included, and there are any number of books on the market.

Dumbbell punch Start with the lightest dumbbells in the set and work up to using the heavier ones. Stand with you feet a little apart and hold the dumbbells at shoulder height. Alternatively lift each dumbbell in the air, straight up from the shoulder and return to shoulder height. Breathe in as you push up the dumbbell and out as you bring it down again. Repeat ten times on each side.

Bicep curl Stand with your feet a little apart and a dumbbell in each hand. Raise the right arm up slowly, bringing the dumbbell to your chest, slowly lower the right arm and at the same time raise the left arm. Repeat whole movement five times.

Upper body stretches

1) Swinging arms. Circle each arm in turn, both clockwise and anti-clockwise. On the clockwise circle, think of backstroke when swimming.
2) Place your left hand up your back between your shoulder blades with the back of your hand touching your back. Bring your right hand over and clasp the fingers of your left hand. Repeat with the right hand coming behind your back. If at first your hands don't meet, a belt or towel can be used.

Stand with your head, shoulders and hips aligned. Clasp your hands behind you. Your knees should be slightly bent. Bring your hands up toward the ceiling until you feel gently tension in your shoulders and chest.

The Cat This stretch is for the lower back. On all fours, make a square shape with hands under shoulders and knees, hip width apart, and under hips. Dip the back and stretch the head back at the same time while breathing out and looking up. Keep the mouth open. Hold for a minute or longer, but not once it becomes uncomfortable. Now breathe in and, at the same time, lower the head and arch the back, keeping stomach pulled in. Once again, hold the posture for a short time.

Lower body stretches

Lie on your back, keeping one leg bent and the corresponding foot on the floor. Raise your other leg up, assisting with your hands or using a towel to assist, until you feel a gentle tension in the hamstring. Repeat on the other side.

While lying on your back, grab the back of your leg just above the knee, gently pull that leg up toward your chest. Keep your opposite leg straight on the ground. Repeat on the other side.

Do the same exercise but draw both legs up to your chest.

While sitting on the floor, place the soles of your feet together and allow your knees to drop down toward the floor. Gradually pull your feet toward you, until you feel gentle tension in your inner thighs and groin. You can lean forward as you become more flexible.

Scissors Lie on the floor on your side. Place your left hand palm down on the floor just above your waist and rest your head on your right hand. Look down your body to see that you are in a straight line. Lift your left leg slowly, and then slowly lower it. Repeat 20 times and 20 times on the other side.

There are many books and videos on stretching and yoga. However, if you are able to attend a class you will have personal help from the tutor and have the additional enjoyment of being with other people.

WB5

Opinions vary on how frequently to exercise. Many experts advise exercising aerobically five to seven days per week. In order to work out the best individual exercise plan for yourself, it is advisable to seek professional advice.

Vary your exercise regime. For example, instead of jogging, cycle or swim. Arrange to run with friends or neighbours sometimes (but remember to always go at your own pace), perhaps arrange a workout group. Listen to music while you exercise, use a gym, or think of other ways to ensure that you enjoy your workouts.

Exercise sessions should last between 20 and 60 minutes.

It is important to ensure that enough water is drunk. Six to eight glasses a day are recommended.

In order to protect your heart, you need to exercise for 20 minutes three times a week at a moderate intensity.

WB6: Getting a good night's sleep

1. A clear conscience

    There may be things troubling us that are beyond our control, such as fears about jobs, but those things that are within our control we should try to deal with. For example, if you have something troubling you, try to sort it out. If there is bad feeling or a misunderstanding with someone, talk to them about it and do your best to sort it out. If you have done something wrong, admit it.

2. Debt

    Being in debt, or not managing to meet the bills, is worrying. For the sake of well-being, it is best not to get into debt. If you are in debt, seek advice, perhaps from the Citizens' Advice Bureau. Once clear of debt, do all in your power to live within your means.

3. Relaxation

    Relaxing can be easier said than done. In order to get a good night's sleep your body must ease off on the stress hormones and increase the sedative hormones. This happens as you relax. Ensure a period of relaxation of at least half-an-hour before you go to bed.

    There are various relaxation methods. Here are a few:

    Lie comfortably and tense then relax your muscles, starting at the feet. Tense your feet as tightly as you can. Hold for a count of eight, then relax, breathing out and saying the word 'relax' in your mind as you do so. Repeat this with your calves/legs, buttocks, stomach, hands, arms, shoulders and face.

    Use a mantra. A mantra is a repeated sound. The most common mantra is the sound "Om". Sit quietly and repeat the om sound in your mind or out loud. If your thoughts stray, it doesn't matter just go back to repeating the sound. Do this for a few minutes and gradually build up the time until you can sit for 20 minutes.

    Make sure that you are comfortable. Visualise breathing out all the stress and tension in your mind and body and breathing in either:

    the word 'peace' or 'trust' or 'calm'
    or breathing in pure, warm, golden light.

    It won't work for everyone, but try improving your maths. While your mind is busy working out a maths problems, it can't be dwelling on other things. Successfully completing a few problems can be very calming for some people.

    Listen to a favourite piece of music.

    Consider buying a relaxation tape.

4. Some people are able to read their body clocks very efficiently, others are not. If you have trouble knowing how to get a good night's sleep, try the following routine:

    Go to bed every night at 10pm, and wake early. If you wake early, you will want to sleep earlier at night. It is believed that the best sleep is had before 2 am, so by going to bed earlier you will be getting the most high quality sleep.

5. Try acupressure. Resting your elbow on your knee, press your thumb between your eyebrows and lean your weight on it. Now hold the pressure for about 10-15 seconds.

    Press your thumb on the slight depression on the inside of your wrist, in line with your little finger, for about 10 seconds.

    Massage your temples – it is said that these are the most powerful acupressure points.

6. Aromatherapy oils can have a profound effect on us. Use lavender to help you to sleep. Many people believe that this is as effective as sleeping pills, and there are no side effects. A few drops can be placed in water in an oil burner; a few drops can be added to bath water or dripped onto the duvet (but not too near your head), or a few drops can be added to a base massage oil and used massaged into the skin.

7. Experts tell us that we should have a new bed ideally every eight years. The bed should be firm enough to support your spine in a straight line, and comfortable. Some French research has shown that people sleep, on average, an extra hour per night on a new bed.

    If your situation permits, you could try sex. This causes a rush of adrenaline followed by calming endorphins that encourage sleep.

8. Proper exercise, raising the heartbeat as suggested at the beginning of this module, helps encourage good, sound sleep.

9. Good nutrition helps sleep, as does not eating for 3-4 hours before going to bed. Many junk foods contain MSG, a chemical that raises adrenaline levels. Try not to drink coffee and tea after 4pm as caffeine has a half-life of six hours, which means that coffee will still affect you six hours after you have drunk it. Try a soft drink, or herbal tea instead.

10. Try fantasy. Imagine the house you would like to live in, a relaxing day at the beach or whatever you find calming, pleasant and interesting. Imagine your fantasy in detail. If it is the house fantasy, think about how you would decorate it, carpet it and so on. If it is a garden fantasy, consider where you would plant a favourite shrub, how the path would wind and so on.

11. Unnecessary worrying. If you can't sleep, don't worry. No-one in the normal course of life has ever died through lack of sleep. You could switch on the light and read, or do a small chore. Perhaps write a list of things to be done the next day. Or you could just rest. However, whilst we can catch up with sleep the next night, we can't build up a reserve of sleep to allow us to keep going without for a night or more.

WB7: Values

Part one – Physical well-being

Consider how important this is to you.

Grade it from 1 not very important to 5 very important.

Grade _____

Part two – Mental well-being

Consider how important this is to you.

Grade it from 1 not very important to 5 very important.

Grade _____

Part three – Social well-being

Consider how important this is to you.

Grade it from 1 not very important to 5 very important.

Grade _____

Now think what each of the above means to you. Try defining what physical well-being, mental well-being and social well-being mean to you. Write your thoughts below.

WB9: Health quiz

True or false

1. Most people in this country are less fit than they should be

2. Being unemployed affects men's health more than women's

3. If the NHS had more money, we would be healthier

4. Smoking is bad for your teeth

5. Health is when you are not ill

6. Unemployed people are more likely to be ill than employed people

7. Working class people are more likely to suffer ill-health than wealthier people

8. Unemployed people are more likely than employed people to suffer from mental illness or stress

9. Unemployed people are likely to have a lower standard of living which can damage their health

10. People could enjoy better health if they looked after themselves

---

WB8: Action plan

1. **Main goal**

Steps:

1

2

2. **Main goal**

Steps:

1

2

3. **Main goal**

Steps:

1

2

3

WB10: Summary

Having completed the course on Exercise and well-being, please complete this form.

Please write down three things you have learned about exercise and well-being:

1. _____

2. _____

3. _____

Please write down three things you want to change in your life as a result of this module

1. _____

2. _____

3. _____

OHP | ## WB11: Metabolic rate

Metabolic rate = the rate at which your body burns calories.

Increase your metabolic rate and you:

i) store fewer calories

ii) have more energy for your body to use

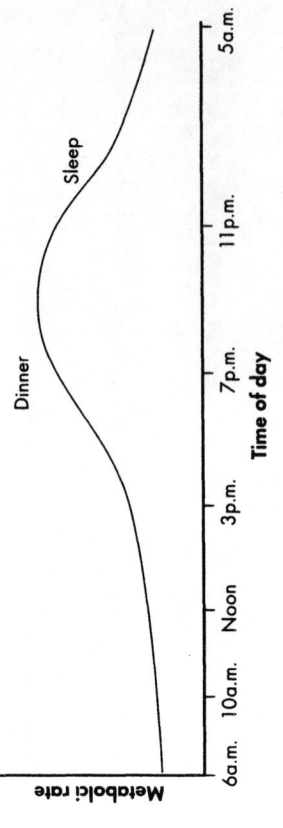

Metabolic rate with no exercise

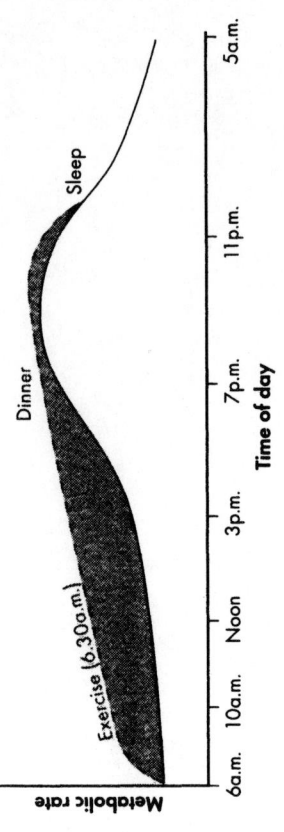

Metabolic rate plus exercise

Shaded area shows raised metabolic rate

Do-It-Yourself: Improve your home, your appearance and your chances

 The module is divided into three main parts, each of which is then sub-divided.

Improve your home

1. Accidents at home and improving safety (1 hour 55 min)
2. Improving comfort (45 min)
3. Housing and rights (1 hour)
4. Planning and summary (20 min)

Improve your appearance

5. Introducing appearance (1 hour 55 min)
6. Keys to improved appearance (6 hours 30 min)
7. Planning and summary (30 min)

Improve your chances

8. Focus on me and my chances (2 hours)
9. Planning (1 hour)

There are some optional areas for example, practical work on washing, ironing and repairing clothes. The sessions on rights and housing and on improving chances may take longer if an outside speaker from a housing or tenants' association or employment services could attend.

 The module uses the learning and training styles of:

- brainstorming
- discussion
- selection and sorting cards
- planning
- self-assessment
- collage and drawing
- practical activities
- mime
- small group activities

 Trainer's notes

This final module introduces some new material, for example health and safety at home, thinking about cheap DIY improvements. It also serves to reinforce some of the earlier material; for example, improving appearance and chances both link to effective money management, exercise and good nutrition.

The emphasis throughout is on resting the responsibility for making changes with the learner.

The module aims to:

- raise awareness about ways the learner can better manage themselves and their environment
- provide some inexpensive suggestions for making such improvements
- provide practical guidance on making changes
- help the learner to explore some key areas of their life and environment in a supportive and structured way
- increase the learners' awareness of health and safety
- increase the learners' sense of the importance of taking an interest in and looking after personal appearance and immediate home environment
- increasing the learners' sense of the need to take responsibility for themselves and their environment

285

Improve your home

 Trainer's notes

The first part of this module aims to raise learners' awareness of some of the things they can do to feel more in control of their home environment. It does not set out to be a handy person course. Some learners will have been in institutional settings and will not have considered ways in which they might take some control over their environment. This module offers some ideas.

Session One: Accidents at home and improving safety

It is said that many accidents happen at home. Accidents happen to children, adults and the elderly. The learners should be aware of how they might take greater responsibility for themselves and others.

This session would be best supported with some public information leaflets on safety in the home. Leaflets can be obtained from:

- The Royal Society for the Prevention of Accidents, 353 Bristol Road, Edgbaston, Birmingham B5 7ST
- Disabled Living Foundation, 380–384 Harrow Road, London W9 2HU
- Help the Aged, St James Walk, Clerkenwell Green, London EC1R 0DE
- Department of Health, PO Box 410, Wetherby LS23 7LN
- local health authority education and public information services
- local fire brigade

Organisations such as the British Red Cross and St John's Ambulance, National Back Pain Association will also offer leaflets and advice.

Brainstorm (30 min)

Ask the learners to brainstorm the types of accidents and reasons for accidents which may occur at home. The lists may include such as:

Burns:	open fires, unprotected electric fires; children playing and pulling irons or fires onto themselves; burning self on oven
Fires:	cigarettes onto fabric, bedding, furniture (not having flame resistant furniture); children playing with matches; chip pan fires (one of the biggest causes of fire in the home)
DIY activities:	balancing on furniture instead of getting a ladder; not having a properly secured ladder; not having the right tools for the job and hurting oneself; not knowing how to properly use a power or hand tool; trying to do electrical work
Cutting:	trying to cut frozen foods; separating frozen hamburgers with knives; children playing with knives/sharp objects; opening packets with a knife; not cutting downwards and away from the body
Slips, trips and falls:	falling over toys; children falling downstairs because there is no stair guard; falling over trailing flexes; slipping on wet floors or spilt liquids; slipping on rugs, slippery floors or torn floor coverings.

Electrical accidents:	trying to do repairs at home; not having appliances checked; ignoring frayed flexes; not turning off the power before doing a job; not having wiring checked at home
Gas poisoning:	blocking air vents; not having gas appliances serviced by a proper engineer; having an 'odd job person' install gas appliances or trying to do it yourself
Swallowing poisons/ pills/objects:	children getting hold of used ashtrays, objects, pills and eating them or their contents; children picking things from floors, the garden or outdoors and eating them
Food poisoning:	unhygienic practices in the kitchen, e.g. poor food storage (check module on nutrition)

Use the ideas above to help you move the learners into new areas for the brainstorm activity.

Risk prevention (20 min)
Ask the groups to work in pairs to generate a list on DI1 of the risks and ways to prevent the risk.

Group feedback (15 min)
Check speedily on some of the answers from the pairs. Then distribute Safety in the Home leaflets. A list of useful addresses is offered above.

The group should be allowed time to read through the leaflets and add to their DI1 worksheet. If there is a new definitive list produced by the group then copies of this could be reproduced for the learners.

Risky environments (15 min)
Give out DI2 and ask the learners to work in pairs to decide what is wrong with the situation and how they would reduce risks.

Feedback (10 min)
Ask for the hazards and their prevention. Check all the pairs were able to find all the hazards and work out what to do about them.

Improving safety: a personal plan (25 min)
Ask the learners to work alone on DI3, to consider what changes they might make to the safety of their own homes. Each learner will have different circumstances, e.g. be a heavy smoker or living with one; have children; have pets in the house or have open fires.

Ask the learners to compare their plans in pairs. Ask for a couple of volunteers to share their plans and invite others in the group to add any more suggestions.

Not all learners will be living at home, so ask them to consider things they do in their residential environment which may be risky and to plan ways not to do these. For example:

- making home-made wiring systems for a radio
- smoking in bed
- making snacks without the proper tools or utensils
- storing food improperly

Session Two: Improving comfort

Opening brainstorm (15 min)

Everyone's idea of what is comfortable will differ. A brainstorm will generate a number of ideas. these may include:

- warmth
- tidiness
- carpet
- nice furniture
- things which match each other

- cheerful colours
- cleanliness
- things being organised
- no draughts
- knowing where things are

Explanation and discussion (30 min)

There are many things which the learners can do to improve their homes. Some will need to check with landlords if they can paint walls/ceilings, paint furniture or change furniture. Others will need advice on how to get their landlords to make basic repairs or to provide basic decorating materials. Advice on and drafting of letters to landlords to draw attention to defects or to seek permission to undertake improvements may be needed.

Work through the following four headings with the learners going through the suggestions and asking the learners what they would do or have done to make improvements in these areas.

1. Increasing warmth

- draught excluders
- paper between cracks in windows
- fill in keyholes
- cover bare floorboards – off-cuts of carpet or second-hand rugs are effective
- draw curtains – get thick curtains from Oxfam and other charity shops or from specialist second-hand curtains shops
- block or cover open fire places which are not used
- drawing curtains to keep in heat
- cover window frames with cling film
- insulate loft spaces

It is important that in trying to reduce draughts the learners do not block air vents needed for gas appliances or find themselves living in overheated stuffy rooms.

The learners should take care about the type of heating they use. Open fires should only be set in swept chimneys and areas open for such fires. Guards should be placed round paraffin, gas or open fires. Electric fires with frayed flexes should not be used. Getting second-hand heating appliances could be risky unless they have been properly inspected.

DIY stores carry many advice leaflets on home improvements and the use of roof and other types of insulation can be found among them. The Department of the Environment produces a leaflet on energy conservation and cutting down fuel bills called *Saving Money on Fuel Bills – Dos and Don'ts*. This can be obtained by phoning 0181 691 9191. It is also worth trying your local authority.

2. Being organised and tidy

One of the ways in which learners can feel more in control of themselves and their environment and save time, is to get better organised. This may be about storing important papers and documents, getting clothes hung up and off the floor, storing other household and personal items. Better storage preserves things, saves time when looking for them and helps make a small living space seem larger and more comfortable.

Learners should consider economical ways to increase their storage facilities. For example, making shelves with bricks and planks, buying self-assembly book cases or cupboards, buying second-hand units and re-painting them. They should think about ways to store things:

- large envelopes for important papers and documents always kept in a certain drawer
- re-use shoeboxes – covered or painted for storage
- buy cheap plastic storage boxes to keep shoes or cleaning materials tidied away
- buy special shoe and clothes tidy cloth storage units from Oxfam

Spending time each day putting things back in their place, will save time and increase feelings of organisation, space and control. With things tidied away it is easier to keep a room, bedsit, flat or house clean.

3. Cleanliness

Consider building regular cleaning sessions into weekly timetables. It will save time, increase a sense of control over the home and creates some structure and routine in the week.

Consider with the learners what basic cleaning materials are needed, what types of materials are used for what jobs, how they can be used to best effect and why named brands waste money. The learners need to be aware of the importance of hygiene for well-being and health as well as improved comfort. Cleanliness of kitchens and bathrooms should be discussed in terms of preventing ill-health.

Consider with learners ways to keep shared living accommodation clean; explore the idea of rotas and the reasons why people sharing accommodation have responsibilities to one another. The importance of taking others into account can be explored by each person listing three things they *hate* to find in:

- a kitchen
- a bathroom

and three things they *like* to find in:

- a kitchen
- a bathroom

After five minutes create a group list asking each person in turn to add one item from each of their two lists to the group list.

4. Creating comfort, or a more ideal home on a budget

Encourage the learners to think about buying second-hand furniture or using their current furniture but painting it and changing cupboard handles to make it more cheerful. Those who wanted could experiment with paint effects or stencilling.

Recycling furniture or making use of second-hand items saves money and will allow a budget for furniture to go further. Painting some items, e.g. wardrobe, chest and table will make them match each other.

Some basic DIY skills and tools could save money for those who are able to assemble DIY furniture from flatpack kits or able to put up shelving.

Learners may need to know about furniture projects which supply donated furniture and white goods. They may need to know how to contact such projects. Some learners will need to know about family credit and how to get help to buy certain essential household items. Encourage learners to consider getting soft furnishings from Oxfam and other charity shops – curtains, cushions and covers. Explain how to measure for curtains and how larger curtains and covers can be cut down or used as throws.

Everyone's ideas of comfort and a nice home environment will differ. Time spent considering what these ideas mean to each individual may help them in deciding what they might like to work towards. Having concrete ideas will help them in planning what they need to do to make their home environment more comfortable or more like their ideal.

For some, it may mean having very little furniture, few ornaments and soft furnishings; for others, it may mean having plenty of personal possessions around them. For those who have had little chance to think about or experiment with their own home environment a collage making session may be of value. Using pictures from magazines the learners should create what is an ideal home environment. They should think about colour, types of furniture, lighting, plants and so on.

While not everything is immediately attainable, having a sense of something to work towards may encourage the learners in thinking about home and life values and goals. Helping the learners with simple tasks and to understand that they can change their environment with some painting skills will help them to save money and feel more comfortable.

DIY stores have many leaflets on simple jobs which can be done at home. Supplies of such leaflets could be offered to the learning groups; for example on changing a washer, safely laying loft insulation or installing basic home security, e.g. door chains or door viewers.

In thinking about creating a more comfortable home the learners should consider what skills they may have to trade for others; for example carpentry skills for decorating or soft furnishing for plumbing skills.

Where a training centre has the resources the session could be supplemented with looking at basic small repairs such as putting on plugs, changing a washer, dealing with stuck ballcocks, changing a plug in a bath or sink. Some chances to experiment with painting and to learn how to paint with emulsion and gloss, and to clean up, would be useful ones to offer the learners. Again, DIY stores often have leaflets about decorating techniques and materials.

Session Three: Housing and rights

This session should be undertaken as an awareness raising session not as a one-to-one advice giving session. Where learners have clear issues or problems these should be noted so referrals can be made.

Each trainer will need to have available lists of housing and advice groups or agencies able to deal with problems such as:
- access to facilities for homeless people
- housing single parents
- advice on rent arrears
- advice on mortgage arrears
- tenant/landlord disputes
- neighbour disputes and conflicts
- what to do if someone is in prison on remand/sentenced
- protected tenancies

- looking for accommodation
- housing benefits
- protected housing and domestic violence
- housing when nearing the end of a sentence
- housing projects for, e.g. ex-offenders, people with mental health problems

In addition to local advice centres, often the local council's Housing Advice Shop and agencies may be worth contacting. Also national agencies such as:

- NACRO
- National Association for Voluntary Hostels
- Langley House Trust
- Mediation UK
- Citizen's Advice Bureau
- Women's Aid Federation

The session should be treated as a group brainstorm about what people want or need to know and this should be followed by a talk from one or more experts about tenants' rights, housing association procedures, mediation or keeping local communities safe.

Session Four: Planning and summary

Ask the learners to each think of three things they have gained from the work on improving their homes and to consider how they will implement what they have learned, use **DI4**.

Ask for a couple of volunteers to go through their learning points and plans. Ensure learners have all the public information, public safety and store leaflets they need and any follow-up addresses which are useful to them.

Thank them for their work.

Improve your appearance

 Trainer's notes

This part of the module will link with other modules on developing positive attitudes, nutrition and exercise.

These learning activities focus on appearance – others' and the learners' own. It is important that this work is handled carefully. Learners may have been or may still be ridiculed about their appearance or cleanliness. The session could re-open painful memories or add to current tensions. These sessions must be managed so that personal comments are disallowed. The trainer needs to be aware of any learners who are stigmatised or ridiculed by others and take them to one side to work through the issues. If the trainer is aware of any learners with personal hygiene or other such problems then again the learner should be taken to one side and such matters discussed.

Depending on the group some of the suggested activities may be more or less relevant than others; for example, work on personal hygiene may not be important for some groups.

There are many leaflets which are available about personal hygiene, cleaning and care of clothes, choice of appropriate footwear, improving posture, the importance of rest and managing stress.

These can be found in supermarkets and chemists, and be supplied by health education authorities and so on. Some of these aspects of work link with health and well-being, stress management and nutrition. All contribute to developing the learners' self-esteem. These leaflets should be available for the learners.

Magazines for collage work will be needed.

Session Five: Introducing appearance

Opening brainstorms (20 min)

Ask the group to brainstorm the question:

> **Why is appearance important?**

They may suggest:

- it helps people decide how to respond to you – positively, negatively, afraid, scared, as an authority figure
- it says things about how you value yourself
- it is a way of showing power/authority
- it is a way of showing status
- it may be part of uniform or may show belonging to a group
- it shows how you want to be treated/regarded
- it says much about how you feel about yourself

Brainstorm the question:

> **What makes up appearance?**

Responses may include:

- posture
- way you walk
- clothes clean or dirty
- head up – or looking at floor
- cleanliness of hair etc.
- type of clothes – fashionable, smart, casual
- clothes well repaired
- shoes shined and repaired

Miming in the manner of ... (20 min)

A pack of playing cards is needed for this mime. Shuffle the cards and ask for a volunteer to pick one. They must not show this card to anyone. They must then act in the manner of the card. For example, a King would be most grand, a five would be an ordinary worker and one might be begging. The person undertaking the mime should not speak. The group has to guess which card (the suit is unimportant) the volunteer has picked. If someone says 'a three' and the volunteer is playing a six, they must alter the role appropriately. Once the group has understood this, ask for more volunteers.

Debrief the learners. What was it that told them that the person was of high rank, middle-of-the-road or down on their heels? Was it something to do with:

- posture – if so, try to be specific. Position of the shoulders etc.
- manner of walking
- facial expression
- how head held
- position of the hands
- manner of sitting
- how they have arranged their clothes

Clearly there are a number of clues about someone other than simply their clothes. These non-verbal clues tell us much about the person, how they feel about themselves and what they expect.

Check how much they would add to the two earlier brainstorms following this exercise.

What's important to you? (45 min)

Ask the learners to work alone for 30 minutes using magazines for collage or doing their own drawing. Ask them to each produce an A1 sheet of what is important to them about appearance – their own and others. They may want to cut out figures, certain clothes, health or beauty products. The may want to write words on their collage. The exercise is to focus them on appearance not to gain a prize for artwork.

For about 15 minutes:

1. Ask one or two volunteers to talk about what they have included in their designs.
2. Discuss with the group what they learned about themselves and appearance from the exercise.

These posters can be displayed for the group if the learners are happy to do so.

Statements (20 min)

Ask learners to work in pairs, and to produce a list of seven statements on which they can agree on to do with appearance. Comments must not be directed to others in the group. Ask them to write these boldly on A1 paper. The posters might include:

- appearance is more important in women than men
- if you look good, you feel good
- only rich people can look really good
- only young people can look really good
- designer labels are important
- you can't be seen in the same clothes too often
- fat people look awful
- cleanliness is very important to how you look
- wearing the right clothes for the occasion helps you feel comfortable
- you've got to look as good as you can, if you want to go out on dates/attract partner
- people are impressed by your clothes

Once the posters are pinned up, ask for comments on each statement from the group. How far do they agree/disagree with the statements? Do not allow any personal comments, not even "I know who wrote…".

Drawing the threads together: trainer explanations (10 min)

Explain that the previous four exercises have focused on appearance and its importance. They should have opened up a number of prejudices about appearance and will have made it clear that appearance is about more than clothes.

Find out if there are particular things which the learners would like to know about appearance. List these and as the sessions progress check points have been covered.

Session Six: Keys to improved appearance

 Trainer's notes

This session looks at key areas to improving appearance:

- cleanliness and personal hygiene
- management of clothes
- buying and wearing the right clothes
- posture
- looking fit and healthy

Brainstorm one: Improving appearance (10 min)

Ask the learners to brainstorm how they could improve their appearance with no restrictions on ideas. They may suggest:

- win the lottery
- have cosmetic/plastic surgery
- buy better clothes
- get hair re-styled
- get fit
- diet
- learn to make-up to suit their face/colouring

- become more confident
- smile more
- being neat
- cleanliness
- buying lots of new clothes
- having jewellery

Brainstorm two: Goals (10 min)

If they look at the suggestions from the first brainstorm could they list out some of the things they could do which would be within their reach. This list may include:

- getting fit
- buying good clothes
- cleanliness

- knowing what suits me
- knowing how to repair/look after clothes
- having better posture

Appearance is more than clothes. Creating a good appearance is about being clean (well groomed), having appropriate clothing for the occasion, having clothes well pressed and repaired, having good posture and looking as if clothes, body and mind fit. Appearance, confidence, feeling comfortable are improved if appearance and situation match.

Lead from these two brainstorms into the areas covered by this session, as is appropriate to the group.

Personal hygiene

Introductory activity (15 min)

It is crucial for a person's acceptability to others, sense of self-esteem and our health to take personal cleanliness seriously. **DI5** is an outline of a person, the learners are asked to consider what needs cleaning, how frequently and why and what are the consequences of not. They should work alone on completing this figure.

Feedback (15 min)

A large outline figure will need to be drawn on the flipchart.

The learners should contribute suggestions during group feedback. Ensure that all body areas are covered no matter the embarrassment; and that the importance of well-being, developing self-esteem, feeling better and acceptance by others are all discussed.

Emphasise that keeping clean does not have to be expensive but it does need to be part of a daily set of activities. It will give a sense of control of self and daily life and taking care will help with a general sense of health and well-being.

Any health education leaflets can be given out at this point as reminders. For example, leaflets on good foot care and health; maintaining healthy teeth and gums; and personal hygiene and food preparation.

Remind the learners that smoking and drinking also contribute to body smells which others may find offensive and which may also be out of place at work. For example, people will not want to be served food or be cared for by people smelling of alcohol or cigarettes.

In pairs: adverts (30 min)

Ask the learners to find a number of adverts which look at body odour, personal hygiene and beauty. Ask them to make a collage and to decide what are the key messages from these adverts.

Feedback (30 min)

Look at the collage work. Record the key messages, for example:

- sex appeal
- not ageing, being eternally young
- being more attractive
- help you to attract the ideal person
- make you beautiful
- are for the beautiful
- having a tan and looking healthy
- eliminating odours

Decide which products:

- are necessary
- seem to be creating problems which do not exist
- are promising the impossible
- are expensive and probably not worthwhile having

Make a list of the key items which everyone should have. Try to cost these items and ensure that, like cleaning materials for the home, these items have a place in the learners' weekly/monthly budgets.

Clothes care
Brainstorm (15 min)

Ask the learners to consider these two questions:

> **Why is it important to take care of clothes?**
>
> **How do you care for clothes?**

Their answers may reveal problems with washing and pressing clothes, with simple clothes repairs or just in being generally negligent about looking after their clothing. Problems may arise because the learners are not storing their clothes properly, have no place to store clothes, are not protecting them from dust or do not have the facilities for or know how to wash and repair their clothes.

Checklist on clothes management (15 min)

Ask the learners to complete DI7.

Ask if any learners are prepared to talk about how they care for their clothes. Find out how their behaviour about their clothes makes them feel, what happens to the clothes and why they do what they do. Stress that looking after clothes helps to maintain them. Find out which areas the learners may have had difficulty with, e.g. repairs or washing.

Find out what learners expect about clothes. Do they think they will last a long time, or just to be worn and replaced. Do they expect to spend a lot of their budget on clothes. Do they expect to buy a lot of cheap clothes and throw them away? Do they expect to own 'designer' clothes?

Care symbols (15 min)

Give out the clothes care symbol quiz DI6 and ask them to work alone for ten minutes. To wash or handle clothes wrongly may lead to expensive mistakes as well as to ruining the appearance of items.

Stress that effective treatment of clothes enhances their life and that they will look better for longer.

Repairs: optional session

If the resources are available then some simple survival sewing activities may be useful. Knowledge and practical experience under guidance of the five following tasks would help any learner to be better in control of their wardrobe:

- replacing buttons
- repairing small tears
- repairing seams
- replacing zips
- turning up hems

Explain that being able to do small repairs will:

- save money
- make the learners feel better about themselves by being more competent
- help clothes to last for longer
- ensure that clothes look better for longer

Find out how many have their shoes repaired and ask them to compare costs of repairs to shoes with replacing shoes. Again find out the learners' expectations about how long shoes should last, what they should cost and whether they expect to buy quality shoes.

Ironing: optional session

If appropriate and if resources are available then a session on ironing may be useful. Check that the learners understand about the effects of heat on different fabrics; how to press in seams they want, how to avoid adding those they do not. Explain the importance of taking care of irons and ironing boards especially where there are other people around.

Buying and wearing the right clothes

Opening exercise (30 min)

Choice and wearing clothes is a matter of taste, budget and about the image which people want to project.

Write these three questions on the flipchart. Ask the learners to answer them on their own.

1. Ask the learners to think and to decide:
   a. what their clothes say about them
   b. what they would like their clothes to say
   c. why there may be a difference between their answers

2. The learners should then compare their answers in pairs. Does the other in the pair agree?

3. Ask for some learners to volunteer their thoughts. Record these on the flipchart.

4. What solutions can the learners find to differences in their answers between a and c.
   Is it about money?
   Not knowing what to buy?
   Not being sure what image they want to project?

Awareness raising (20 min)

Using magazines ask the learners to find images to illustrate a range of different types of appearance. They should work in pairs and agree what they think each image is. These can be stuck on A1 sheets for display. Ask for one or two pairs to go through their image poster explaining their choices and decision to the others.

Purchasing and choice of clothing explanation and discussion (20 min)

Clothing is a matter of personal choice. It is wrong to be prescriptive. There are some things which the learners might consider when assembling their wardrobe.

1. The range of activities they undertake and so the clothes they may need; for example what is needed for work as well as home.

2. The amount of money they have to spend on clothes and so how best to balance needs; for example something for work, desire for fashionable items, and making clothes last.

3. Buying something which will be useful for formal occasions, e.g. an interview, seeing a solicitor, a court appearance, going to see a bank manager.

4. Thinking how to make their money stretch by buying clothes which could be worn with each other.

5. Wearing what is appropriate for an occasion.

6. Finding out about good retail outlets.

Ask the learners what they think of any of these six points. Discuss with them their spending habits, expectations of clothes and the types of clothes they like.

Inject reality into the discussions by speaking of budgets, working clothes and the need to have some formal clothes.

Posture

Opening brainstorm (10 min)

Ask the learners to brainstorm:

> **What can someone's posture tell us?**

Ask for examples; these should include:

- being lonely – being hunched up, keeping away from others
- feeling afraid – looking away or down
- feeling shy – looking down, shuffling feet, fiddling with things
- feeling confident – smiling, looking others in the eye
- feeling in control – walking tall, ready to shake hands etc.

 Trainer's notes

Remind the learners of the mime exercise with the cards which will have made the learners aware of the effects of looking up and outwards or shuffling and looking at the floor. People who appear nervous or intimidated are ones who look downwards.

Body language, or things you can tell about others from posture and body positioning is looked at in the manual *Developing Social Skills*. This section considers the importance of developing good posture for looking good and feeling good, for helping reduce back problems and encouraging good breathing.

Feeling in control of how a person holds their body is a way of encouraging greater confidence and self-esteem.

Trainer's explanation (10 min)

Explain why this session looks at posture by taking some of the ideas from the notes above.

Awareness raising (30 min)

Ask learners to work in fours and to take turns to:

- observe each group member walk across the room and sit in a chair
- observe the remaining three seated as a group talking about the weather, football or some topic of interest

DI8 should be completed by each learner and the box for self-analysis completed.

Feedback in small groups (20 min)

Ask each learner to share their thoughts about the other three and themselves. There should be no personal criticism and observations should be offered as supportively as possible.

- How many in the group agreed with each other?
- How many were accurate about themselves?

Group feedback (15 min)

Ask the group to share what they learned from the exercises, what may have surprised, pleased or disappointed them.

Practical work: improving posture (40 min)

Explain the following three exercises will be a way to improve posture and to make them conscious of what they do. They are adapted from the Alexander Technique. There are books on the Alexander Technique and classes are run in many areas.

Ask for a volunteer (it is best to have someone wearing trousers) to lie on the floor on their back. Put two or three books under the person's head, ask them to bend their knees and then to relax completely and let you take the weight of their legs. Hold each leg in turn just above the knee and at the back of the knee and let the foot fall naturally. The feet should be about hip-width apart. Ask the person to bend their arms and place their hands on their hips. The spine should settle and, if this is practised for 20 minutes a day, their posture should improve. Learners can try this in pairs.

Learners should try to remember this body position at all times. When sitting the position should be reflected. That is, feet both on the floor, hip-width apart knees bending where they naturally fall, head in the same relative position. Again in pairs they should try sitting well.

When walking, legs do the work and the body remains upright (again same as the position on the floor). Tell the learners to look down with their eyes (keep head upright – imagine a thread from the crown of the head tugging gently upwards) and see their feet moving ahead of them. Again ask them to practise in pairs. Remind them how it looks to see people walking bent at the waist. This position increases tension and does not get you there any faster. Get them to watch people walking. Ask whether they see more women or men walking badly. What may be the reason for this?

Actors talk about 'stage presence'; that is holding yourself well and moving well, not slouching, and not fidgeting. Fidgeting about with your hands is distracting – watch people in power, they do not fidget. Fidgeting can be caused by stress, insecurity or just habit.

Looking and feeling fit and healthy (40 min)

This is an important part of feeling good about oneself, therefore having higher self-esteem and impressing others. It is important to look healthy and fit when applying for work.

Looking and feeling fit will have an impact on the way you appear to other people and how you feel about your own appearance. A fitter person is more likely to:

- feel clothes fit better
- walk taller
- look healthy
- be less stressed and look less stressed
- react more calmly, take more in their stride
- feel and look more rested

Becoming fit and healthy was considered in the module on Health and Well-being.

The key points to consider with the learners are:

- How much excess fat do they feel they carry?
- How well are clothes fitting?
- How hard are their hearts having to work?
- How much work are their lungs doing?
- What are they eating to help their bodies work well, e.g. eliminate waste?
- What are they eating to increase their weight?
- How much exercise are they taking to help them feel more active, slimmer and in greater control?

Feeling fitter and looking more healthy can be tackled by a simple month long programme of:

1. *Eating a more balanced diet* – see Food Guide Pyramid
   - cutting out sugar and salts
   - cutting down alcohol
   - increasing water intake
   - decreasing fats
   - decreasing refined carbohydrates
   - decreasing proteins
   - increasing fibre

2. *Ensuring vitamins are taken.* B and C are water-based, others oil-based. The body does not make or store B and C and these are needed to deal with stress and promote a healthy nervous system.

3. *Taking simple exercise such as walking* can increase the heart rate and ensure that the lungs are working properly by taking in more air and therefore more oxygen.

4. *Increased oxygen makes the body* work more effectively, burning fuel and producing energy.

5. *Improved cardio-vascular system* means that the heart becomes stronger and blood levels more elastic. Muscles, ligaments, joints all improve in efficiency. The heart being stronger has to work less hard to achieve the same results. It can take more rest and will not wear out so fast.

6. *Attention to diet and to simple exercise will mean weight loss;* better fitting clothes, a positive sense of self and a sense of well-being or vitality.

7. *Attention to a stress reducing diet* i.e. one which does not keeping stoking up the body with a false sense of well-being – alcohol, caffeine, tannin and nicotine – will improve energy levels, allow proper rest.

8. *Reducing smoking and drinking* and increasing water intake will do much to improve skin texture.

9. *Exercise helps to deal with stress, helps relaxation and sleeping,* all of which encourage looking healthy and behaving in a more in control way.

Walking as an aid to better appearance, fitness and health should be aerobic walking; that is walking at a pace which pushes up the learners' heart rate. Walking should be 4 mph or more for 20–30 minutes each day. The walking will burn calories, stretch hips, encourage breathing and it will put up the metabolic rate so the body burns foods more effectively for the rest of the time.

Learners should build up to the 30 minutes of brisk walking from 20 minutes, alternated for the first week with a slower than 4 mph rate.

Walking requires no equipment or experience. It is easy to do, requires no special skill or confidence, and creates no sense of being watched doing something unusual. It cannot cause damage as you are not asking the learner to take exercise or use equipment for which they have not been trained. Walking is habit forming and will give the learners time out during which other problems or issues may resolve themselves.

Walking will improve posture by encouraging a straighter back and striding out. The learners will be lifting their heads to look ahead rather than walking with a shuffling pace while looking on the floor.

Session Seven: Planning and summary

Ask the learners to close these sessions on DIY: Improve appearance by completing the handout they have already completed for DIY: Improving my home **DI4**.

They should take 20 minutes to complete the sheets and a further ten minutes should be spent in discussing their conclusions. Help anyone with issues which have arisen.

For example, the need to lose weight may require something more structured than a walking and better eating regime.

Improve your chances

 Trainer's notes

These two sessions encourage the learners to take stock of the attitudes and behaviours which will help them to help themselves and those forces which will prevent them from making the changes and choices to improve their situation. The two sessions are designed to encourage the learners to take themselves seriously and to lay plans for change.

Session Eight: Focus on me and my chances

Opening brainstorm

Ask the learners what it means to:

> **Improve my chances**

The suggestions should cover making changes, thinking about aspirations and how to meet them, and dealing with things which hold them back such as habits, lack of qualifications, fears and insecurities. Record the many and leave the list displayed. This exercise should have generated many ideas and should prepare the learners for the next activities where they work alone.

Me and my chances (40 min in total)
 Trainer's notes

This exercise involves sorting through three different sets of statement cards.

DI9, DI11 and DI12. The statements encourage learners to think about things they should do and want to do, should do but are less inclined to do and then to identify those forces which will help them and those which will hold them back.

Having collected and sifted through this amount of information they will be able to prioritise and target areas for activity.

1. Ask the learners to read through the choice cards **DI9**, select and put into piles:
   - those cards which are about improving chances which the learner wants to do
   - those cards which would be about improving chances but which learners feel would be harder to do

There are some blank cards for the learners to write down other things which they feel would help them improve their chances.

2. Ask the learners to prioritise their cards into the five key things they should do, irrespective of wanting to do them or not.

   This information should be recorded on **DI10**. A ✓ can be placed by things the learners want to do.

3. Ask the learners to review the statement cards **DI11** and **DI12** selecting their helping and hindering factors. Their findings should be recorded on **DI10**.

At the close of the exercise they have much information about themselves.

Group feedback explanation (20 min)
Find out from the groups what surprised them about what they found out and what it pleased them to know.

List on the flipchart:
- some of the areas the learners identified for improving upon
- some of their helping forces
- some of their hindering forces

These lists will help in planning revision of some areas in earlier modules, developing the individual and group programmes for those who have not taken earlier modules and for planning other activities from the Russell House companion volumes *Developing Social Skills* and *Addressing Anti-Social Behaviour*.

Take one example of an area which would improve chances and work through on the flipchart the analysis on **IC05** making use of the helping and hindering forces diagram. Show the group how they can analyse helping and hindering forces for each area they would like to work on and how they can analyse the best ways to develop the helpers and weaken the hinderers.

Explain that this type of analysis – force field analysis – can be used for other types of problems.

Helping and hindering analysis (20 min)
Ask the learners to work though **DI13** on their own. Check on progress and on the answers to the questions.

Pair work (20 min)
Ask the learners to work together to review their two diagrams and their three answers. The pairs should generate questions, requests for more information etc. in readiness for a whole group feedback session.

Task feedback (20 min)
Ask a volunteer to talk through their plan with the group. Ask the group to help the learner with other suggestions. Collect group list of questions or areas which require more information to support changes. This session could usefully inform inviting in expert outsiders to speak and adding more guidance and information leaflets to those already available.

Session Nine: Planning

 Trainer's notes

If possible have outside help but certainly have a ready and easily accessible supply of leaflets for the learners covering:

- training provided in the area
- grants and funding
- information about benefits
- basic skills programmes
- developing skills with computers
- fitness and exercise classes
- leisure facilities
- marriage and relationship counsellors and guidance
- advice on stopping drinking, taking drugs, gambling etc. Addresses of counsellors in these areas
- help with money management
- information on job seeking

Allow time for the learners to consider leaflets which interest them, to read, take down interesting details or addresses.

Check on how they find the material – accessible, useful, too simplistic, too difficult, not detailed enough. Find out what they think is missing and address this in building up an improved data collection for subsequent groups. Ask the learners to work on their Improving their Chances Plan (**DI14**). The headings should be familiar but review what is wanted in the exercise. The plans can be completed alone and compared with a partner. There may be some learners who will work in the longer-term with a partner to support them. Check on individual progress and on any need for further referral or guidance.

Close the session with a game such as Counting to Ten or Rainforest to bring the group back together.

D12: Risky environments

Look at the sketch below and decide what constitutes a risk.
What should be done about the risk?

From *The Foster Carer's Handbook* by Ann Wheal (RHP, 1995)

D11: Accidents and injury at home

Name of risk	Why is it a risk?	How to prevent it

D13: Planning

List six areas of risk in your home

1.

2.

3.

4.

5.

6.

Work out action steps to reduce these risk areas

1.

2.

3.

4.

5.

6.

D14: Summary points

Three new things I have learned are:

1.

2.

3.

I plan to use the following ideas:

To help me do this I will need:

D16: Clothes care symbols

Symbols Quiz

1.

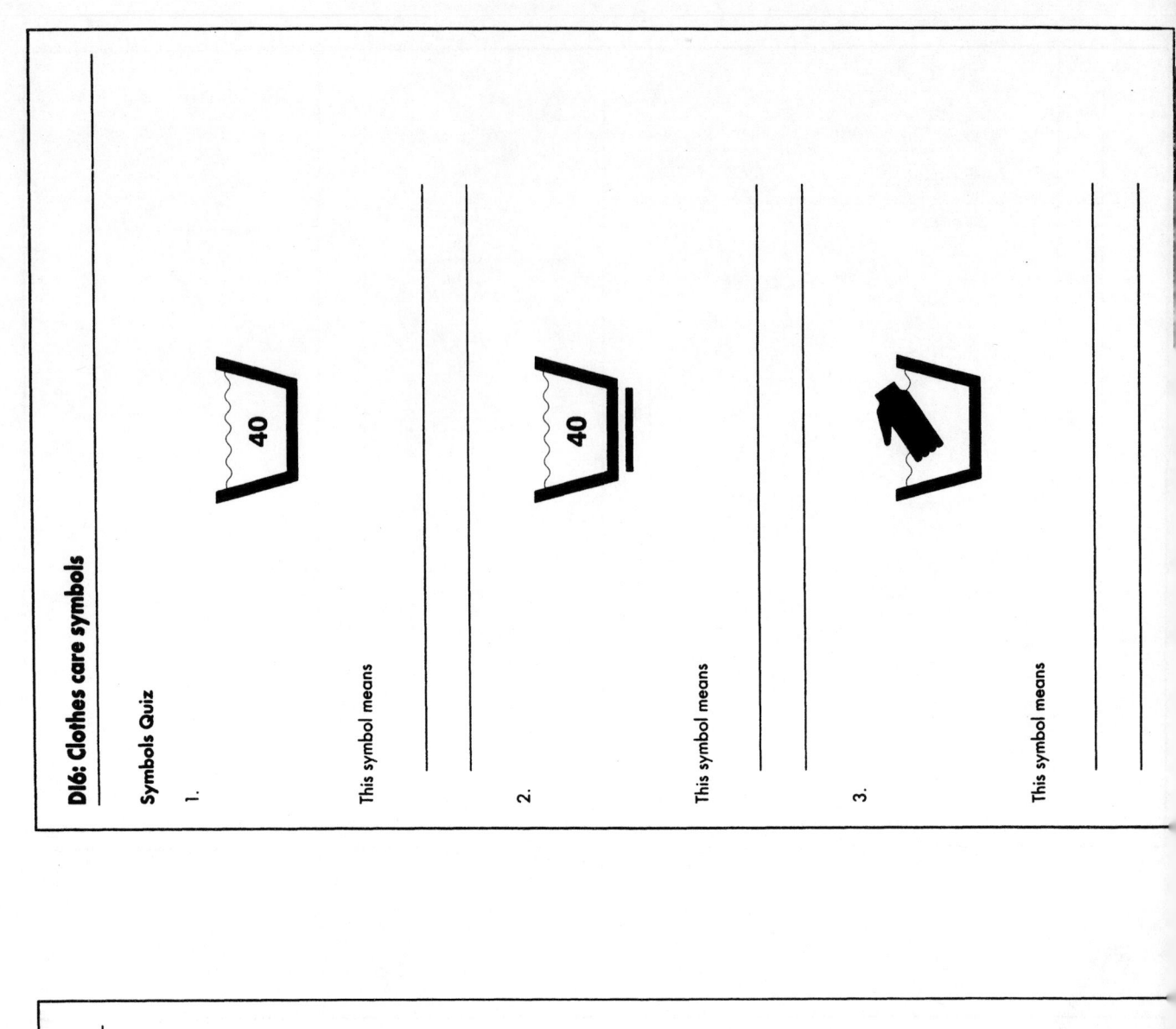

This symbol means _____

_____

2.

This symbol means _____

_____

3.

This symbol means _____

_____

D15: Personal hygiene

Look at the figure below and decide which parts need washing, how frequently and why cleanliness is important for health and well-being, appearance and self-esteem. Some arrows have been added to get you started

Teeth – brush twice daily because ...

Ear clean with water/flannel. Don't clean with sharp/hard object. Risk of puncturing ear drum

Clean and dry between toes, have clean socks/tights. Risk of fungal infections

4.

This symbol means _____

5.

This symbol means _____

6.

This symbol means _____

7.

This symbol means _____

8.

This symbol means _____

D18: Observation of posture

Record how each person walks; for example, how do they hold their head, carry their shoulders, who or what are they looking at, are they standing straight, are their steps sure or shuffling, etc.

1

2

3

Decide what impression the walkers 1 - 3 above create.

1

2

3

Record how each of the three group members is sitting; how are they holding themselves, what impression are they creating? For example, interested, stressed, bored. Do they appear confident or shy?

1

2

3

Decide how you think that you have appeared walking and sitting as part of the group. Record your impressions of yourself so that you can then compare these with those other people have written about you.

D17: Clothes care

Tick the statements which apply to you

Statement	✓
I have ruined clothes by ironing them wrongly	
I know how to wash clothes properly	
I can repair clothes	
I don't really care what my clothes look like	
I fold clothes carefully	
I always wash everything on the same wash cycle number	
I think I can iron well	
When I pack clothes I just put them in the bag	
I clean my shoes regularly	
I hang up my clothes each day	
I take my shoes for repair	
I leave my clothes on the floor	
I only look after my best clothes	
What is the point of taking care of clothes you can always buy more	

Have better control over my emotions	Get help with my depression	Stop holding myself back
Take stock of my values	Ask my boss what I could do to get on	Value myself and decide I am worth it
Make more effort with my appearance	Give myself time out from worrying	Look at my lifestyle and decide what to change
Like myself more	Think creatively about myself and my future	Improve my self-confidence
Try to get in with another group of people	Find someone to help me be less anxious	Move away from my current friends
Save some money	Try to expand what I know about/what interests me	Find out about training/re-training opportunities
Learn how to get on with others in the workplace	Improve my communication skills	Have a strategy for looking for jobs

DI9: Taking stock of myself

Read through the statements below and select those which:
i) are things you should do and want to do to improve your chances
ii) are things you should do but don't want to do very much to improve your chances

There are some blanks for you to add your own ideas

Learn how to control my temper	Look at my bad habits and tackle them	Acknowledge problem with drink/drugs/gambling etc.
Stop dragging myself down with guilt	Make an effort to get myself in a better state of mind	Try harder to look for work
Try to tackle my need to worry all the time	Develop positive thinking	Get counselling
Find a goal I want and I can stick to	Confront my problems	Decide to do something about my problems
Get help with my education	Try to find a better job	Get vocational training
Stop wasting my time	Try to get fitter	Get people around me who can help

Photocopy onto thin card and cut out each of the cards

D110: Improving my chances – taking stock

To improve my chances I should:		
Item		**Reason**
1.		
2.		
3.		
4.		
5.		

Key skills/qualities/factors to support me are:

Key things holding me back are:

DI9: – continued

Stop being so critical	Learn about computers	Make an effort with my partner and family
Find ways to deal with my shyness	Take time to think about the future	Take up some voluntary work
Learn a new skill	Stop being so abrupt with people	Find out about money management
Decide what's important to me	Get out of damaging relationships	Stop watching TV so much
Do something instead of the pub	Get a CV organised	Take some interest in other people

I don't get put off easily	I want to improve my chances	I will take risks
I can tackle and solve problems	Getting on is important to me	I can put up with hardship for a while
I don't mind trying new things	I will ask others to support me in my plans	I know when I have a problem
I have imagination	I will be honest with others	I don't expect immediate success
I can count on others because they can count on me to help them	I want to make changes	I'm not afraid of making changes
I know when I have to leave people/situations	I can imagine myself being successful	I take myself seriously
		I have shown in the past I can learn new things

DI11: Things which help me

Read through the statements below and decide on those skills or qualities which you have which will help you to improve your chances. There are some blanks for you to add your own ideas.

Get on well with new people	Like to be successful	Can collect and make use of information
I am honest with myself	I'm not afraid to ask for help	I have a supportive partner/family
I'm keen to try new things	I like learning new things	I'm willing to travel for work/training
I'm able to admit I need help		I'm determined
I'm open and outgoing	I like to get to the bottom of things	People like to help me
I will work hard to achieve what I want	I will work hard to achieve what I want	I think I am worth it

Photocopy onto thin card and cut out each of the cards

I have problems with my drinking	I don't see why others should have more than me	I'm not able to control my own feelings
I don't think I'm worth it	I get bothered about meeting new people	I have too many responsibilities to others to think about myself
My partner has to come first	I haven't got the money to do...	I don't really like new situations
Why bother to make the effort?	I'm afraid I'll fail	I tell myself things like – why would anyone want me...
I don't want to take myself and my future seriously	I wouldn't know where to start to...	I don't want to think about the future
People like me just don't get on	I feel bad that I can't spell	What I do always depends on what someone else does
My future means changes and I don't like change	It's easier to do nothing and wait and see what happens	Once you're down it's hard to do anything about it

---

DI12: Things we hinder me

Read through the statements below and select those which best describe those things which hold you back.
There are some blanks for you to add your own ideas.

I tend to get distracted easily	I don't like to take risks	I feel bad that I have problems with numbers
I have no idea where to look for help	I find it hard to push myself forward	I'm easily influenced by others
I can't manage aggressive feelings	I don't have much faith in myself or my ideas	I give up easily
My family/partner are not supportive	I'm driven by guilt	I don't want people to know my problems
I can't break old habits	I'm afraid of change	I get put off by setbacks
I feel I need to make up for what I did in the past	If something is difficult I stop trying	I want someone else to take the responsibility of making changes

Photocopy onto thin card and cut out each of the cards

DI13: Helping and hindering forces

Complete the statements about something you need to do to improve your chances, and the forces which help or hinder you in doing this. Add as many arrows as you need on the helping side or hindering side.

Working to help me are:

↓   ↓   ↓

To improve my chances I need to:

↑   ↑   ↑

Working against me are:

DI12: – continued

			I feel bad that I am confident when writing letters			
	I feel bad that I don't understand about money				I feel bad that my reading is so poor	
I feel bad that I can't read timetables						

DI14: DIY improving my chances

Key areas to target are:

The goals for improving my chances are:

Goal 1

Goal 2

Achieving these will mean to me that...

Action steps	Timescale
Goal 1	
Goal 2	

Success in Goal 1 means:

Success in Goal 2 means:

Review date:

DI13 – continued

Look at your diagram and think about these questions

Have you more factors helping or holding you back?

Why is this so?

Which forces are particularly strong and why?

How can you support the helpers and weaken those forces which hinder you?

This concluding section is divided into:

1. Evaluation and self-assessment
2. Acknowledging the learners' contributions
3. Trainer's techniques and strategies

More information can be found in the manual *Becoming an Effective Trainer* (Russell House Publishing, 1998). The following pages offer some key points and should not be considered an exhaustive discussion of these issues.

Evaluation and self-assessment

This part briefly addresses some of the tools and strategies to support you as a trainer to improve upon the design and subsequent delivery of the learning activities. It addresses learners' evaluations and your own assessment of your performance.

Learners' evaluations

Given that the only purpose in creating and providing learning opportunities is for the learner to derive something of value and meaning for them in either the long- or the short-term, it is imperative to understand how the learning activities have been received by the learners.

Evaluation should cover some of the following:

1. At the outset of the learning activity:
   - Find out how the first session has been received and perceived by the learner.
   - Is it meeting learner identified needs?
   - Are the learning styles appropriate?
   - Is the pace of the session right and is it pitched appropriately?

2. During the learning programme:
   - Find out what have the learners gained from the session.
   - Is the content and style what they expected?
   - Is the learning programme useful and in what way?
   - Does it meet their needs?
   - Are they finding the activities too difficult or insufficiently demanding?
   - What is its value and use?
   - How much is thought to be not useful and why?
   - Does anything appear muddled or confused to the learner and what?

3. At the end, find out:
   - What do they feel they have learned?
   - What has been of value?
   - What would they like more of or less of within the programme and why? – this may apply to content or to types of learning activity
   - If they were designing a module, what would they do, include or exclude and why?

Some example forms of evaluation are at the close of this section.

Evaluation may be undertaken on paper, during a group brainstorm, orally, or one-to-one. Evaluation should not be confused with individual learner's progress reviews. The focus of evaluation should be on the programme, its integrity, the types of training and learning styles and materials used. Evaluation should not be thought of by either trainer or learner as likely to lead to punitive action. It should be part of the learning experience for learner and trainer. Encouraging the learner to reflect upon the learning experience, the types of materials, the activities and how they may be experienced by others helps to make the learning activity a more conscious and serious one.

It is good for the trainer to be confronted with suggestions for change, improvements and with the thoughts, experiences and perceptions of the learners. It encourages the trainer to appreciate the importance of the learner, their critical judgements and perhaps to respect the learning role more fully. The learner, in offering feedback through an evaluation and seeing it accepted and probably used, will gain practical experience of the value and role of feedback.

Trainer self-assessment

For trainers to gain the most from the training role and be most effective in discharging the role for the learners they need to become reflective. This means taking note of what happens and analysing why something happened and the reasons for this. The trainer may want to reflect on a single session, or the course as a whole, select a particular theme or analyse the ways in which certain activities are received and enacted and why this may be so. The trainer may consider:

- why the group dynamic develops as it does
- the trainer's own role in encouraging or inhibiting learning
- how the trainer's attention is shared among the learners and with what effect
- why a particular or critical incident evolved as it did
- how thye have developed a particular training skill

Self-assessment can be undertaken by keeping an after-session log, completing a checklist about key aspects of the session, or by undertaking a trainer's SWOT analysis and reviewing progress.

Acknowledging the learners' contributions

Throughout the sessions learners should have been thanked for their input and hard work or for trying what may have been a new type of learning activity. Learners will have been completing and discussing their learning and action plans and these discussions with the trainer should have generated positive feedback from the trainer about effort, attention, aspiration and good work, as appropriate.

The life skills modules and their learning activities are underpinned throughout the manual with self-assessment and action planning activities. These engage the learner in self-directed and formative learning and often require that the learners' ideas, aspirations and insights are shared and valued within the learning group.

Other more formal assessment activities such as accreditation for learning or end of module tests may be the appropriate culminating activity for learning in some situations. Accreditation would not be appropriate for these types of learning activities unless the accreditation was grounded in the learning process and not preoccupied with outcomes. These activities are very much awareness-raising exercises, ones for which there are no right answers and ones which should engage the learner in ongoing learning. These activities seek to stimulate the learners' sense of personal control and self-esteem. People should be judged against their own criteria, performance and on the ways in which they create their own meaning.

These activities all emphasise making small changes and building upon such changes. Valuing the learners' work and their completed activities and contribution should be done by encouraging the learner to maintain a learning portfolio and by sitting and reviewing it with them. Valuing learning should be undertaken by peers commenting on each others' contributions in learning sessions.

End of module statements or end of programme statements can be prepared to draw together what the learner has undertaken. These statements will describe the range of learning activities and areas covered. They will not specify success or failure or make statements about competence. Such statements of completion are a formal and official summary of a learning activity. They are not certificates or awards. Learners know the difference between an institutionally created certificate and one which rests within national frameworks of accreditation. Such statements of completion can be supported by the learners own statement of learning. These can be housed in the learner's course or programme portfolio and can be a part of the learners' National Record of Achievement/Progress File (Achievement Planner).

If the institution or organisation for which the trainer works is going to assess the learner; for example, for contribution to sessions, punctuality, attendance or competence in the learning activities, then this should be explained to the learners at the outset. They should be made aware of the criteria for assessment. The trainer and institution should consider most carefully how trying to assess competence fits into the spirit and intention of these learning activities for awareness raising, personal development and the fostering of personal life skills. Learners who think that there are institutional hoops or hurdles to negotiate are often most adept presenting their public selves.

Trainer's techniques and strategies

Throughout the learning activities guidance is given to assist delivery. The trainer does need to read at greater length how to manage various training and learning styles or to consider the reason for such activities. This section outlines some of the most common learning activities in these modules.

Brainstorming

This is frequently used as a way to introduce a topic. The groundrules for this activity need to be made clear to participants. It is a session where, in large or small groups, the learners tackle a problem or an issue by making as many suggestions or comments about the topic as possible. The intention is to try to explore what the topic means, what may be done and what its implications may be. The emphasis throughout is:

- on the volume of ideas, not necessarily their feasibility or accuracy
- on exploring a range of ideas about and associated with, the issue
- on generating the speedy flow of ideas
- on getting the sparks of ideas but not fully discussing them
- on everyone being able to join in

There should be no censure of anyone or their ideas. All suggestions should be written up clearly and in the speaker's own words. It is important that the group leader or other person writing up the suggestions does not translate the ideas into their own language. The implications of ideas can be discussed later. The trainer will have to decide when to tackle any outcomes from the brainstorming which contravene group groundrules or equality of opportunities issues.

Once generated the ideas can be used to stimulate role-plays, as starting points for discussion of learners' expectations, as a stimulus to move onto a subsequent activity or explored to find patterns about, for example, beliefs, or discussed as strategies for managing a situation.

Group discussion

Group discussions are another frequently used learning tool in these modules. Discussions are useful but they need careful managing to be successful. Effective discussion will not simply or spontaneously happen. All group members need the skills to manage their participatory roles and to understand that the discussion is an opportunity to explore ideas. Discussion should not become an opportunity for personal comment or criticism.

Managing discussion activities should not be confused with controlling the content of the discussion.

Discussions can become:
- unfocused leading away from the topic and onto the participants' concerns. This can drain energy from the group and frustrate many who then gain nothing from the discussion but feelings of wasting their time
- an opportunity to attack a fellow course participant
- a chance for one or two to monopolise the session
- a time when the trainer dominates the session
- a time when the trainer tries to give a short lecture

Group discussions do have many benefits:
- they bring the group together to share ideas
- give everyone a broader range of insights into an issue
- give the trainer and group members a clear sense of people's starting points or entrenched ideas which then need to be worked on to realise learning goals
- they break up a learning day or session
- they bring the group back together after individual or pair work
- they can be a structured chance to report back on other learning activities to the whole group
- they are a chance to explore understandings of material being worked with
- they can re-focus the group
- successful discussions can re-energise the group and offer it new leads for further thought and work

Managing the discussion
Some actions need to be taken to ensure success. These include the following:
- clear groundrules about lengths and frequency of individual contributions. There should be opportunities for all to participate
- no personal attacks or undermining of others
- equality of opportunities should be observed
- objectives of the discussion should be clarified from the outset
- these should be re-visited if the discussion drifts
- the trainer or other group member should summarise the key points part way through the discussion and set out questions or areas to be covered to keep the discussion on course for the remainder of the time allocated
- the trainer should not be afraid to guide the discussion
- people should have some time for reflection or other stimulus

Goldfish bowl
There are two versions of this activity. In both versions the room is set out with two circles of chairs, an inner circle with more chairs and these closer together and an outer circle with fewer chairs spread apart.

Version One: The inner circle is for those who opt to discuss the issue. The outer ring is for those who observe the discussion and its conduct. The observers need to have some guidelines about what to look for. It may be that they observe the way the members of the inner group allow participation in the discussion, allowed or disallowed a range of ideas, how certain ideas were dealt with and the types of language and body posture used by group members and to what effect.

Version Two: In this, there are two empty chairs in the inner circle. These can be used by anyone observing from the outer circle who wishes to add to the discussion if they feel points are not being raised or that someone in the inner circle is not getting a fair hearing.

As with all exercises, the conduct of the exercise and what various group members gained from it should all form part of the debriefing.

Role-play

As an activity this has many advantages for the learner and offers the learner fairly immediate and significant engagement in the learning. It is often assumed, like discussion activities, that anyone can do this. Role-play needs thoughtful preparation, needs to be clearly explained to the participants along with any groundrules to follow, and the activity needs on-going management.

Role-play takes problems or situations as their focus and they offer the opportunity for those involved to explore the issues, to gain insights into how others perceive the same problem, and see how others experience the behaviours they may themselves engage in. The role-play situation can give people the chance to experience a new or unfamiliar situation and help them to prepare to face it; e.g. an interview, a court appearance or a review. It can help people to try out behaviours which are not their usual ones. It allows them to feel what it is like to be a victim, to behave considerately to others, or to act out the anger they feel towards someone. To set up the role-play the trainer needs to establish some parameters with the group. These may include:

- the extent and nature, if any, of physical contact
- the possible role or use of shouting, swearing or offensive language
- understanding that the role-play is a fiction and that the participants are in role. It needs stressing that they are not really those people
- that the exercise will be challenging and may open up a number of memories and issues and that these should be talked through with the trainer or other appropriate person

The trainer needs to prepare for the role-play, to have the physical space cleared for the action, to provide a few props if these are necessary, to outline the situation on which the role-play is centred and to outline the brief roles for each player.

The trainer needs to decide how much time will be available for preparation of the role-play or whether people are to react to a given situation in their role straightaway. If there is only one role-play to be enacted:
- what will happen to the rest of the group members while the role-play is being rehearsed?
- what should the rest of the group do while the role-play is taking place?

The trainer needs to decide how to manage the debriefing. There are many options for the trainer.

De-roling

In every instance it is important for those who have been in role to come out of role. They may do this by:
- commenting on what it felt like to play the part
- commenting on how and why there are differences between the real self and the role-play self maybe commenting on the ways their real self would have managed the situation.

See *Becoming an Effective Trainer* for greater discussion of role-play, de-roling and hot seating.

The continuum

One way of making choices and an especially good way because it is highly visual, involves quite literally the whole person and the whole group, is that of using the continuum. The group members are asked to place themselves on an imaginary and graduated line in a position which represents the view, opinion or feeling which they hold.

Within a group setting draw an imaginary line across the room. One end represents one extreme of an opinion or state, and the other end the opposite extreme or state. The group members are asked to place themselves on the line where they think that their point of view or set of feelings are best represented. They should do this without taking much notice of anyone else in the room and to react to the statement fairly spontaneously.

The result may be an even scattering along the line or a bunching of people at certain points on the line. It is a way of asking people to declare their starting points and to think about where they would place themselves. It is interesting for the group to see where people place themselves and to discuss the reasons for this. The exercise can help define understanding about issues, to see if everyone shares a definition and under what circumstances certain group members may change their position.

Ranking exercises

A familiar way for people to confront issues and raise awareness of their own priorities is that of undertaking ranking exercises. Group members are asked to confront a particular issue or aspect of themselves and to mark their responses on a graduated line, by giving a number from one to five or by selecting pre-printed statements on cards. The cards may then need further ranking into priority order.

Learners are then asked to consider patterns or themes which may emerge from their ranking activities.

Talks or presentations by the trainer

If infrequent and interspersed with other activities these add to the variety of learning activities and enable the transmission of information. Talking at learners can however be damaging, it may remind them of past experiences or encourage them to absent their minds from the session.

Talks should be accompanied by clear signposting to assist the listener to know what is happening and should be little more than 20–30 minutes unless broken up with activities and questioning. The talk needs:

- a clear structure
- a clear purpose and defined outcomes
- to be supported with simple phrases or key words on handouts or OHTs

The trainer should say what the session is going to be about and summarise the areas to be covered. Part way through the learners should review what they have heard and then be told briefly what comes next. At the close, the talk should again be summarised and the key points displayed.

The review and repetition will ensure that the trainer maintains the discipline to stick to key points and a clear structure and will enable the learners to understand the links between the ideas.

Hearing a lecture is fairly passive unless the listener can make notes on handouts or can perhaps complete the gaps in pre-made notes. This task gives an additional reason to listen and to seek out information.

Material from the lecture should be used soon afterwards so that learners are forced to revisit it, use it and internalise it.

Drawing or collage work

Learners can work alone or in small groups to make representations of feelings, relationships, issues or ideas. They can work through drawing, painting, collage, or making models. The groups and individuals should understand that the skill in execution and the quality of outcome are not at issue. The exercise, which some will find hard, should stimulate a flow of thinking and feelings, some of which may not have yet come to the fore.

If undertaken in small groups the pictures or models will spark discussion, as they are being made, about how to represent their thoughts and feelings.

Once all are completed:
- they can be presented to the full group and discussed
- they can be left as items, as in a gallery, to be looked at by individuals
- the process, as well as the feelings and thoughts can become the meat for a group discussion

Using and managing checklists
There are a number of checklists in the manual. These help the learner to undertake some systematic self-analysis and appraisal of skills. They are a useful way to prompt a learner to think about current levels of skill and any areas of difficulty. Checklists can be helpful in encouraging learners to examine ways in which they see themselves and the world around them, the types of assumptions they make, the ways in which they often behave and reasons which might lie behind their assumptions and behaviours.

Checklists should be a prompt to self-reflection. They are *only* of value if something is done with the findings of a checklist. The findings may be used in discussion with other group members to think of ways ahead, to highlight areas on which learner and trainer could usefully work to develop skills or to change behaviours or ways of perceiving the world.

In using checklists it needs to be emphasised that there are not right or wrong answers or value judgements being made. They only have a role in learning if they are used honestly and provoke an individual learner's thinking.

Checklists are not a way to silence a group. They should be a precursor to discussion. They should certainly not be used as a means of making anyone feel they are without skills or positive qualities; they are merely a rather crude indicator that change may be useful in some areas or that certain patterns or tendencies are present.

Checklists should be worked on alongside the learner. This is essential in instances where learner may have literacy problems. This will mean:
- that the learner clearly understands what each item is about
- that the learner's answer can be discussed and evidence can be sought by the trainer. This process will ensure clear understanding and will enable both learner and trainer to appreciate what the learner needs to do next
- that the findings from the checklist can inform the process of planning the learning programme

There is a danger that checklists given to the learner to complete in an unsupported way will mean:
- little is understood
- the checklist is completed perfunctorily. This will mean little thought goes into it and little stimulus is gained from it
- the learner may feel defeb=nsive at the end of the exercise
- the learner has a false sense of current levels of achievement not having any sense of standards nor appreciation of what is asked

The most likely way checklists will be used successfully in a group situation will be for the trainer to:
- explain the purpose of the activity
- explain what the content is about, perhaps picking one or two questions and asking the group to explain what they mean

- be on hand to help, to review and to question as the learners undertake the task of completing the checklists
- know why the activity is being undertaken and to have clear intentions about how the information or/and raised self-awareness will be used next

If you reflect on surveys or checklists you have completed you may remember feelings of boredom, questioning why something was asked or why the data was collected. These negative feelings are not ones to encourage in learners. Learners should be engaged, should be able to find out much about themselves from such activities and should be stimulated to consider the issues and to perceive patterns and trends in their own experiences and behaviours.

Games

Fruit bowl

The aim of this game is to get the group moving around the room and to concentrate on something else, have some fun, focus on being in the training room and on those around them. Only have enough chairs for each member of the group to sit on. Take away your chair.

Then, stand in the middle of the group and name each member one of three fruits, any fruit. Give yourself a fruit name too. Explain that when you call the name of a fruit, those named must move to another chair, the one without a chair stands in the middle and calls out a fruit name. To begin the game you should use your fruit name. This will get you onto a chair and a learner into the centre.

Name game

The group sits in a circle. The first person names themselves. The person to his or her right has to say the previous name and their own. The next person to the right has to give the two preceding names plus their own. And so on. It is amazing how as it gets closer to being your turn panic sets in and names become muddled or forgotten. The group is likely to bond around this common task and to feel sympathetic and helpful.

Throwing the ball to me

Everyone needs to be in a circle with easy eye contact. All names need to be known to each group member. An object needs to be used as a 'ball'. Someone has the 'ball' and throws it while calling out a name and making eye contact with that person. The ball however is not thrown to that person but to someone else in the group.

It encourages concentration and the knowledge of group members' names.

African rain forest

The leader makes noises such as rubbing hands together, gentle clapping like rain, hissing, tapping feet and finally clapping hands on thighs louder and louder then quieter etc. The sounds have to travel around the circle until everyone is making the sound, then the leader changes the sound until all sounds have been made.

The game aids concentration and increases attentiveness on the activities taking place.

Counting to ten

The group members stand in a circle. They may look at each other or not as they choose. Everyone needs to be quiet and then it should be explained that:

- as a group the learners, including the trainer, will count to ten
- each person should speak at least once (if there are less than 10 in the group)
- the learners have to concentrate on who has spoken, who is preparing to speak and try to sense when it is appropriate for them to speak.

If two or more people speak at the same time, then the group must begin again at one.

Closing rounds

At the close of a course or workshop you could go round the group asking each learner to answer a question like one of the following. It should make the learners think about their experiences on the course and as part of the group.

- *What I am taking away with me from this group is ...*
- *What I'll think of afterwards and wish I had said was ...*
- *The most boring/exciting part of this group for me was ...*
- *Something I have discovered is ...*
- *I plan to ...*

All these techniques for encouraging learning need to be clearly understood. The reasons for them, the outcomes they are seeking and the ways in which learners can be best managed. The trainer needs to feel confident about what tools are to be used and why.

These are tools to provoke learning; they are not an end in themselves. The trainer needs to confidently manipulate techniques and be comfortable with such strategies as hot seating and detailed and guided questioning to enable them to fully exploit the materials created and explored by the learners. The trainer should help the learners explore what they mean, to discover that there are other ways of viewing a situation, to reflect upon experiences, to reframe their pasts and to find other strategies for managing their futures.

The trainer will need to be able to manage difficult situations in the training room; for example, conflicts between learners, a learner threatening to get into conflict with the trainer or even the trainer generating conflict situations. The trainer will need to establish groundrules with the group before starting so that there are agreed and commonly accepted behaviours which can be referred back to as and when needed. For example, as a way to cajole the overly noisy or potentially violent participant to think about how they are not conforming to group expectations, or to encourage the learner who wants to make personal comments or to be critical to appreciate they are contravening a group agreement.

Ways to manage groups are discussed in the manual *Becoming an Effective Trainer*.

Learner's activity sheet: learners' views 2

Name of course: ....

1. When I came to this course, I had hoped to achieve:

2. I wanted to achieve this because:

3. Now that I have taken the course, I feel that I have gained/achieved:

4. Now that I have taken the course, I feel that I have not gained/achieved:

5. One or two things I plan to use from this course is/are:

   i.

   ii.

6. My suggestions for the improvement of the course are:

   i.

   ii.

Name .... Date ....

Learner's activity sheet: learners' views 1

Title of session/workshop ....

1. The three most important things for me which we covered today were:

   i.

   ii.

   iii.

2. A key idea I gained from today was:

3. I am still unsure about:

4. I would like to find out more about:

5. From this session I would like to make use of:

Name .... Date ....

Learner's activity sheet: learners' views 3

Title of programme: ....

How many sessions have you been to?

What have you enjoyed most so far?

   – Why is this so?

What have you enjoyed least so far?

   – Why is this so?

What do you think will be of greatest long-term use to you?

   – Why is this so?

What would you like to find out more about?

Name .... Date ....